MW01224285

TEACHING THEM OBEDIENCE IN ALL THINGS
Equipping for the 21st Century

Edgar J. Elliston, Editor

Evangelical Missiological Society Series # 7

William Carey Library
Pasadena, California

EMS Series #7

Published by
William Carey Library
P. O. Box 40129
Pasadena, CA 91114
(626) 798-0819

ISBN 0-87808-381-2

Library of Congress Cataloging-in-Publication Data

Teaching them obedience in all things: equipping for the 21st century/Edgar J. Elliston, editor.
     p. cm. -- (Evangelical Missiological Society series; #7)
    Ten papers presented in Evangelical Missiological Society meetings in 1998.
    Includes bibliographical references and index.
    ISBN 0-87808-381-2 (alk. paper)
    1. Obedience--Religious aspects--Christianity--Congresses.
    2. Missions--Congresses.
I. Elliston, Edgar J., 1943- II. Evangelical Missiological Society. III. Evangelical Missiological Society series : no. 7.

BV4647.02 T43 1999
266--dc21
                                           99-046670
                                                CIP

Second Printing 2000

PRINTED IN THE UNITED STATES OF AMERICA

TABLE OF CONTENTS

iii

iv

LIST OF TABLES

TABLE

LIST OF FIGURES

FIGURE

PREFACE

This book consists of a collection of ten papers that were presented in Evangelical Missiological Society meetings in 1998. John Piper presented his paper in a joint plenary session of the Evangelical Theological Society and the Evangelical Missiological Society. The text is organized into four major sections: 1) Biblical/missiological foundations with chapters by Kenneth Mulholland, John Piper, Michael Wilkins and Rick Love. 2) Two views of Christian higher education and its role in addressing the theme of teaching obedience in all things with chapters by Sherwood Lingenfelter and Larry Poston. 3) Case studies in two post-modern settings and one traditional context with chapters by Jonathan Campbell, Rick Sessoms and Abdella Usman Muktar. 4) Finally, I raise curricular issues in the final chapter to aim the trainer of cross-cultural missionaries toward a contextualized design.

While each chapter has undergone some editing to bring the style into more of a print style than an oral style, my desire has been to maintain the individual authors' perspectives and content.

TEACHING THEM...ALL THINGS:
THREE DOTS AND A PILGRIMAGE
Kenneth B. Mulholland

Thesis: Teaching them all things begins with obedience.

The Evangelical Theological Society (ETS) celebrated its fiftieth anniversary in 1998. This year also marked the tenth year since the Evangelical Missiological Society began to meet jointly with ETS. Up until then, the Evangelical Missiological Society met nationally only every three years and then not with the academic community (even though we called ourselves at that time the Association of Evangelical Missions Professors). Instead, we met jointly with missions executives from the Interdenominational Foreign Mission Association and what was then called the Evangelical Foreign Missions Association.

This arrangement changed when the executive committee decided that missiologists needed to engage the academic community as well as what Ralph Winter likes to call the "Missions Industry."

After all, are not biblical and theological studies founda-tional for the discipline of missiology? Moreover, do not biblical scholars and theologians need to be informed about the missiological implications of their discipline? Is not Christian mission rooted in the nature of God Himself? Does not every doctrine of our faith have missiological implications? Are not God's people a missionary people? How ironic it is that in the current issue of the *International Bulletin of Missionary Research*, Frederick Dale Brunner, reviewing Andreas Kostenberger's book, *The Missions of Jesus and the Disciples According to the Fourth Gospel*, comments, "Kostenberger is that rare biblical scholar who is interested in world missions" (Bruner 1998:181). Were not missionaries the principal authors of the New Testament? Were they not writing to faith communities established by missionaries? Is not the God of the Old Testament a missionary God? Is not the Christ of the gospels a missionary Christ? Is not the Holy Spirit of the book of Acts a missionary Spirit? Is not the church of the epistles a missionary church? Is not the consummation of the book of Revelation a missionary consummation? Or to put it another way, if you believe in God, He is a missionary God. If you are committed to Christ, He is a missionary Christ. If you are filled with the Holy Spirit, He is a missionary Spirit. If you belong to the church, she is a missionary church. If you await the consummation from heaven, it is a missionary consummation both in terms of God's ultimate victory and of the universal representation before the throne of God of every tribe and people and tongue and clan (Stott: 321-334).

Missiology as a discipline bridges both the academic community and the missionary sending structures. Missiology encompasses both reflection and action. It bears both upon the teaching and the practice of mission.

Sometimes our theme is markedly different than that of the Evangelical Theological Society. On those occasions, we have pursued our own course. At other times, there has been remarkable convergence. This is one of those years. The ETS has chosen the theme "Teaching Them. . . All Things." That's our terrain! How much more missiological can you get than Matthew 28:19? The Great Commission itself! I am grateful that John Piper was one of the plenary speakers this year. Nevertheless, look at the meeting program: "Teaching Them All Things." In the original publicity, it was "Teaching Them . . . All Things."

Three Dots

What has been left out? The words "to obey." Obedience has been left out—a fatal flaw. Dare I suggest that often what has been taught in our schools and even to the converts in our churches is content rather than the attitude of obedience?

I have a concern: the three dots. The question that I bring to this gathering is: How shall we exegete the three dots? Certainly not by ignoring them!

Will scholars uninformed by missiological insight, in violation both of the message of the gospel of Matthew as a whole as well as the very grammar of Mt 28:19, seek to interpret the teaching ministry described as an end in itself whose object is the impartation of content, the more the better?

Let us look at the text from which our theme is abstracted. The grammatical structure involves four activities, indicated by the verbal terms go, make disciples, baptizing and teaching. Only the second term "make disciples," is an imperative, second person plural verb: the other three are nominative plural participles all related to the plural subject of the main verb. The construction thus stresses the focal point in the commission, namely the assignment to make disciples of all nations. The participles grammatically dependent on the main verb denote activities related to the accomplishment of a central assignment. They are the means by which disciples are made. Going--teaching--baptizing. The imperative in this verse is "make disciples."

These words refer to the initial enrollment of persons in the school of Christ--not the process making average students into honor roll students. However awkward McGavran's vocabulary has proven to be, his distinction between discipling and perfecting is helpful (McGavran 1959:93-101).

Going, because nobody thinks up the gospel for himself or herself. Going is the means by which access to the gospel is created. The gospel comes to us from someone outside of ourselves whether the harbinger of good news arrives from across the street or across the sea.

Baptizing--because incorporation into the Christian community is an integral part of becoming a disciple. After all, how can you accept Christ and reject his people?

Teaching--because it is in learning to submit our lives to the known will of God which facilitates spiritual maturity and growth. Matters related to going and baptizing are not an issue at this meeting. Teaching is an issue and although the content of Christ's commands is important, knowledge of that content cannot be divorced from obedience. Obedience is more than an afterthought in the Great Commission. It is integral to the entire gospel according to Matthew. The central thrust of our theme for this gathering is that the purpose of Great Commission instruction is not to impart knowledge alone, but to enable obedience to the known will of God.

Peter Cotterell has pointed out: "Matthew has intentionally climaxed his record of the life of Jesus with the commissioning of the disciples for mission. This is the high point of Matthew's gospel as 20:31 is the high point of John's gospel" (Cotterell 1990:95).

In his masterful chapter on "Mission in Matthew" in the book, *Mission in the New Testament: An Evangelical Approach*, John Harvey points out that throughout his gospel, Matthew says a great deal about what is involved in discipleship.

From the call of the first disciples comes three important truths: First, discipleship leads to mission; not only will they have a passive role as followers, they will have an active role as "fishers of men" (4:19). Second, discipleship demands obedience: when Jesus calls, both sets of brothers follow him "immediately" (4:19-22). Third, discipleship involves sacrifice: Peter and Andrew leave their livelihood (4:20); James and John leave their livelihood *and* their father (4:22) (Larkin 1998:130).

Harvey identifies additional traits of true discipleship which emerges near the conclusion of the Sermon on the Mount. First, disciples enter in by the narrow gate. Second, they produce good fruit. Third, they obey the Father's will. Finally, they act on Jesus' words (Larkin 1998:130).

Harvey emphasizes that "For Matthew, obedience is *the key* quality of a disciple who is on mission" (Harvey, 133). We see this not only in Matthew 28 where it cannot be separated from Christ's claim to have authority in all of heaven and earth, but throughout Matthew's gospel beginning in the first chapter with Joseph who "did as the angel commanded him" (Mt 1:24). As mentioned previously, the four fisherman--Peter and Andrew, James and John--obey immediately Jesus' summons to follow Him (Mt 4:18-22). And in the account of his own call (9:9), Matthew obeyed in the same way. In Matthew 21:6 and then in 26:19, Matthew notes the disciples "did just as Jesus had directed them." When the angel instructs the women to tell the story of the resurrection, they "ran to tell it to the disciples" (28:8). Finally, after Jesus rose from the dead, the eleven "proceeded. . . to the mountain where Jesus had designated" (28:16) (Larkin 1998:133).

I do not want to minimize the content of teaching in the production of disciples. The focus of the Great Commission is on the sort of teaching that trains--not alone on the wholesale impartation of religious information. To teach a person to observe the truth of God may demand a deliberate withholding of truth until that which has already been presented has been incorporated into his or her life.

Three dots and a pilgrimage. Let me share with you some incidents of my own pilgrimage that have reinforced the significance of obedience.

A Pilgrimage: Honduras

There are three experiences where the truth of Matthew 28:19 was dramatically and increasingly reinforced in my own life. The first occurred early in my missionary career that dates back to the mid-1960's. My initial assignment as a missionary was to head a small theological institute in northern Honduras in the city of San Pedro Sula. What I did not know at that time was that the institute was located midway between two neighboring veteran missionaries. On the one side was Ralph Winter. On the other side was George Patterson. Innocently and inadvertently,

I found myself on the ground floor of an emerging new movement called Theological Education By Extension. From Ralph Winter and his colleagues Ross Kinsler, Jim Emery, Chepe Carrera, and Nelly de Jacobs, I learned the philosophy and strategy of TEE. However, it was from George Patterson that I learned what I have come to believe what is the very soul of theological education itself.

Early in 1968, I invited Patterson to give a weekend workshop on the relationship between theological education and church growth. He and his national colleagues had linked theological education by extension to church planting in a remarkably creative and effective way. I wanted him to share that story with our own student body, which, through the application of TEE principles, had now grown from six resident students to a total of about fifty persons studying by means of a variety of delivery systems. It turned out that this was the first time that anyone had ever asked Patterson to organize a presentation for what he had been doing so effectively. He rose to the challenge and accepted.

What I learned about was "Obedience Oriented Education." Later, Patterson put his thoughts in a little booklet by that title. Let me share with you from that booklet. Whether you agree with everything he writes or not, the theme is powerful.

In this "tract for the times," Patterson argued that neither the communication of content nor the development of skills are the foundational objectives of theological education, but rather obedience to the commandments of Christ. " God does not bless *methods*," insisted Patterson in his introduction. "He blesses loving, faithful obedience" (Patterson n.d.:i).

So Patterson forged his educational philosophy in the context of pastoral training ministry which accompanied a church planting ministry.

He differentiated between levels of authority. The lowest level consists of human traditions--things like Sunday School, choirs, pulpits, public invitations to go forward, candles, and wearing a tie while preaching. While these are not required (some people think they are), they may be prohibited if they impede obedience. Any authority they may have arises from the voluntary agreement of a congregation to adopt the tradition to further its ministry. Such traditions should not be imposed by one congregation on another.

The middle level of authority consists of apostolic practices. Paul traveled by ship. The Jerusalem congregation shared its goods in common. Apostles communicated to churches and individuals not by e-mail, but by hand carried letters. Patterson held that apostolic practices, while they were not to be prohibited (How can you prohibit what the apostles do?) were not to be required either. He affirmed that only Christ has the authority to order what we must do and not do as churches.

The highest level of activities for a church is derived from the commandments of Christ. Based on Mt 28:18-20, they are required and they can not be prohibited. Patterson (Winter and Hawthorne 1992:D-85) asked his converts to memorize the following list of Christ's basic commands: Repent and believe (Mark 1:15); Be baptized and continue in the new life it initiates (Mt 28:18-20, Acts 2:38, Rom. 6:1-11); Love God and neighbor in a practical way (Mt 22:37-40); Celebrate the Lord's supper (Lk 22:17-20); Pray (Mt 6:5-15); Give (Mt 6:19-21, Lk 6:38); Disciple others (Mt 28:18-20).

Thus, the way in which Patterson constructed his curriculum was to direct all subjects toward obedience. Training was tied to a responsible ministry in a congregational context. Patterson (n.d.:4) reasoned "We have an obedience oriented pastoral course when our immediate educational objectives fulfill the commandments of Christ, but to guarantee a permanent orientation to obedience, we must secure the act of cooperation of the churches."

Patterson's emphasis on obedience orientation as central to theological education extended to congregations equally committed to a life of obedience to Christ. He said, "The obedience oriented churches grew, multiplied, maintained discipline and showed discernment in doctrine" (n.d.:17).

A Pilgrimage: Liberia
(With Help from Papua New Guinea)

Years later, this same emphasis on obedience oriented education was reinforced while ministering in Liberia among a people group which did not yet have the Old Testament in their language. In addition, many were not literate. Nevertheless, I was astounded at the vitality of the church and their commitment to do whatever they understood to be the will of God. I recall in particular how they hung on to every word as Philip Steyne preached and taught his way through Old Testament passages which had not yet been translated into their language. They had never read those passages. They were hearing them for the first time and many were eager to obey what God's word taught.

I recall among those in attendance one blind evangelist whose family, all newly converted Christians, accompanied him as he went from village to village to share the good news of

Christ. They even rejoiced at the inconvenience they experienced for the sake of the privilege of participating in the communication of the gospel.

Again, it became clear to me that growth in godliness comes not so much from the accumulation of theological knowledge, but from obedience to the known will of God. The practice of immersing oneself in biblical and theological content with the thought of putting it into practice in our lives some time in the future creates spiritual hardness. The attitude that somehow I can be encountered by the Word of God and yet defer action on that Word of God does not work. The idea that I do not really have to conform my life to it now--I can store it up for later and think about it at some future time only blinds one's heart.

Leaders who think that growth in grace comes by knowing the Word of God without doing it will produce congregations of passive Christians which resemble human beings that eat too much and exercise too little.

Then help came from Papua New Guinea. Just last month, I led a Global Challenge group in which we observed the video "EE-TAOW: The Next Chapter." It is the story of how through a people movement to Christ among the Mouk people in Papua New Guinea, resulting from the chronological Bible teaching method, the believers immediately determined to share the Good News with neighboring tribes. And, they did it.

A Pilgrimage: Pretoria

Still another instance where I encountered the significance of obedience was at the gathering of the Global Consultation on World Evangelization (GCOWE) in Pretoria, South Africa in 1997. From one of the tracks in that group, the presidents' and deans' track, emerged the PAD declaration (Johnstone 1998:201-02).

PAD Declaration

Two hundred and fifty Presidents and Academic Deans (PAD) representing theological schools from fifty-three nations gathered at the Doxa Deo Church in Pretoria, South Africa, July 1-3, 1997 to consider ways in which the schools they lead can further the goal of "a church for every people and the gospel for every person." Theological educators have tremendous potential to bless, but also to damage the church; to enhance but also to hinder the fulfillment of the commission.

Out of the worship, plenary addresses, workshops, testimonies, prayer, discussion, and informal fellowship the following ten theses have emerged:

1) The primacy of missiological concern for world evangelism must be recognized and focused in the total curriculum of ministry training.

2) Partnership at all levels and in multiple forms is essential for reaching the unreached people of the world.

3) Formal, non-formal and relational approaches to learning are to be seen as complementary rather than competitive.

4) The content of ministry training must uphold the uniqueness of Jesus Christ and the necessity of personal faith in Him as Lord and Savior. This commitment is especially imperative in the light of the increasing pluralistic environment which has been brought about by the resurgence of non-Christian religions hostile to the advance of the

gospel, by the erosion of historic Christianity in the West, and by the increasing prevalence of secularism almost everywhere.

5) Ministry training must aim to produce practicing supernaturalists who minister effectively in the power of the Holy Spirit, relying on prayer and complete trust in the Word of God.

6) Basic to all ministry training is spiritual and character formation in the life of the student, in part facilitated by the examples of the teacher.

7) Approaches to ministry training must reflect concern for the whole counsel of God wisely contextualized and sustainable by local and national resources.

8) Academic accreditation may serve to guarantee quality control and encourage institutional effectiveness. At the same time, it should not be allowed to impede the spiritual and missiological thrust of theological education. Every effort must be made to assure that accrediting structures affirm and promote commitment to world evangelization.

9) Serious consideration should be given to the training of both husband and wife for their mutual effectiveness in ministry, and accessibility to ministry training broadened to include all who can benefit from it.

10) A permanent PAD track should be incorporated into the AD2000 Movement and another Consultation convened.

Looking to the future, we call upon college Presidents and Academic Deans and commit ourselves to put the vision of *"a church for every people and the gospel for every person* at the heart of ministry training. We resolve to explore together new paradigms of partnership in theological education that training schools share their distinctives and resources to accomplish the goal of global evangelization. We shall continue to press the claims of the kingdom as we move towards the consummation of history and the coming of our Lord in the glory of God.

In his marvelous book, *The Church is Bigger Than you Think,* Patrick Johnstone (1998:202) challenges theological institutions to have a greater impact on world evangelization. After hearing the PAD declaration read for the very first time (he was present at the meeting), he wrote, (1998:202) "For the first time in history, a significant and representative body of theological trainers set up a peer pressure accountability structure to insure their schools become Great Commission centered schools. I pray," he continued, "that it might become as powerful a defining instrument in the theological world as the *Lausanne Covenant* has become for evangelicals since 1974."

Thesis six in the PAD Declaration declares that basic to all ministry training is spiritual and character formation in the life of the student in part facilitated by the examples of the teacher. One of our faculty loves to say that the curriculum is the teachers. Teachers are the curriculum which models obedience to Christ.

As my eye glances over the program for this particular day, I am delighted to see highlighted the words "teaching them to obey all things" which are so prominent in our foundational biblical studies and making disciples through the teaching of obedience which are so central in the case studies. Wherever we are in our own spiritual pilgrimage, may this same prominence be reflected in our lives, our ministries and the church.

Teaching Them...All Things.

I have a little granddaughter. She has an activity book. I do not get to see her very much because she lives in Venezuela. Her parents are missionaries. And when I am with her, sometimes she opens the activity book and says, "Grandpa, let's fill in the dots." Let's fill in the dots with obedience to Christ.

References Cited

Bruner, Frederick Dale
    1998   Book Review of "The Missions of Jesus and the Disciples According to the Fourth Gospel: With Implications for the Fourth Gospel's Purpose and the Mission of the Contemporary Church." *International Bulletin of Missionary Research.* 22:4 (October).

Cotterell, Peter
    1990   *Mission and Meaninglessness.* London: SPCK.

Johnstone, Patrick
    1998   *The Church is Bigger Than You Think.* Geanies House, Fearn, Rossshire: Christian Focus Publications.

Larkin, William J, Jr. and Joel F. Williams, eds.
    1998   *Mission in the New Testament: An Evangelical Approach.* Maryknoll, NY: Orbis Books.

McGavran, Donald Anderson
    1959   *How Churches Grow.* London: World Dominion Press.

Patterson, George

    Obedience Oriented Education. Cucamonga, CA: Church Planting Int'l, n.d.

Stott, John R.W.

    1992   *The Contemporary Christian.* Downers Grove, IL: InterVarsity Press.

Winter, Ralph D. and Stephen C. Hawthorne, eds.

    1992   *Perspectives on the World Christian Movement.* Pasadena, CA: William Carey Library.

TRAINING THE NEXT GENERATION OF EVANGELICAL PASTORS AND MISSIONARIES

John Piper

Thesis: Knowing God and enjoying Him is the greatest need

The greatest need of the next generation of pastors and missionaries is exactly the same as the greatest need of every generation of pastors and missionaries that has ever or will ever exist. Therefore, the central task of those who would train them never changes.

In fact, this great need is so central to all of life, and so definitive for all ministries, and so relevant to all cultures, and so ultimate compared to all other values, that it should be the all-absorbing passion of every Christian scholar and teacher. This fire should especially drive those who train pastors who shepherd the church and missionaries who plant it among the unreached peoples of the world. This need is the need of pastors and missionaries to know God and to find in him a Treasure more satisfying than any other person or thing or relationship or experience or accomplishment in the world. It should satisfy more than the honor or speaking to a plenary session of the ETS, more than the publishing of articles and books, and more than the preciousness of friends. The greatest need of every pastor and every missionary is to know God better than they know anything and enjoy God more than they enjoy anything.

Therefore, the supreme challenge of every scholar and teacher who would prepare these pastors and missionaries is clear: How shall I study, how shall I teach, and how shall I write, and how shall I live, how shall I give my seminar paper in Orlando, how shall I speak of sacred things over supper tonight, what will be my vigilance regarding television in the privacy of my room, will I rise early enough to pray concerning the magnitude of truth that is at stake in the workshops of this meeting so as to help pastors and missionaries know God better than they know anything, and delight in God more than they delight in anything? That is the supreme challenge of your life.

I know of other demands on us in the pastorate and on the mission field, if we are to do our job well. There are hundreds of them. In addition, they change from year to year, even month to month, and from city to city, and church to church, and mission to mission, and people to people, and culture to culture, but one demand never changes. It is the main demand, and it is the hardest demand of the ministry to fulfil. It is the most crucial demand if we are to do our jobs well. Pastors and missionaries need to know God better than we know anything and must be more satisfied in all that God is for us in Jesus than in anything else – including our wives or husbands or children or ministries.

We could address hundreds of other things in the ministry if we are to do our job well, but nothing comes close to the magnitude of the importance of this need to know God. I stress it for at least five reasons.

Five Reasons for Focusing on the Primacy
of Knowing and Enjoying God

1. Doing our job well as pastors and missionaries means mainly bringing more and more people, among more and more peoples, to know God and to delight in him above all things is what our job *is*. Therefore, the most fundamental, essential, pervasive need of our lives and our ministries is that we ourselves know God and enjoy God above all things. The absence of other skills and knowledge in ministry may *hinder* this job, but the absence of this all-pervasive necessity *destroys* our job.

2. The second reason I stress the need to know God is when pastors and missionaries know God better than they know anything and delight in God more than they delight in anything, all the other important relationships and practices of ministry are sustained by God-exalting motives. Furthermore, these relationships and ministry practices are refined in the fire of God-centered truth, and empowered by the energy of God-saturated spiritual life. All that is secondary and good and important in ministry is sustained and refined and empowered by focusing on something else, namely, God. God does not destroy secondary things when he is known and loved above them.

3. The third reason I stress the centrality of knowing and enjoying God is a tremendous, relentless, almost irresistible pressure in the churches, the academy, and in mission agencies today to take God for granted. While we give ourselves to other things that are perceived to be strategic, urgent, or practical, a strange tendency exists today to say, "Yes, yes, of course, knowing and loving God is supremely important. How could anybody disagree?" Then to say, as if it were a tribute to God, "We take that for granted in all of our seminars and courses and syllabi and lectures and books and mission conferences and leadership gatherings. It is foundational for all we do," but the problem with this approach is that you cannot take it for granted that students or pastors or missionaries or teachers know God better than they know anything and find more satisfaction in him than in anything else in their lives. You cannot assume that. The foundation simply is not there.

The evidence for this lack is the emergence of the spiritual formation movement. It would not have occurred to anyone to add courses in spiritual formation if students were walking out of their Biblical classes aflame with a passion for the glory of God standing forth in the exegesis of his Word. It would not have occurred to anyone to add courses in spiritual formation if students were coming out of systematic theology and church history with their minds amazed at the majesty of God and their hearts burning within them like the men on the road to Emmaus (Luke 24:32).

In 1905, J. Gresham Machen experienced something in Germany that almost swept him away from orthodox Christianity. He wrote home from Germany about the incredible impact of Wilhelm Hermann, the systematic theologian at Marburg. Hermann represented the modernism that Machen would later oppose with all his might. However, that was not all. Machen wrote:

> My chief feeling with reference to him is already one of the deepest reverence. . . . I have been thrown all into confusion by what he says–so much deeper is his devotion to Christ than anything I have known in myself during the past few years. . . . He believes that Jesus is the one thing in all the world that inspires *absolute* confidence, and an *absolute*, joyful subjection; that through Jesus we come into communion with the living God and are made free from the world. . . . His trust in Christ is (practically, if anything, even more truly

than   theoretically)   unbounded   (Stonehouse
1987:106-108).

It simply would have been unintelligible to Machen if
someone had said: "What the seminaries need is courses in
spiritual formation so that students can experience communion
with God and learn about unbounded trust in Jesus and see
examples of absolute, joyful submission to the purposes of
Christ." Machen would have simply said, "You do not need
special courses. Just take systematic theology with Wilhelm
Hermann." If that could be said of a course from the likes of
Hermann, what should be said of ours who esteem the Scriptures so much more highly? The spiritual formation movement
in our day is a symptom of failure, as much as a sign of hope.

So when we hear this response: "Yes, yes, knowing
God better than we know anything and delighting in God more
than we delight in anything is foundational, we take that for
granted. We assume it in our seminary courses and in our
church growth seminars and in church planting workshops, and
in our cross-cultural missionary training. Yes, yes, it is foundational, we assume it, we take it for granted." However, we
may very calmly say, "It is not to be taken for granted, because
it is not there."

Moreover, even if it were there *as a foundation*, a
deeper reason remains why we should not take it for granted,
namely, God does not like being taken for granted, and he
never intended that knowledge of himself or delight in himself
be the quiet, hidden foundation for something else. The
problem with the metaphor of "foundation" is that foundations
are unsightly structures, out of sight and forgotten. While they
hold up all the rooms where we do what we like to do: the
kitchen where we like to eat, and the den where we like to
watch television, and the bedroom where we like sex, and the
living room where we like to meet with friends, we never think

about them. They all depend on the foundation, but whoever thinks about the foundation?

The metaphor is Biblical. It is true. And, it is utterly inadequate. God is not just our foundation. He is the food we eat. He is the entertainment of the eyes of our hearts. He is the lover of our souls. And, He is the all-satisfying friend for our deepest loneliness. He does not mean to be taken for granted as the ground of our being while we enjoy other things. He means to be pervasive in every room and every course and every syllabus and every book and lecture and sermon and seminar and workshop and conference. "Whether, then, you eat or drink or whatever you do, do all to the glory of God" (1Corinthians 10:31). "Whoever serves, let him serve in the strength that God supplies that in everything God may be glorified through Jesus Christ to whom belongs the glory and the dominion for ever and ever" (1 Peter 4:11).

4. The fourth reason why I am stressing that the greatest need of pastors and missionaries is to know and enjoy God above all things is his purpose for our labor. When you smile and moan with delight at the Thanksgiving table next Thursday, you will not be glorifying the chair that holds you up, but the turkey in your mouth. If you multiply your pleasures that evening with the ecstasies of your marriage bed, these delights will not be a tribute to the mattress on which you lie, but to the person in your arms.

The point: the purpose of God in all pastoral labor and all missionary service is to be glorified publicly. God's aim is to be admired and magnified and honored in all the churches and in all of culture and among all the nations. God is most glorified in us when we are most satisfied in him. This truth is the overarching point of all the Scriptures. I was struck again with this truth a few days ago in reading the prophet Ezekiel. Sixty times he tells us that God does what he does so that Israel and the nations will know that he is the Lord.

For example, in chapters 38 and 39 – the prophecies concerning Gog and Magog – God says to this mysterious ruler, Gog, "I will bring you against my land that the nations may know me, when through you, O Gog, I vindicate my holiness before their eyes" (38:16). Notice the zeal of God that the nations "know" him and that his holiness be vindicated "before their eyes." Not in a corner or quietly or secretly, not taken for granted, but publicly and for all to see.

Then when Gog has done his work against Israel, the wrath of God will turn and be kindled against Gog himself. So the Lord says, "I will summon every terror against Gog, says the Lord. . . . So I will show my greatness and my holiness and make myself known in the eyes of many nations. Then they will know that I am the Lord" (38:21,23). "I will send fire on Magog and on those who dwell securely in the coast-lands; and they shall know that I am the Lord" (39:6). "And my holy name I will make known in the midst of my people Israel; and I will not let my holy name be profaned anymore; and the nations shall know that I am the Lord, the Holy One in Israel" (39:7). "And I will set my glory among the nations; and all the nations shall see my judgment which I have exe-cuted, and my hand which I have laid on them. The house of Israel shall know that I am the Lord their God from that day forward" (39:21f).

I cite the witness of God in Ezekiel as typical of all the Bible. The uniform witness of Scripture is that the ultimate aim of God in all judgment and all mercy is that his glory might be magnified publicly among all the peoples of the earth. The very meaning of missions and the ultimate aim of all pastoral labor is to display the glory of God in all things for the joy of all peoples.

Now, of course, I am assuming something. I am assuming that knowing the glory of God and enjoying the glory of God is the way that God intends for us to display and magnify the glory of God. My great guide among the mountain ranges of the Scriptures on this matter has been Jonathan Edwards, who says,

> God glorifies Himself toward the creatures . . . in two ways: 1. By appearing to . . . their understanding. 2. In communicating Himself to their hearts, and in their rejoicing and delighting in, and enjoying, the manifestations which He makes of Himself. . . . *God is glorified not only by His glory's being seen, but by its being rejoiced in.* When those that see it delight in it, God is more glorified than if they only see it. His glory is then received by the whole soul, both by the understanding and by the heart. God made the world that He might communicate, and the creature receive, His glory; and that it might [be] received both by the mind and heart. He that testifies his idea of God's glory [does not] glorify God so much as he that testifies also [of] his approbation of it and his delight in it (emphasis added) (Edwards 1994:495).[1]

The greatest need for pastors and missionaries today is that we know and enjoy God – that we see and savor the glory of God. This savoring of God is essential for displaying the glory of God and is the goal of all ministry and missions. Let me illustrate the need.

Charles Misner, a scientific specialist in general relativity theory, expressed Albert Einstein's view of preaching:

> I do see the design of the universe as essentially a religious question. That is, one should have some kind of respect and awe for the whole business. . . . It's very magnificent and should not be taken for

---

[1] See also #87, 332, 679 (Edwards 1994:251-252; 410), (not in the New Haven volume).

granted. In fact, I believe that is why Einstein had so little use for organized religion, although he strikes me as a basically very religious man. *He must have looked at what the preachers said about God and felt that they were blaspheming. He had seen much more majesty than they had ever imagined, and they were just not talking about the real thing* (emphasis added) (1991:63).

Einstein died in 1955, when I was nine years old. If he were alive today, his indictment would be even stronger, because today we have the Hubble telescope sending back infrared images of galaxies (of the fifty billion that may exist) from as far away, they say, as twelve billion light years (twelve billion times six trillion miles). And over against this majesty we have a steady diet on Sunday morning of practical "how to's" and psychological soothing and relational therapy that betrays, sooner or later, that the preachers do not know God as they ought and do not regard him as infinitely glorious and worthy of one focused hour a week. "They are just not talking about the real thing."

Even though God himself has spoken to them and said, "To whom then will you compare me. . . ? [I] bring out their host [all the stars – in all 50 billion galaxies] by number, calling them all by name; by the greatness of his might, and because he is strong in power not one is missing" (Isaiah 40:25-26). Einstein felt instinctively: If the God of the Bible exists, and if pastors and missionaries really know him and count him their greatest treasure, then something is profoundly wrong. "They are just not talking about the real thing."

What is wrong is that knowing God better than we know anything else and treasuring God more than we treasure anything else is not the passion of many pastors and missionaries. We have been driven and deceived into feeling that reading the next book by Barna or Drucker or Schaller is more crucial for ministry than understanding the visions of Ezekiel or the mysteries of God in Romans 9-11 that catapult Paul into song:

O the depth of the riches and wisdom and knowledge of God! How unsearchable are his judgments and how inscrutable his ways! "For who has known the mind of the Lord, or who has been his counselor?" "Or who has given a gift to him that he might be repaid?" For from him and through him and to him are all things. To him be glory for ever. Amen.

The aim of the pastorate and the aim of missions is the glory of God. And knowing God and enjoying God above all things is the indispensable and all-important pathway to this end. That is the fourth reason for making it the centerpiece of my message.

5. One additional reason (out of many!): knowing God and being satisfied in him above all earthly pleasures frees us for the kind of love that will suffer the loss of all things for the sake of every good deed and for the sake of finishing the great commission. The great commission will not be finished without martyrs (Revelation 6:11). And churches will not make God look like our all-sufficient, all-satisfying treasure if pastors and people have all the same values and priorities and lifestyle commitments that everybody around them has. Unless we become a lot more radical in the risks we take and the suffering we embrace, why should anyone believe that our treasure is in heaven – in God – and that he is more valuable than anything here?

The key is being utterly certain and utterly satisfied that "in his presence is fullness of joy and at his right hand are pleasures for evermore" (Psalm 16:11). Or as Paul said, that "to live is Christ and to die is gain" (Philippians 1:21). This truth is the key to the sacrifices demanded by love. No sequence of texts in the Bible makes it plainer than Hebrews 10-13. Here is a portrait of the people we need in the pastorate and on the mission field today.

First, the case of the early Christians in Hebrews 10:34, "You had compassion on the prisoners, and you joyfully accepted the plundering of your property, since you knew that you yourselves had a better possession and an abiding one." They suffered the loss of their property with joy in order to show compassion to the prisoners. How? What released such love? – "Since you knew that you had a better possession and an abiding one." They treasured God more than anything.

Then the case of Moses in Hebrews 11:24-26, "By faith Moses, when he was grown up, refused to be called the son of Pharaoh's daughter, choosing rather to share ill-treatment with the people of God than to enjoy the fleeting pleasures of sin. He considered abuse suffered for the Christ greater wealth than the treasures of Egypt, for he looked to the reward." He suffered the loss of all that Egypt could offer in order to embrace suffering as a leader of the people of God. How? What released such love? – "For he looked to the reward." He treasured God more than anything in Egypt.

Then the case of Jesus Christ himself in Hebrews 12:2, " who for the joy that was set before him endured the cross, despising the shame, and is seated at the right hand of the throne of God." Jesus embraced the suffering of the cross and gave shame no sway in his life so that he might die for his people. How? What released such love? – "For the joy that was set before him."

Finally, the case of the readers – you and me – in Hebrews 13:12-14, "Jesus suffered outside the gate in order to sanctify the people through his own blood. Therefore, let us go forth to him outside the camp and bear the abuse he endured. For here we have no lasting city, but we seek the city which is to come." Here is a call to every Christian, but especially to every pastor and every missionary: Let us go to him outside the securities and comforts of the camp and bear abuse for the sake of his name. How? What will release such love? For "here we have no lasting city, but we seek a city which is to come." The city of this world is not our satisfaction, God is.

Where does the love come from that can suffer the loss of all things and make plain to the world that God is gloriously more to be desired than life itself? It comes from being certain and being satisfied that God is a better possession than all our goods. It comes from the surety that the reward of his presence is vastly better than the fleeting pleasures of Egypt. It comes from the assurance that the suffering of our cross is not worth comparing to the joy set before us, and that the city which is to come will last forever and will be the habitation of God.

In other words, the lever that unstops the river of love for pastors and missionaries is knowing God better than you know anything and delighting in God more than you delight in anything. Knowing God is the greatest need in the next generation of pastors and missionaries, just as it has always been the greatest need of every generation of pastors and missionaries.

Concluding Exhortations

Someone might ask me now, "Why didn't you talk about your assigned topic, *training* the next generation of pastors and missionaries?" If I took the few minutes that I have to talk to you – and I may never stand before you again – and devoted my time to giving you my list of practical ideas about how I think theological education should be done, I would betray one of my basic convictions, namely, that knowing and being *comes before* doing and *shapes* doing. The problem we face in theological education is not technique, it is not curriculum, it is not time, it is not the busy-ness of our students; it is not pragmatic administrators; it is not lack of funds for research. The problem is that we do not have an all-consuming passion to know God in the fullness of his perfections and to enjoy him more than we enjoy anything in the world. Until your studies of God's word and God's ways fill your head with wonders and fill your heart with joy and your life with love, students will probably leave your classes feeling like they need some course on spirituality or some church experience to make the magic thing happen.

So I would only close with three exhortations and look to God to do the rest.

1. First, in all your studies seek to know God, the Creator of the universe, the Ruler of all things, the Savior of the world, the Sustainer of all being, the Guide of all history. Seek to know him as a Person with a character. Labor not to treat him as an idea. Fix your gaze on his glory in the face of Christ. Resist the vague, cloudy image and strive for a clear, sharp spiritual portrait with lines and contours that make him this and not that. Ask with every chapter of Scripture and every article and every book you read: what can I learn of my God from this? Where is God in this? Moreover, resist the addiction of methodological narcissism that never finds the treasure because you never look up from the map.

2. Second, saturate your studies with the prayer of Psalm 90:14, "Satisfy us in the morning with thy steadfast love, that we may rejoice and be glad all our days." Plead with God that he not leave you unmoved by the glories revealed every day in the sky, and in the Scriptures. When you are drawn away from the greatness of your work by some silly financial scheme, pray earnestly the words of Psalm 119:36, "Incline my heart to thy testimonies, and not to gain!" When you feel the page go blank in your hand, plead the words of Psalm 119:18,

"Open my eyes, that I may behold wondrous things out of thy law."

Paul said in 2 Corinthians 1:24 that he was a worker with them for their joy." Spiritual joy – joy in God – is not native to the fallen human heart. It is a fight from start to finish. So be like Warfield when it comes to mingling prayer and study. When he was challenged that "ten minutes on your knees will give you a truer, deeper, more operative knowledge of God than ten hours over your books." "What!" he responded, "than ten hours over your books, on your knees" (Warfield 1983:263)? In addition, be like John Owen who knew the secret of communion with God in the very act of study and theological controversy.

When the heart is cast indeed into the mould of the doctrine that the mind embraceth – when the evidence and necessity of the truth abides in us – when not the sense of the words only is in our heads, but the sense of the thing abides in our hearts – when we have communion with God in the doctrine we contend for – then shall we be garrisoned by the grace of God against all the assaults of men" (Gould 1965: lxiii-lxiv).

I would add, then will our students be set aflame by the authenticity of our knowledge of God and the intensity of our delight in him.

3. Finally, "take your share of sufferings as a good soldier of Christ Jesus" (2 Timothy 2:3). Do not begrudge the day of your affliction. Luther noticed that, in Psalm 119, there were three rules for understanding the Scriptures and knowing God: *Oratio, meditatio, tentatio* (Prayer, meditation, trial) (Plass 1959:1359). And trials (*Anfechtungen*) he called the "touchstone." Psalm 119:67,71, "Before I was afflicted I went astray, but now I keep Thy word. . . . It is good for me that I was afflicted, that I may learn Thy statutes." Do not begrudge your sufferings in the school of Christ, he said, "[They] teach you not only to know and understand but also to experience how right, how true, how sweet, how lovely, how mighty, how comforting God's word is: it is wisdom supreme" (Plass 1959:1360)

He proved the value of trials repeatedly in his own experience. He writes,

> For as soon as God's Word becomes known through you," he says, "the devil will afflict you, will make a real doctor of you, and will teach you by his temptations to seek and to love God's Word. For I myself . . . owe my papists many thanks for so beating, pressing, and frightening me through the devil's raging that they have turned me into a fairly good theologian, driving me to a goal I should never have reached" (Plass 1959:1360.

Have not most of us in this room seen our God more clearly and loved him more dearly because of the meditations and prayers and sufferings of this great man! And so it can be with you. May God make it so – for the sake of the pastors and the missionaries and the churches and the nations, who need to know God and enjoy him above all things.

Bibliography

Edwards, Jonathan
    1994   "The Miscellanies," in Thomas Schafer (ed.),
          The Works of Jonathan Edwards, vol. 13. New
          Haven: Yale University Press, pp. 495.

Gould, William, (Ed.)
    1965   *Works of John Owen*, Vol. 1. Edinburgh: Ban-
          ner of Truth Trust.

Misner, Charles
    1991   *First Things.* 18:63.

Plass Ewald M., (Ed.)
    1959   *What Luther Says*, Vol. 3 St. Louis: Concordia
          Publishing House,

Schafer, Thomas, (Ed.)
    1994   "The "Miscellanies," *The Works of Jonathan
          Edwards*, Vol. 13. Pp. 251-252, 410, 495,

Warfield, B. B
    1983"The Religious Life of Theological Students," in
          The Princeton Theology, ed. by Mark Noll
          Grand Rapids: Baker Book House.

Teaching Them to Obey All Things:
A View from the Matthean Account of the Great Commission

Michael J. Wilkins

Back in the 1960's, prior to my conversion to Christ, I was a drill sergeant in the Army, training men and women for combat roles in Vietnam. Before long, it was my turn to be sent to Vietnam. After serving for a year with an airborne infantry combat unit, I came back a very different kind of person, and I was a very different kind of drill sergeant. I had much the same content as I trained new men and women, but that year in combat changed the way that I applied the content to their training.

In analogous fashion, I come to you by invitation with two background elements that I hope will contribute to the theme of this book: "Teaching Them To Obey All Things." First, my academic and research interest has focused on Jesus and His disciples, the theme of master-disciple relationships in antiquity, and Matthew's gospel. I have spent much of the past twenty years studying and writing on these themes.[1] Second, I have over twenty years of "combat" experience in the pastorate, evangelism, and mission teaching that helps me to understand the application of my research. So I come to you as one who is passionate about this theme of making disciples who are taught to obey all things that Jesus instructed the original disciples.

The Question in Fulfilling the Great Commission

Recently, I have been called into a variety of settings as a consultant to missiologists, educators, and pastors who are committed to fulfilling the Great Commission of Matthew 28. These groups have settled themselves into the task, and have marvelous strategies for accomplishing their objectives.

I enter the discussion not as one to critique their *methods*, but rather as one who hopes to help clarify their *objectives* in the light a *biblical theology of discipleship*. As simplistic as this may sound, the most basic of all questions needs to be reexamined. I could put the most basic question this way, *What is a "disciple," how does one become a disciple, and how does this relate to "discipling" and "discipleship"?* And especially, in the light of our theme—"Teaching them to obey all things"—we need to ask specifically, *whom are we teaching to obey what?*

For example, Sherwood Lingenfelter elsewhere in this book assesses the relationship between the Christian University and the Church, asking the question whether they were "Prisoners of Culture or Partners for the Great Commission?" It is a

---

[1] For extended discussion, see Wilkins (1988; 1992a; 1992b; 1992c, 1995, 1997). See also the forthcoming volumes on Matthew's gospel: Wilkins (n.d.a; n.d.b)

marvelous paper, but one of my criticisms in its development related to his use of terminology. Significant for the underlying thesis of his paper is his concept and use of the terms "convert" and "disciple," and further, the use of the expressions "world evangelization" and "making disciples." At one place he states: "Within that same context the local community invites new believers to join in an adventure of pilgrimage, which serves to transform those *converts* into *disciples* of Jesus Christ." In another place he discusses the relationship between, "The Church, the University and Culture," by asking the question: "How can and should these two institutions, united in their commitment to Jesus Christ and to His mission, partner in the task of *world Evangelization* and *making disciples?*"

Some underlying assumptions here need to be given strict attention. We see here what is a widely held use of terminology (especially in older parachurch circles) that suggests there is two-stage process in the Christian life: a person becomes a *Christian (convert),* and then at a later stage of commitment becomes a *disciple.* So articulated, a *convert,* when committed, becomes a *disciple*; a person who is evangelized later is made into a disciple.

However, this perspective does not seem to square with the intent of the Great Commission: we are to make disciples of all *nations*, not make disciples of *Christians.*

On the other hand, Lingenfelter states later in the same paper,

> The task for university and church, then, is to lead the next generation to conversion and transformation in the Lord Jesus Christ. Conversion occurs when people hear the gospel, understand it, and receive Christ; transformation occurs when people engage the universal Word of God, and follow the Living Word to become like Christ.

This statement is an excellent description of the relationship between conversion and growth, but my question to him was, how does this square with your earlier statement and understanding of "making disciples"? There seems to be a confusion of concepts, which can lead to a confusion of methods.

In another fascinating study, entitled *The Missionary Movement in Christian History*, Andrew Walls attempts to draw an analogy to Christian disciple making in ancient rabbinic models. He looks to the ancient rabbis, such as Rabbi Johannan ben Zakkai, for whom a "disciple" was a "student" who was in training to become a "rabbi" (Walls 1996:49-50). However, Jesus himself said to his disciples that they were not to be called "rabbi," since they will always be disciples of Jesus (see Mt 23:8-12). So, Walls' comparison of Rabbi Zakkai's disciples to Christian discipleship is only a partially appropriate analogy.

We all need a clearer historical perspective of master-disciple relationships generally in the ancient world, and then how Jesus' form of discipleship was continuous and yet discontinuous with those other forms. In Jesus' distinctive form of discipleship, a disciple is always becoming more fully a disciple, which indicates that every disciple is in the process of discipleship. When Walls (and others) speaks of *world evangelization and making disciples,* he seems to make a distinction between those expressions. Actually, they both address the beginning point of conversion, but how does that relate to "discipleship"? "Discipleship" is the on-going process of growth as a disciple. How does that relate to "making disciples"? One could accurately speak of world evangelization and discipleship, if one does not separate "making disciples" from discipleship. There is much fuzzy use of terminology, as we will now see.

Discipleship Models

A disciple of Jesus—a phenomenon simple to appreciate, yet incredibly complex to comprehend fully. In the last thirty-plus years, actually since the end of World War II, a virtual flood of discipleship studies has swept over the church. Yet people may be more confused now than ever. The reason? No consensus reigns in understanding what Jesus was doing, and what we should be doing, in making disciples. What is a disciple of Jesus? What should we be like as disciples? Who are to be the objects of discipleship?

Different answers are given to those questions today. As we look at the various responses, we can see several models of discipleship that result from those who have studied the biblical data. While some diversity is to be found within each model, distinct characteristics mark each one. I have isolated five models here (Wilkins 1992 and 1997). Each view of discipleship has both strengths and weaknesses. Which of the following discipleship models represents your own understanding of what it means to be a disciple of Jesus?

Disciples are Learners

Some suggest that a disciple is a learner who follows a great teacher. They suggest that the term "disciple" refers to one who puts himself / herself under the teaching authority of a great teacher, but that it has no reference to whether or not the person is a Christian (E.g., Ryrie 1989; Blauvelt 1986:41; Wuest 1966:25). For example, one author suggests the following general definition for a "disciple": "a follower of a teacher and his teachings, involving, in Bible times, traveling with that teacher wherever he went" (Ryrie 1989:155). Another author states,

> The word merely refers to one who puts himself
> under the teaching of someone else and learns
> from him. . . . In the case of the word 'disciple'
> the context must rule as to whether the particu-
> lar disciple mentioned is saved or unsaved, not
> the word itself (Wuest 1966:25).

This view is instructive because it emphasizes the early linguistic relationship between the noun "disciple" and the verb "learn." Further, this model emphasizes the fact that a variety of different kinds of followers were called disciples. In the gospels we find that a disciple may be a believer in Jesus Christ, or may be a follower of someone else, such as John the Baptist (Jn 1:35) or the Pharisees (Mt 22: 15-16).[2] This model also indicates the historical development of the "disciples" of Jesus within His earthly ministry. At an early point in Jesus' ministry, people became "disciples" of Jesus even though it was revealed later that they were not believers.

This model has two basic difficulties. In the first place, the Greek term for "disciple" ($\mu\alpha\theta\eta\tau\eta\varsigma$) is used in Scripture in a manner different than simply to designate a "learner." For example, the followers of John the Baptist are more like adherents to the prophet and the movement surrounding him than students of a teacher. The second difficulty appears when we note the normal use of the term disciple in the book of Acts. In Acts the term is normally used without any qualifiers simply to designate "Christians." For example, Acts 11:26 says

---

[2] A variation on this view suggests that discipleship was appropriate to Jesus' day, while people could follow Him around physically. However, today, since Jesus has ascended to heaven and believers can no longer follow Him physically, it is inappropriate for us to speak of ourselves as disciples. See for example Rickards (1976:5-18 and Fisher (1972).

simply "the disciples were called Christians first at Antioch."
The disciple appears to be more than simply a learner.

Disciples are Committed Believers.

Several others suggest that a disciple is a committed
Christian, a believer who has made a commitment to follow
Jesus and obey his radical demands of discipleship (See
Coppedge 1989:40-42; Eims 1978:61ff, 83ff, 181-188;
Henrichsen 1974:18, 40; Hodges 1981:36-45; 1989:67f., 87;
Kuhne 1978:15; Ortiz 1975:9; Pentecost 1971:14; Powell
1982:11-12; Sanders 1962:108-109). One author answers one
of our original questions by saying, "What is a disciple? A
disciple is one who follows Jesus Christ. But because we are
Christians does not necessarily mean we are his disciples, even
though we are members of his kingdom. Following Christ
means acknowledging Him as Lord; it means serving Him as a
slave" (Ortiz 1975:9). Another author similarly asserts that
"there is a vast difference between being saved and being a
disciple. Not all men who are saved are disciples although all
who are disciples are saved. In discussing the question of
discipleship, we are not dealing with a man's salvation. We
are dealing with a man's relationship to Jesus Christ as his
teacher, his Master, and his Lord." (Pentecost 1971:14).

This discipleship model emphasizes Jesus' radical
challenge to count the cost of discipleship. It points to the
small group of disciples who followed Jesus and emphasizes
that when they left all to follow Jesus they became models of a
higher spiritual calling. It compares Jesus' disciples with the
crowds around Him, and concludes that the difference lay in
responding to Jesus' call to commitment. The beginning point
of discipleship, therefore, was commitment. This model
suggests that there are two levels within the church today:
disciples and ordinary believers. A disciple is a more commit-

ted Christian than the average Christian. This model of discipleship is quite widespread, being found in several different forms. This model also encounters difficulties. One difficulty lies in the interpretation of Jesus' discipleship messages and the spiritual nature of the audiences to whom He directs His messages. For example, when Jesus gives a message directed to the "crowds" which calls them to count the cost before they become His "disciples" (Lk 14:25-33), or when He tells the rich young ruler to go give all his riches to the poor before he can enter into eternal life (Mt 19:16-22), what is the spiritual nature of the crowds? of the ruler? Are they already believers or not? What is the meaning of the message? Is it a call to deeper commitment, or a call to salvation?

Disciples are Ministers

Another model of discipleship suggests that a disciple is the believer who has been called out from among lay believers in order to enter into ministry. Discipleship means to be with Jesus in order to learn from Him how to serve the crowd, the church (See Degenhardt 1965; Schelkle 1965; Sheridan 1973:235-255; Minear 1974:28-44; Thysman 1974; Lohfink 1984:31-33; Trakatellis 1985:271-285; Sweetland 1987). Focusing on the distinction between the crowds and the disciples in the gospel of Matthew, one author maintains that because the crowds represent followers of Jesus, His disciples "form a much more limited and specialized group than is usually supposed. They are those chosen and trained as successors to Jesus in His role as exorcist, healer, prophet, and teacher" (Minear 1974:31). Another author has a similar perspective when he says, "Everyone is called to participate in the reign of God, but only some are called to be followers of Jesus...The disciple of Jesus is called to serve other members of the eschatological community (cf. Mk 1:31) and, through the missionary enterprise, those outside the community as well (Sweetland 1987:17, 35).

This model results from observing the close relationship of the twelve disciples with Jesus in His ministry, and their later ministry to the early church.[3] It concludes that the radical call to discipleship was intended to be a model of how a believer today is called into ministry. This model of discipleship is also quite widespread, found especially in church traditions that emphasize a hierarchical order within their denominational structure, and usually emphasizes a distinction between the clergy and the laity. This model is also employed quite often by those who point to Jesus' training of His disciples as examples of how Christian leaders should be trained today (Chandapilla 1974; Drushal 1988:47-62; Eims 1978:61ff, 83ff, 181-188).

The same difficulties encountered in the second model apply here, but an additional difficulty is encountered because the twelve disciples are often used as the example. A problem arises when a clear distinction is not made between the Twelve as *disciples* and the Twelve as *apostles*. Most scholars agree that the terms "disciple" and "apostle" point to significantly different aspects of the Twelve. When do the Twelve function as *disciples* and when do they function as *apostles*? That is a crucial distinction for us to make.

---

[3]This is the implication of Gerd Theissen's study, when he distinguishes "wandering charismatics" (the disciples) from the "sympathizers" in the local communities (Theissen 1978:8-23).

Disciples are Converts with
Discipleship Following

Others propose that disciples are converts to Jesus, and that discipleship comes later. A disciple is one who has been evangelized, and the later process of growth is called "perfecting" or "discipleship" (McGavran and Arn 1973; Wagner 1974:79). One author says, "Church-growth men use the word 'discipling' to mean the initial step by which people come to Christ and become baptized believers. We go on and say that the second part of church growth is 'perfecting' or growing in grace" (McGavran and Arn 1973:80). Another leader in the church growth movement similarly declares that

> a person is not a disciple just because he has been born in a Christian country or in many cases, even if he is a church member. . . . The basic meaning of disciple in the New Testament is equivalent to a true, born-again Christian. . . . Some have confused 'making disciples' with 'discipleship' (Wagner 1974:79-80; 1973:285-293). Making disciples is the right goal of evangelism and missions according to the Great Commission. Once disciples are made, they then begin the lifetime road of discipleship.

This discipleship model emphasizes that the meaning of the Great Commission's imperative, "make disciples" of all the nations, is to make converts out of non-Christians. It stresses conversion as the beginning point of the Christian life, which means that conversion is the beginning point of becoming a disciple. Further, it recognizes that the term disciple is the most common designation for a "believer" in the Gospels and Acts.

The difficulty with this model is that it seems to separate the imperative of the Great Commission, "make disciples," from the following participles, "baptizing" and "teaching." The discrepancy may lie in the use of the English terms disciple, discipling, and discipleship. Is it possible to be a *disciple* without being on the road of *discipleship*? Is *discipling* different than *discipleship*?

Disciples are Converts
In the Process of Discipleship

Still others suggest that a disciple is the true believer who enters the life of discipleship at the time of conversion. In this model, as with the prior view, conversion is the beginning point of becoming a disciple. But this model stresses that discipleship is vitally linked to conversion as the natural result. Discipleship is not a second step in the Christian life, but rather is synonymous with the Christian life. At conversion one becomes a disciple of Jesus, and the process of growth as a Christian is called discipleship. For one author, to speak of entrance to the Christian life without recognizing the fact that it also means entrance into the life of discipleship, is to cheapen the grace of God. He says,

> Cheap grace is grace without discipleship, grace without the cross, grace without Jesus Christ, living and incarnate.... Happy are they who know that discipleship means the life which springs from grace, and that grace simply means discipleship. Happy are they who have become Christians in this sense of the word. For them the word of grace has proved a fount of mercy (Bonhoffer 1963:47, 60).

Similarly, another author asserts that

> ... discipleship is not a supposed second step in Christianity, as if one first becomes a believer in Jesus and then, if he chooses, a disciple. From the beginning, discipleship is involved in what it means to be a Christian" (Boice 1986:16).

This model of discipleship emphasizes that as Jesus called men and women to Him, and as He sent His disciples out to make other disciples, He was calling men and women into a saving relationship with himself which *would* make a difference in the new disciple's life. Therefore, Jesus' purpose in the Great Commission included both conversion and growth; i.e., "making disciples" meant that one became a disciple at the moment of conversion and that growth in discipleship was the natural result of the new disciple's life. As Jesus sent the disciples out to make converts, the demands for discipleship made by Jesus in His teaching were directed not only to His first followers, but to all true believers. This model of discipleship is quite widespread, appearing in several different contexts.

This latter model is the most consistent with early Christian usage. It is not without its problems, which I have addressed elsewhere, but once we attempt to overcome those difficulties, the definitions become clearer.

Overcoming Difficulties
In Discipleship Studies

Each of these models is represented by sincere men and women of God who are serious about heeding Jesus' call to discipleship. Each model has correctly accented--at least partially--biblical teaching. Why the different models? Why the problems?

These various models have come about as people have attempted to get at the heart of Jesus' conception of discipleship and then have attempted to apply that conception to present-day ministry. The major problems surface when each model attempts to reconcile seemingly contradictory passages. These problems especially occur in four different contexts:

1. when reconciling Jesus' gracious call to discipleship with His stringent demands of discipleship,
2. when reconciling Jesus' ministry to the crowds with His ministry to the disciples,
3. when reconciling general discipleship passages with the role of the Twelve, or
4. when reconciling the portrait of disciples in the Gospels with their occurrence in the Acts and the non-occurrence of the term "disciple" in the Epistles.

The strength of each discipleship model lies in its emphasis upon a particular type of discipleship teaching. The weakness of each discipleship model lies in its de-emphasis of other types of discipleship teachings. Several observations should be kept in mind.

Enter Jesus' First Century World
Before Following Him In Ours

Many difficulties can be overcome if we try to understand, first, the dynamics of discipleship as they occurred within the cultural setting of the first century, before we try to apply those dynamics to our own ministries and lives.

With each new class studying the gospels I like to perform a fun exercise. I take a few volunteers and ask them to stand on the platform in the large auditorium in which the stand on the platform in the large auditorium in which the lecture is held. I inform them that when I was a drill sergeant in the Army one of my responsibilities was to teach the new recruits how to march. "So," I tell them, "I'm going to teach you how to march through the gospels." As the volunteers line up, I call out, "Forward, march!" They go a few steps and then, after they stop, I ask them to tell me which foot they started out on. Some say right, some say left, others do not remember! Then I tell them how it is that military people always stay in step with each other: They always start out on the same foot, and that is always the *left* foot.

The application to discipleship study? Basic hermeneutics. When walking through the gospels, we must always start out on the same foot, the left foot. The left foot represents starting with understanding the gospels first from the standpoint of what was happening in the first century as Jesus walked and taught all around Palestine. What did the discipleship saying of Jesus mean to those who first heard it while Jesus was with them? What was Jesus' intention in His first century setting? Then, after our left foot is solidly planted, we can go to the right foot, which represents applying the passage to our lives today.

Once we understand what the discipleship sayings meant to Jesus' original audience we will be able to take the essential principles and apply them to our own setting. If we start with the right foot, we run the risk of reading our own set of values and circumstances back into the gospels. We must allow the original intention to interpret our own application.[4] Several difficulties found in the above discipleship models result from

---

[4]On the technical side, this reveals my hermeneutical approach, which flies in the face of much contemporary hermeneutics, especially certain literary-critical approaches that deny the reality of authorial intention.

starting with the right foot! We must be as clear as possible in our understanding of what it meant to follow Jesus in the first century if we are to be clear about what it means to follow Jesus in our modern world. We must start with the left foot!

Identify With the Appropriate Audience

Several difficulties in the discipleship models result from a lack of precision concerning the audiences who heard Jesus' teachings. Even as preachers and teachers today try to know their audiences so that they can minister to appropriate needs and circumstances, Jesus gave teaching that was appropriate for the spiritual state of His listeners. He gave teaching and offered invitations that were uniquely suited for the particular audience that surrounded Him. For example, in His parabolic discourse Jesus gave parables which had one intention for the crowds (hiding the mysteries of the kingdom) and one intention for the disciples (revealing the mysteries of the kingdom) (cf. Mt 13:1-2, 10-17; Mk 4:1-12). If we do not specify precisely the audience, we will not identify with the audience and teaching that is appropriate for our spiritual state. Overall, discipleship teaching that is directed to the *crowds* deals with the act of becoming a disciple (evangelism), whereas teaching directed to the *disciples* deals with growth in discipleship (Christian growth).

Distinguish Between The Twelve As Disciples And The Twelve As Apostles

Throughout the history of the church a certain tension has been felt when looking at the lives of the Twelve. Special comfort has been drawn from recognizing that they are really not that much different than we are. If Jesus could make something of their lives, then He certainly can with ours! Yet, on the other hand, they seem so different than we are. The Twelve were used in the founding of the early church in ways not duplicated. When have we experienced such a ministry?

This points to a special difficulty which was observed when the Twelve were used in the above discipleship models: a clear distinction was not always made between the Twelve as disciples and the Twelve as apostles. Although the Twelve were both disciples and apostles, scholars agree that the terms "disciple" and "apostle" point to significantly different aspects. Indeed, while in the gospels the Twelve are usually called disciples, in the book of Acts the Twelve are never called disciples. In Acts they are only called apostles, to emphasize their leadership role in the early church. Therefore, our preliminary observation is that as disciples the Twelve give us an example of how Jesus works with all believers, and as apostles the Twelve give us an example of how Jesus works with leaders of the church.

Acts Helps Interpret Meaning
Of Discipleship Terminology

Several difficulties have already been mentioned which are best resolved when we allow the book of Acts to help us interpret the meaning of discipleship terminology. By the time of the early church, as recorded in Acts, the term disciple was synonymous with the true believer in Jesus. Luke speaks of the multitude of "believers" in Acts 4:32 and the multitude or congregation of "disciples," in Acts 6:2. In Luke's writings, the expressions "those who believe" and "the disciples" signify the same group of people (cf. Acts. 6:7; 9:26; 11:26; 14:21-22). Acts clarifies for us that the common word for a believer in the early church was *disciple*. *Disciple* was also the earliest synonym for Christian (Acts 11:26).

Luke also clarifies the use of the terms disciple and apostle with reference to the Twelve. Unlike in his gospel, Luke in Acts never calls the Twelve "disciples." Since the Twelve are only called apostles in Acts, Luke stresses the distinctive role that the Twelve played as apostles in the early church. In Acts the Twelve are called apostles to accentuate their leadership role, and the common name for a believer is disciple.

The book of Acts also helps us see the transitions that took place in discipleship terminology. In the gospels "disciple" is the most common word used to designate the followers of Jesus, but the word does not occur at all in the epistles. Instead, other terms, such as *brother/sister*, *saints*, *believers*, and *Christians* came to be the prominent terms used to designate followers of Jesus. Although the *term* disciple does not occur in the epistles, the book of Acts allows us to see that at the same basic historical period as the writing of the epistles the terminology and concept of discipleship flourished.

Disciples in Historical Context

Today the English terms, "disciple," "discipleship," and "discipling," imply different things to different users, depending upon the background of the user and the context of use. This confusion is part of the problem behind the different discipleship models in existence today. We need standardized definitions of these very important terms, or else we will not be talking about the same things. As we define them we must keep in mind three categories of usage: 1) How were the terms used in the general context of the first century world? 2) How were the terms used in the biblical context? and 3) How are the terms used today?

Behind our English word "disciple" lie the Latin terms *discipulus* (masculine) / *discipula* (feminine) and the Greek words μαθητης (masculine) / μαθητρια (feminine). Since these Latin and Greek nouns have a linguistic relationship to verbs for "learn"[5] in their earliest history, they were used to refer to "learners" and "students." Eventually the meaning broadened so that they were used to refer to "adherents" of a great master. The Greek term especially, by the late Hellenistic period during the time when the NT was written, was used increasingly to refer to an adherent. The type of adherence was determined by the master, but it ranged from being the companion of a philosopher, to being the follower of a great thinker and master of the past, to being the devotee of a religious figure. Therefore, in most common usage, whether in the Roman or Greek world, a "disciple" was a person who was committed to a significant master.[6] To say that a disciple is a learner is true, but this over emphasizes one aspect of the term's meaning and misses what the term primarily signified in the New Testament era. For example, the disciples of John the Baptist were not primarily learners, since John was not primarily a teacher, but a prophet. A disciple was one who made a life commitment to a particular master and his way of life. The type of "disciple" and the corresponding life of "discipleship" was determined by the type of master, but commitment to the master and his ways was central.

Therefore, it is not enough to ask "what is a disciple?" Rather, we must ask, a disciple of whom, and at what period of time? A disciple of Jesus during His earthly ministry was one who made a life commitment to Him. Among those who made an early commitment were some who gave up following Jesus around when His Way proved to be different than what they

---

[5]Latin, *discere*; Greek, *μανθανειν.*
[6]For a discussion of the classical and Hellenistic background to these terms see Wilkins (1988:11-42).

had expected (cf. Jn 6:60-66). There was also one who finally was proven to be a false disciple (Judas Iscariot). But as Jesus increasingly revealed His messianic identity, those who believed in Him claimed Him as their Savior and God, and those who remained with Him were Jesus' true disciples.

Definitions

We are now prepared to give basic definitions for some crucial terms. These definitions will be fleshed out as we go through the biblical data, but at this point they should provide some orientation for our journey.

Disciple

When we come to the New Testament, the primary word for "disciple" was the Greek term μαθητης (pl. μαθηται). The definition of a disciple must be given in a general sense as well as in a specific sense with reference to what Jesus intended His disciples be. This specific sense is seen most clearly toward the end of Jesus' earthly ministry, in the Great Commission, and in the use of the early church Acts (Louw and Nida 1988:I:471).

In the general sense, we may define a disciple as a committed follower of a great master. The general sense of the term has two common applications. 1) It was used in non-referentially to distinguish the disciple from the teacher (Mt 10:24-25; Lk 6:40). 2) It was also used to designate the followers of a great leader or movement. Thus, we find disciples of Moses (Jn 9:28), disciples of the Pharisees (Mt 22:16; Mk 2:18; Lk 5:33), disciples of John the Baptist (Mt 9:14; Mk 2:18; Lk 5:33; Jn 1:35; 3:25), and disciples of Jesus.

In the specific sense, a disciple of Jesus is one who has come to Jesus for eternal life, has claimed Jesus as Savior and

God, and has embarked upon the life of following Jesus. "Disciple" is the primary term used in the Gospels to refer to Jesus' followers, and is a common referent for those known in the early church as "believers," "Christians," "brothers/ sisters," "those of the Way," or "saints," although each term focuses upon different aspects of the individual's relationship with Jesus and others of the faith. The term was used most frequently in this specific sense; at least 230 times in the Gospels (e.g., Jn 6:66-72) and 28 times in Acts (e.g., Acts 9:1, 10, 19-20).

The English term "disciple" has undergone much the same development as did the Greek and Latin terms. Although "disciple" has roots in the Latin noun *discipulus,* which is related to the verb "to learn" *(discere),* present English usage only secondarily associates "disciple" with a person who is a student or learner. The English noun is now associated most often with the words "supporter, follower, or adherent." The word disciple in contemporary usage "pertains exclusively to someone devoted to a master or patron. Most strictly, *disciple* suggests a religious situation: the *disciples* of Buddha who codified his teachings. In general usage, the word refers to someone's ardent advocacy of any prominent figure or theory: an early disciple of Freud. . ." (Hayakawa 1979:596-597). The words supporter or follower are perhaps the nearest synonyms: "Supporter is the general term for one who allies himself with a cause or shows allegiance to its leader...Follower and disciple are related in that they emphasize devotion to a leader rather than to its doctrine or cause" (Hayakawa 1979:607). Hence, in the Christian sense, a disciple of Jesus is one who has come to Him for eternal life, has claimed Him as Savior and God, and has embarked upon the life of following Him.

Discipleship and Discipling

The terms "discipleship" and "discipling," are English word derived, obviously, from disciple. The nearest equivalent to these expressions in the New Testament is the verbal form μαθητευω, "make or become disciples," which occurs only four times (Mt 13:52; 27:57; 28:19; Acts 14:21). In common parlance, "discipleship" and "discipling" today relate to the ongoing life of the disciple. "Discipleship" is the ongoing process of growth as a disciple. "Discipling" implies the responsibility of disciples helping one another to grow as disciples. Therefore, discipleship and discipling can be narrowly understood as a technical discussion of the historical master-disciple relationship, but these terms can also be understood in a broader way as Christian experience, that is, the self-understanding of the early Christian believers as believers: what such a way of life requires, implies, and entails (Segovia 1985:2). Therefore, when we speak of Christian discipleship and discipling we are speaking of what it means to grow as a Christian in every area of life. Since "disciple" is a common referent for "Christian," discipleship and discipling imply the process of becoming like Jesus Christ. Discipleship and discipling mean living a fully human life in this world in union with Jesus Christ and growing in conformity to His image.

This definition is much broader than what many conceive of discipleship and discipling. Most conceive of discipleship as a more narrow program or training time. But when Jesus says that "a disciple is not above his teacher, but everyone when fully trained, will be like his teacher" (Lk 6:40), He enunciates a principle common to all master-disciple relationships: a disciple is involved in a natural process which will bring him or her to be like the master. That principle is central to biblical discipleship: in this life a disciple is always in a discipleship process, the process of becoming like the Master, Jesus. This establishes a link between explicit discipleship sayings in the Gospels and Acts with similar concepts in the rest of the New Testament, such as Paul's statement that the goal of God's calling in the life of the Christian is to be conformed to the image of Christ (cf. Rom 8:28-30). As one author says, "Indeed, full discipleship and full Christlikeness are the same thing" (Parker n.d.:845). Hence, all who are called to be His disciples are in the process of becoming more like the Master, Jesus Christ, i.e., discipleship. Each disciple also has the responsibility to be involved in helping other disciples grow, i.e., discipling.

An Overview of the Great Commission
(Mt 28:18-20)

As Jesus concluded His earthly ministry, He explicitly commanded His disciples to address themselves to worldwide evangelism. At the heart of the church's commission is the command to "make disciples." Jesus had focussed His ministry on making disciples, and His goal was for the disciples to make what He had made of them. Jesus is the supreme Lord and Teacher of the historical disciples and the post-resurrection community. Matthew's gospel is at least in part a manual on discipleship. With all of the major discourses directed to the disciples, with the term arranged in such a way that most sayings directed to the disciples have become teachings on discipleship, with the positive yet realistic enhancement of the picture of the disciples, and with disciples called and trained and commissioned to carry out the climactic mandate to "make disciples" in the conclusion of the gospel, Matthew has constructed a gospel that will equip the disciples in the making of disciples (Wilkins 1988:172). Through the "Great Commission" of Mt 28:16-20 Jesus focuses his followers on the ongoing importance of discipleship through the ages (Wilkins 1992b, 1992a: 188-191).

"Make disciples of all the nations"

Make Disciples

Jesus committed his earthly ministry to "making disciples" within Israel (cf. Jn 4:1), and he commissions his disciples to "make disciples" among the nations (Mt 28:16-20). The obvious meaning of "making disciples" is to proclaim the gospel message among those who have not yet received forgiveness of sins (Lk 24:46-47; Jn 20:21). The command[7] finds remarkable verbal fulfillment in the activities of the early church (e.g., Acts 14:21), where they went from Jerusalem to Judea, to Samaria, to the ends of the earth proclaiming the message of Jesus and making disciples. In the early church, to believe in the gospel message was to become a disciple (cf. Acts 4:32 with 6:2). The injunction of the Great Commission is given at least to the Eleven (cf. Mt 28:16), but in their own role as disciples they are paradigms for all disciples (Carson 1984:596). As he addresses the disciples and commands them to "make disciples of all the nations,"[8] Jesus is telling them to make more of what he has made of them.

All The Nations

The object of "making disciples" is *"all the nations."* All nations, now including both the Gentiles and Jews, receive

---

[7]Μαθητευω occurs as an aorist active imperative.

[8]μαθητευσατε παντα τα εθνη.

the opportunity to become Jesus' disciples. Although some suggest that "all the nations" means only "Gentiles," not the "Jews," since Matthew invariably only refers to Gentiles by this title (e.g., Kio 1990:230-239 and Hare 1967), most recognize Matthew's overall intention is to include the Jews. The full expression "all the nations" is used four times in Matthew in settings which more naturally include all peoples, including Jews (Mt 24:9, 14; 25:32), including here. Most importantly, Matthew returns in the commission to the universal theme of the introductory verse to the gospel (Mt 1:1). There the blessings promised through Abraham and through him to all people of the earth (Gen 12:3) are said now be fulfilled in Jesus the Messiah. When the original covenant promise to Abraham (Gen 12:3) is reiterated in Genesis 18:18; 22:18, the Septuagint uses the same words found in Mt 28:19: "all the nations." Matthew's purpose has been to show how Jesus is the Messiah of all peoples. His theme of universal salvation through Jesus (e.g., Mt 1:1; 2:1-12; 4:15-16; 8:5-13; 10:18; 13:38; 24:14 et al.) thus climaxes this gospel in the command to "make disciples of all the nations" (Plummer 1982:430; Carson 1984:596). When we see Matthew's commission to make disciples of "all the nations" in the light of Luke's commission, that "repentance and forgiveness of sins will be preached in His name to all nations, beginning at Jerusalem" (Lk 24:47), we understand that Jesus' ministry in Israel was to be the beginning point of what would be later a universal offer of salvation to all the peoples of the earth (Wilkins 1992:188-189; Fitzmyer 1985:1583-1585).

"Baptizing "and "teaching disciples to obey"

However, Jesus' Great Commission implies more than securing salvation as Jesus' disciple. Implied in the use of the imperative "make disciples" is both the call to and the process of becoming a disciple (Osborne 1984:91). Matthean contextual usage points to this conclusion, rather than theologizing based on the occurrence transitive verb; cf. the note in (Silva 1978:256). Even as one is "called" from among the nations to start life as a disciple, one must in turn "follow" the Lord through baptism and through obedience to Jesus' teaching. As He addressed the disciples and commanded them to "make disciples of all the nations," Jesus tells them to make more of what He has made of them. Jesus spent a great deal of time guiding and instructing the disciples in their growth. As He sends them out to make disciples, Jesus tells them to make more of what He has made of them. The process will not be exactly the same as what Jesus did with them, because the circumstances after Pentecost will change the process (cf. Wilkins 1992).[9] However, the process will be similar in many ways.

Specifically, the process of growth is implied in the phrases, "baptizing them in the name of the Father and of the Son and of the Holy Spirit, and teaching them to obey everything I have commanded you" (Mt 29:19-20). As a person responds to the invitation to come out of the nations to start life as a disciple, she or he begins the life of discipleship through baptism and through obedience to Jesus' teaching.

The participle *"baptizing"* describes the activity by which the new disciple identifies with Jesus and the participle *"teaching"* introduces the activities by which the new disciple grows in discipleship (DeRidder 1975:190) For a recent discussion of the meaning of baptism as "adherence" see William B. Badke's article (1990:195-204). We should note that the process of growth does not include only instruction. Growth in disciple-

---

[9]See my discussion of the process after Pentecost in *Following the Master*, chapter 12 on Acts.

ship is accomplished as the new disciple is obedient to what Jesus commanded. Obedience was the hallmark of Jesus' disciples, as we see in an incident in Jesus' earthly ministry. "Pointing to His disciples, He said, "Here are My mother and My brothers. For whoever does the will of My Father in heaven is My brother and sister and mother" (Mt 12:49-50). H. N. Ridderbos says succinctly, "The apostles had to teach people to obey all that Jesus commanded them during His ministry on earth. Their listeners had to be brought under His commandments so that they could show by their lives that they really belong to Him. That is the final purpose of the preaching of the gospel" (Ridderbos 1987: 555-556).

Teaching them to obey all things: Matthew as a Manual on Discipleship

Matthew's gospel was the favorite Gospel of the church for much of church history, because of the theme of this book: "teaching them to obey all things." However, the theme needs to be expanded to include the full phrase in Matthew 28:20: "teaching them to obey everything that I have commanded you" (NRSV). In other words, everything that Jesus taught the original disciples in turn they were now to pass on to new disciples. Moreover, Matthew's gospel presents the most extensive and most intentionally organized collection of Jesus' teaching.

Therefore, Matthew's gospel is intended, at least in part, as a resource tool to help Jesus' disciples in their task of making and developing future disciples. I refer to it as "a manual on discipleship." Matthew points to Jesus to be the supreme Lord and Teacher of the disciples. Although the disciples were still susceptible to incomprehension and misunderstanding in His earthly ministry, Matthew emphasizes that Jesus' teaching

brought them understanding and obedience. That same understanding and obedience will continue to be the hallmark of
disciples in the ongoing age. Matthew's gospel is readily
usable for this purpose, because the growth-process of discipleship is comprised in large part of teaching new disciples to
obey all that Jesus had commanded the original disciples.

First, we see that all five major discourses are directed toward the development of the disciples. These discourses are
intended as instruction in, and clarification of, what it meant to
be Jesus' unique kind of disciple, as opposed to, or distinct
from, other kinds of disciples.

Secondly, there is a progression of teaching in the discourses that addresses the fullness of the disciple's life—i.e.,
discipleship. Matthew was the favorite gospel of the early
church throughout much of church history because it was a
natural catechetical tool designed to develop wholistic disciples. The basic thrust of each discourse points to that kind of
intentional well-roundedness, as we can see briefly:

1) Kingdom life. The Sermon on the Mount (Mt 5-7) addresses all aspects of what life lived in the presence and
   power of the kingdom would be like in this age, including ethical, religious, marital, emotional, economic,
   etc.

2) Missionary disciples. The Missionary discourse (Mt
   10) gives principles for all disciples, both in the original
   missionary outreach of the Twelve and the on-going
   missionary endeavor throughout the ages. It explains
   life as a *mission-driven disciple* in an alien and often
   hostile world until the coming of the Son of man.

3) Presence of the kingdom. The Parabolic discourse (Mt
   13) explains that the kingdom would not manifest itself
   in the political, militaristic, dominant cultural kingdom
   that much of Israel expected to arrive with Messiah.

Jesus explained for the disciples then, and now, that the mysteries of the kingdom of heaven will result in a very different kind of expectation; how the kingdom will grow, what is its value, and how we are to live in the kingdom while still in this world.

4) Community life. In the Community discourse (Mt 18) declared how the community life of the kingdom is expressed through the church, with an emphasis upon purity, accountability, forgiveness, and restoration.

5) Expectation of Jesus' return. The Olivet discourse (Mt 24-25) explains how Jesus' disciples are to live with an appropriate kind of expectation of Jesus' return, the end of the age, and the establishment of Messiah's throne.

Matthew is indeed a wonderful gospel to help us fulfill the theme of the conference: *"Teaching Them To Obey All Things."* How will this flesh out in our teaching, ministry, and mission contexts? Let me suggest the following in conclusion.

◆ Develop a clear articulation of Jesus' form of discipleship, which includes conversion and transformation, evangelism and follow-up. We must be more precise in our use of biblical terminology.

◆ Jesus, through Matthew's gospel, envisions the intentional development of disciples through using the discourses as a catechetical tool.

◆ Develop outcomes that achieve the objective of each discourse, and develop a regular schedule that rotates through these discourses as a teaching base.

◆ The objective of the Great Commission must be achieved in *community*, because it is not enough simply to impart data; disciples must be taught how to obey through *modeling*. They must be held accountable to obey through *mutuality*.

♦ We need to develop a strategy whereby everything Jesus taught His disciples becomes the guiding force in the transformation process of disciples into the image of Christ (For the development of a full "paradigm" of transformational discipleship see Wilkins 1997). Only then can we truly say that we are "teaching them to obey all things."

Bibliography

Arnold, Clinton E. (ed.)
     In press   "Matthew," *The Zondervan Illustrated Bible Backgrounds Commentary*. Grand Rapids: Zondervan, Vol. 1.
Badke, William B.
     1990   "Was Jesus a Disciple of John?" *Evangelical Quarterly* 62:3:195-204.
Boice, James Montgomery
     1986   *Christ's Call to Discipleship.* Chicago: Moody.
Carson, Donald A.
     1984   "Matthew," *EBC.* Grand Rapids: Zondervan. 8:596.
Coppedge, Allan
     1989   *The Biblical Principles of Discipleship.* Grand Rapids: Zondervan.
Bonhoeffer, Dietrich
     1963   *The Cost of Discipleship,* trans. R. H. Fuller (1937; 1949; 1959; 2nd rev. ed.) New York: Macmillan.
Chandapilla, P. T.
     1974   *The Master Trainer.* Bombay: Gospel Literature Service.
Coppedge, Allan

1989   *The Biblical Principles of Discipleship.* Grand
Rapids: Zondervan.

DeRidder, Richard
1975   *Discipling the Nations.* Grand Rapids: Baker.

Drushal, M. E.
1988   "Implementing Theory Z in the Church:
Managing People as Jesus Did," *Ashland
Theological Bulletin* 20.

Degenhardt, H.-J.
1965   *Lukas--Evangelist der Armen. Besitz und
Besitzverzicht nach den lukanischen Schriften:
Eine traditions- und redaktionsgeschichtliche
Untersuchung.* Stuttgart: Katholisches
Bibelwerk.

Eims, Leroy
1978   *The Lost Art of Disciple Making.* Grand
Rapids/Colorado Springs: Zondervan/NavPress.

Fisher Fred L.
1972   *Jesus and His Teachings.* Nashville: Broadman.

Fitzmyer, Joseph A.
1985   *The Gospel According to Luke (X-XXIV), AB* 28A
Garden City, N.Y.: Doubleday, pp. 1583-1584.

Green, Joel B. Scott McKnight, and I. Howard Marshal (eds.)
1988   "The Concept of Disciple in Matthew's Gospel:
As Reflected in the Use of the Term μαθητης,"
Novum Testamentum Supplements. Leiden, The
Netherlands: E. J. Brill
1992   *Dictionary of Jesus and the Gospels.* Downers
Grove: InterVarsity Press.
1995   *Discipleship in the Ancient World and in
Matthew's Gospel* (2nd ed.); Grand Rapids:
Baker

Hare, Douglas R. A.

1967   *The Theme of Jewish Persecution of Christians
        in the Gospel According to St. Matthew.*
        Cambridge, U.K.: Cambridge University Press.

Hayakawa, S. I. *et. al.*

1979   "Student: pupil, scholar, learner, disciple,
        protége," *Use the Right Word: Modern Guide
        to Synonyms and Related Words.* Pleasantville,
        N.Y.: Reader's Digest Association

Henrichsen, Walter A.

1974   *Disciples Are Made--Not Born.* Wheaton, IL:
        Victor Books.

Hodges, Zane C.

1981   *The Gospel Under Siege: A Study on Faith and
        Works.* Dallas: Redención Viva.

1989   *Absolutely Free: A Biblical Reply to Lordship
        Salvation* (Grand Rapids/Dallas: Zondervan /
        Redención Viva.

Kio, Stephen Hre

1990   "Understanding and Translating 'Nations' in Mt
        28:19," *The Bible Translator* 41:2:230-239.

Kuhne, Gary W.

1978   *The Dynamics of Discipleship Training: Being
        and Producing Spiritual Leaders.* Grand Rapids:
        Zondervan.

Livingston, Blauvelt, Jr.

1986   "Does the Bible Teach Lordship Salvation?"
        BibSac 143:41

Lohfink, Gerhard

1984   *Jesus and Community: The Social Dimension of
        Christian Faith.* Philadelphia: Fortress.

Louw, Johannes P. and Eugene A. Nida, (eds.)
    1988   *Greek Lexicon of the New Testament: Based on
           Semantic Domains.* 2 vols. New York: United
           Bible Societies.
McGavran, Donald A. and Win Arn
    1973   *How to Grow a Church.* Glendale, CA: Gospel
           Light.
Minear, Paul S.
    1974   "The Disciples and the Crowds in the Gospel of
           Matthew," *Anglican Theological Review.*
           Supplemental Series, III, March, pp.28-44.
Ortiz, Juan Carlos
    1975   *Disciple.* Carol Stream, IL: Creation House.
Osborne, Grant R.
    1984   *The Resurrection Narratives: A Redactional
           Study.* Grand Rapids: Baker.
Parker, Pierson
    n.d.   "Disciple," *IDB,* I:845
Pentecost, J. Dwight
    1971   *Design for Discipleship.* Grand Rapids:
           Zondervan.
Plummer, Alfred
    1982   *An Exegetical Commentary on the Gospel
           according to St. Matthew.* Grand Rapids: Baker.
Powell, Paul W.
    1982   *The Complete Disciple.* Wheaton, IL Victor.
Rickards, Donald R.,
    1976   "Discipleship: A Biblical Doctrine?" *Voice*
           Vol. 55, pp.5-18.

Ridderbos, H. N.
    1987   "Matthew," *Bible Student's Commentary*, trans.
             Ray Togtman. 1950; *E.T.* Grand Rapids:
             Zondervan, pp. 555-556.

Ryrie, Charles C.
    1989   *So Great Salvation: What It Means to Believe*
             In Jesus Christ. Wheaton, IL: Victor Books.

Sanders J. Oswald
    1962   *Spiritual Maturity.* Chicago: Moody.

Schelkle, Karl Hermann
    1965   *Discipleship and Priesthood,* trans, Joseph
             Disselhorst, (Rev. ed.; *E.T.*) New York.

Segovia, Fernando F. (ed.)
    1985   "Introduction: Call and Discipleship--Toward a
             Re-examination of the Shape and Character of
             Christian Existence in the New Testament,"
             Discipleship in the New Testament.
             Philadelphia: New York: Fortress.

Sheridan, Mark
    1972   "Disciples and Discipleship in Matthew and
             Luke," *Biblical Theological Bulletin.* 3:235-
             255.

Silva, Moisés
    1978   "New Lexical Semitisms?" *ZNTW* 69:9:256

Sweetland, Dennis M.
    1987   *Our Journey with Jesus. Discipleship*
             according to Mark, GNS 22. Wilmington, DE:
             Michael Glazier.

Theissen, Gerd
    1878   *Sociology of Early Palestinian Christianity.*
             trans. John Bowden. Philadelphia: Fortress.

Thysman, R.
    1974   *Communauté et directives éthiques: la*
             catéchèse de Matthieu, Recherches et

Synthèses: Section d'exégèse, no. 1.
Gembloux: Duculot.

Trakatellis, Demetrios
1985 "'φακολουⲧθει μοι/Follow Me' (Mk 2:14):
Discipleship and Priesthood," *Greek Orthodox
Theological Review.* 30:3:271-285

Walls, Andrew F.
1996 *The Missionary Movement in Christian
History: Studies in the Transmission of Faith.*
Maryknoll, NY: Orbis Books.

Wagner, C. Peter
1973 "What is 'Making Disciples'?" *Evangelical
Missions Quarterly* 9:285-293
1974 *Stop the World I Want to Get On.* Glendale, CA;
Regal.

Wilkins, Michael J.
1988 "The Concept of Disciple in Matthew's Gospel:
As Reflected in the Use of the Term μαθητηs,"
Novum Testamentum Supplements, Vol. 59.
Leiden, The Netherlands: E.J. Brill.
1992a *Following the Master: A Biblical Theology of
Discipleship.* Grand Rapids: Zondervan.
1992b "Discipleship," in *Dictionary of Jesus and the
Gospels.* (eds.) Joel B. Green, Scott McKnight,
and I. Howard Marshal. Downers Grove:
InterVarsity. Pp. 188-191.
1992c "Disciples," in *Dictionary of Jesus and the
Gospels.* (ed.) I Howard Marshall. Downers
Grove: InterVarsity.
1992d "Sinner," in *Dictionary of Jesus and the
Gospels.* (ed.) I Howard Marshall. Downers
Grove: InterVarsity.

1995   *Discipleship in the Ancient World and in Matthew's Gospel.* (2nd ed.) Grand Rapids: Baker.

1997   *In His Image Reflecting Christ in Everyday Life.* Colorado Springs: NavPress.

In Press   *Matthew The NIV Application Commentary.* Grand Rapids: Zondervan.

In Press   "Matthew," *The Zondervan Illustrated Bible Backgrounds Commentary,* (ed.) Clinton E. Arnold, Grand Rapids: Zondervan. vol.1.

Willard, Dallas, (ed.)

1997   The Spiritual Formation Line. Colorado Springs: NavPress.

Wuest, Kenneth S.

1966   *Studies in the Vocabulary of the Greek New Testament,* Vol. III, *Wuest's Word Studies.* Grand Rapids: Eerdmans. p.25

TEACHING THEM TO OBEY ALL THINGS: A LUKAN PERSPECTIVE ON CONFRONTING MAGIC IN POWER-ORIENTED SOCIETIES

Rick Love

Power Ministry and Story Telling

The topic of this year's Evangelical Missiological Society meeting actually misquotes Scripture. Our commission is not to "teach them all things" (a cognitively-oriented message), but rather to "teach them to obey all things" (an obedience-oriented message). Since Jesus' obedience-oriented discipleship curriculum includes everything that he commanded, surely it includes some lessons on "power ministry." For while he gave numerous ethical commands (e.g., the Sermon on the Mount), he also commissioned his disciples to preach, heal, and cast out demons (Mt 10:7-8). Robert Gundry's summary of Matthew 28:20 makes this important connection: "To his disciples Jesus gives authority to replicate his ministry in word and deed. They are to teach the word . . . heal the sick and cast out demons. Thus Matthew pictures the disciples as Christian scribes . . . and as Christian healers and exorcists" (Gundry 1982:8; cf. Greig and Springer 1993:399-403; Williams 1989:131).[1] Power ministry is part of the church's discipleship curriculum.

Not only is power ministry included in the Great Commission, it is also illustrated throughout Acts.[2] In other words, while we need to teach *panta ta ethne* to obey all that Jesus commanded, we also need to teach them to obey all that Jesus narrated! Luke's account of power ministry in Acts does more than merely recount the miraculous outreach of the early church. Luke has carefully crafted his narrative to equip the church to confront magic in power-oriented societies.[3] One of the ways Luke chose to teach these important lessons was through stories.[4] If we are serious about teaching *panta ta ethne* to obey all things, then we need to teach them about

---

[1] In addition, in John 20:21, Jesus commissions his disciples to minister in the same way he did: "As the Father has sent me, I also send you." Both preaching and healing are to characterize their ministries. This two-fold emphasis is graphically illustrated in Matthew 10, Mark 6, and Luke 9 as Christ sends out the twelve to preach and heal (cf. Luke 10 in which he sends out the seventy to do the same). I. Howard Marshall rightly notes regarding the preservation of the commands to preach and heal in the sending of the twelve (as recorded in all three synoptic gospels): "Their preservation ... indicates that the basic principles in them were regarded as of lasting value for the church" (1978:351). Acts 1:1 also implies that the church is to carry on the ministry of Christ; the remainder of Acts confirms it (Harrison 1975:36).

[2] Moreover, the very first verse in Acts ("all that Jesus began to do and to teach") implies that Luke understood that Jesus ministry of signs and wonders continues through the church.

[3] James D.G. Dunn rightly notes, "Magic is one of the main secondary themes in Acts" (1996:175).

[4] See Tom Steffen (1996) for the missiological significance of narrative. See Ben Witherington (1994) for an insightful look at how narrative shaped Paul's theology.

power ministry. And, we need to teach them from the narrative portions of Scripture.[5]

The signs and wonders movement has done an excellent job of promoting kingdom theology as the basis for power ministry (Wimber 1986; 1987; Williams 1989). However, as I learned in Indonesia, doing power ministry in America and actually confronting magic in a power-oriented society differs. Most Americans do not live in fear of demons or curses. They do not use charms or amulets. They are not dominated by a power-oriented worldview. However, most of the world lives in such fear and domination. The majority of the world are animists or folk religionists of some kind. For example, while more than one billion people embrace the religion of Islam, approximately three-quarters of these Muslims (more than 800 million) are what missiologists describe as folk Muslims (Love 1996).

Missiologists have noted our ineffectiveness at dealing with syncretism in power-oriented societies. The chronic problem of dual allegiance is found throughout the world. Christians in these societies go to church to worship but to shamans to be healed. Charles Kraft ably describes this problem and offers a balanced approach to these issues (1992).

However, my point is that Luke has intentionally addressed these very issues before the modern signs and wonders movement! In fact, he has developed a "curriculum" for dealing with power-oriented societies—in story form. In

---

[5] Grant Osborne correctly notes, "Narrative is not as direct as didactic material, but it does have a theological point and expects the reader to interact with that message. My argument is that biblical narrative is in some ways even better than the teaching applied to similar situations in the lives of people (1991:172). See also Liefeld (1995) and Klein, Blomber and Hubbard (1993:344-351).

some circles, the topic of this paper is general knowledge. The message about power encounter is well known. However, even if my *message* is well known to some, the *medium* is not. As Evangelicals we tend to downplay narrative in our teaching ministries. And these very stories are often most relevant to our audience!

Magic in Acts

The church encounters magic in four separate accounts in Acts. Philip's confrontation with a magician was one aspect of the breakthrough in Samaria (Acts 8:4-24). A power encounter with a magician was also the first door opener for Paul and Barnabas in Cyprus (Acts 13:4-12). The birth of the church at Philippi involved Paul casting demons out of a girl who had a spirit of divination (Acts 16:16-18). Finally, at Ephesus, are Paul's most dramatic power encounters (Acts 19:11-12).[6]

Luke's broader redactional purposes in Acts are polemical and missiological.[7] Because magic was a widespread and recurring problem facing the church,[8] Luke seemed to

---

[6] See Love (1998) for a comprehensive summary of Paul's ministry at Ephesus.

[7] According to Kurz, "The narrator [of Acts] engages in a major polemic against all forms of magic" (1993:152). See also Dunn (1996:175), Witherington (1998:98, 222, 397, 578), and Talbert (1997:176-177) for similar conclusions.

[8] The majority of the people in the first century were also folk religionists from power-oriented societies. Magic flourished in the first century. Hans Dieter Betz writes regarding the New Testament era, "magical beliefs and practices can hardly be overestimated in their importance for the daily life of the people" (1992:xIi). According to David E. Aune, in the first century, A.D., "magic was a phenomenon which pervaded the various Graeco-Roman cults, Judaism and Christianity" (Aune 1980:1519). Edwin M.

intentionally selects key stories and develop them to: (1)
clarify the difference between magic and miracle,[9] (2) equip the
church for spiritual warfare against the forces of darkness most
focally expressed in magic, and (3) make a clear connection
between pioneer missions and power ministry.

Luke describes these four events, climaxing at Ephesus,
not only to show the supernatural confirmation of the gospel
through signs and wonders, but also to contrast satanically-
inspired magic with spirit-empowered miracle.[10] As Howard
Kee notes, "There is clear evidence that the power of the Holy
Spirit and that of magic are seen to be in competition, begin-

---

Yamauchi says that Christians "lived in a world which was steeped with
occult beliefs and practices" (1983:199; cf. Love 1998). Aune describes
four types of magic prevalent in the Graeco-Roman world:

> (1) protective and apotropaic magic, (2) aggressive and
> malevolent magic, (3) love magic and magic aimed at the
> acquisition of power and control, and (4) magical divina-
> tion. . . . The goals of Graeco-Roman magic then, very
> generally, may be characterized as providing protection,
> healing, success and knowledge for magical practitioners
> and their clients, and harm for their opponents. Formu-
> lated in this way, it can be seen at once that the goals of
> magic are very similar to the goals of religion. The dif-
> ference lies primarily in the way in which goals are
> achieved (1980:1517-1518); cf. Arnold (1993:580-583).

[9] According to Howard Clark Kee, "The antithesis between miracles done in Jesus' name and magic ... was already taking shape in the
narrative of Acts" (1983:217). This is especially apparent in Acts 19 which
"serves to contrast Christianity with the various magical practices, and so
underlines the supernatural power of Christianity" (Newman and Nida
1972:361).

[10] "Luke's renunciation of magic ... is part of a trajectory continuing into
the ancient church" (Talbert 1997:177; cf. Didache II.2; III.4; Barnabas
XX. Ignatius to the Ephesians IXX.3).

ning with the launching of the mission of the church to the
Gentiles" (1986:119). Sir William Ramsay also underscores
the importance of magic in Acts:

> There is no class of opponents with whom the
> earliest Christian Apostles and missionaries are
> brought into collision so frequently, and whose
> opposition is described as being so obstinate and
> determined, as the magicians. *They play a very
> considerable part in the book of the Acts"*
> (1953:113, emphasis added).

Susan Garrett from Yale, concurs, "Luke's particular
treatment was extensive and consistent: he demonstrated that
magicians have no chance of success in the new era inaugu-
rated by Christ's resurrection. . . . *Luke's treatment of magic
and magicians bears upon the interpretation of all of Luke-
Acts"* (emphasis added) (1989a:10).[11]

Six Components of Magic

To understand how Luke's narrative actually addresses
magic in power-oriented societies, it will be helpful to briefly
outline a model of magic developed by J. Dudley Woodberry
(1990).[12]   His model emerges in a folk Islamic context;

---

[11]John M. Hull's monograph, *Hellenistic Magic and the Synoptic Tradition*,
also affirms the importance of this motif. "Luke is the only New Testament
writer who specifically refers to the church's attack on magic. . . . The
magical episodes are an aspect of Luke's world-view. They follow from his
view of angels, demons, of spiritual reality in general, from his view of the
cosmic conflict and its weapons. . . . This is the framework of a magical
universe. . . . The dramatic story which Luke-Acts unfolds is largely the
description of this clash of rival powers" (1974:87, 105).

[12] In this article, Woodberry does not use these components as a model for
analysis.

nevertheless, his categories fit power-oriented societies in general. He specifies six components of folk Islam: 1) power(s) (beings, such as demons or *jinn* or impersonal forces such as *mana*); 2) power people (imams and shamans); 3) power objects (charms and amulets); 4) power places (Mecca, saints' tombs); 5) power times (Muhammad's birthday, the night of power during Ramadan, the pilgrimage); and, 6) power rituals (prayers and incantations using portions of the Quran). This taxonomy helps us analyze accounts in Acts.

TABLE 1
THE SIX COMPONENTS OF FOLK ISLAM

The Six Components	Examples from Folk Islam
Power(s)	Demons, Jinn, Mana
Power person(s)	Imam and shamans
Power object(s)	Quranic verses
Power place(s)	Mecca, saints' tombs
Power time(s)	Muhammad's birthday, the pilgrimage
Power ritual(s)	Prayers using portions of the Quran.

In this paper, I will analyze four "showdowns" between missionaries and magicians. These power encounters function like windows into power-oriented societies. These "duels" illustrate various aspects of magic as well as portray different approaches to defeating the Devil.

Acts 8:5-24

Philip's ministry in Samaria is the quintessential model of what John Wimber calls "power evangelism" (1986). Truth encounter was coupled with power encounter. This spirit-filled evangelist (Acts 6:3-5) proclaimed the gospel with signs following. The *manifestations* of the kingdom pointed to and corroborated the *message* of the kingdom.

Philip's gospel centered around Jesus and the kingdom of God (8:5, 12).[13] The fact that Philip proclaimed the kingdom of God indicates that he preached a Godward and a Satanward gospel (cf. Kallas 1961, 1966, 1968). This kingdom orientation means he not only spoke of *reconciliation* with God, but also *release* from Satan. He emphasized *forgiveness* through Christ, as well as *freedom* from Satan.

Luke says that the Samaritans *heard and saw* the signs Philip was performing. They saw God heal many who were paralyzed and lame. They also heard the signs because those with unclean spirits were shouting with a loud voice (vs. 7; see Mark 1:26; 5:5, 7)! This was a boisterous evangelistic meeting!

---

[13] I. Howard Marshall's comments on Acts 8:12 are notable: "This is an interesting combination of themes [the kingdom of God and the name of Jesus], showing how the early church saw the message of Jesus being continued in its own message but at the same time increasingly spoke about the means by which God's kingly power was being manifested in their own time, namely, through the mighty name of Jesus (Marshall 1983:156).

Philip was engaged in what C. Peter Wagner refers to as ground level spiritual warfare—healing and casting demons out of ordinary people. But Luke indicates that Philip also engaged in occult-level spiritual warfare, which means confrontation with magicians, witches, or shaman (1994:217). Philip met Simon (a power person), the first magican mentioned in Acts.

Luke underscores important facts about Simon through the use of repetition. Twice he mentions that Simon practiced magic (vss. 9, 11). Two times he says that Simon astonished the people of Samaria with his arts (vss. 9, 11). Simon's self-acclaimed greatness (vs. 9) as well as the public affirmation of his greatness ("the great power of God") is also recorded (vs. 10). He was a kind of "Muhammad Ali" of magic.

The description of Simon as the great power of God must be understood against the backdrop of a magical world-view. The word power, *dunamis*, is described in Moulton and Milligan as "one of the most common and characteristic terms in the language of pagan devotion. 'Power' was what the devotees respected and worshipped" (1929:172). (This is similar to the pursuit of power among folk religionists today).

Some commentators believe that these affirmations of greatness imply that Simon was regarded as some kind of a god (Newman and Nida 1972:175). Even if he was not, these words smack of idolatry and self-deification. At the very least, these facts also suggest that Simon was no mere novice or underling in the realm of darkness. He was a powerful servant in Satan's kingdom.

Simon believed the gospel and was baptized (vs. 13). He then followed Philip around, "like a fan of a rock star" (Witherington 1998:285), watching him minister. Luke highlights important differences between Simon's power and Philip's power. The greatness of Philip's signs (vss. 6, 13) are contrasted with Simon's magic (vss. 9, 11), for Philip's power astonishes even Simon (vs. 13).[14] In addition, the very terms he uses underscore the difference. While Simon's power is described as magic, Philip's power is described as a "sign." It points to the kingdom. The miracle points to the message.

Simon's astonishment grew to greed, however, when Peter and John joined Philip's outreach. Simon saw Peter and John lay hands on people to receive the Holy Spirit.[15] He mistakenly assumed that the laying on of hands was some kind of new power ritual.[16] Although there is no mention of tongues (as there is elsewhere in Acts), something visibly supernatural was clearly taking place that demonstrated the Holy Spirit had come upon people. Simon tried to "bargain" with Peter for his power: "Give this authority to me as well, so that everyone on whom I lay my hands may receive the Holy Spirit" (vs. 19). Simon the magician, the power person, reverted to his old ways. The one who was used to being called "the great power of God" now wanted the same power demonstrated by the apostles. As a magician he was looking for customers, not converts (Talbert 1997:85). He wanted power for the wrong reasons and sought it through the wrong methods. Susan Garrett sums up the situation:

---

[14] This is the same Greek word translated as "astonished" in vss 9,11. It is translated as "amazed" in the NASB.

[15] Why the Holy Spirit did not fall on the Samaritans prior to the coming of Peter and John remains one of those classic puzzles of New Testament interpretation. See Marshall (1983:157-158), Longenecker (1981:359-360) and Larkin (1995:127-129) for good summaries of the issues.

[16] "The Christian practice of laying on of hands or exorcism, may look very much the same, and indeed have a similar effect (cf. 8:9-11 with 8:6,8,13), but one of Luke's primary concerns in relating the episodes of 8:17-24 and 19:13-16 is to make clear the difference" (Dunn 1996:109).

> Simon's offer of money to Peter is for Luke not
> only blasphemous but absurd: The magician
> wanted to purchase divine authority while
> himself still trapped under diabolical
> authority.... Christian authority is in no way
> like magical-satanic authority, for the latter can
> be bought but the former is solely a gift of God.
> The Holy Spirit can be used and is used by God
> to confirm the word proclaimed by God's
> servants, but it cannot be used to bring glory to
> an individual (1989:72, 77).[17]

Peter's meaning is "To hell with you and your money!"
(Dunn 1996:112).[18] This condemnation is stern, but appropriate for a magician like Simon. Peter was not rebuking an overzealous new believer. He was confronting a seasoned veteran of the kingdom of darkness. Peter's scathing rebuke and pointed call to repentance exposes the deeper issues of Simon's heart (vss. 21,22). He was not right before God; he was wicked, in the gall of bitterness and in the bondage of iniquity. Thus, "the story ends with Simon, the magician, depicted as one who is baptized, but not changed and as one with whom God is not pleased" (Talbert 1997:87).

While it would be best to read this story and then discuss it with one's target group, here I can merely suggest some practical implications. I see at least three practical points emerging from this story.

1. *A magical view of power is incompatible with the gospel.* First, magical power exalts the magician rather than the messiah. Second, magical power has no meaning beyond

---

[17] Witherington writes: "God's gift is in God's control" (1998:288).

[18] This statement appears to be a curse.

itself. It is not a sign confirming a message. Third, magical power has monetary motivations, whereas the message of the kingdom and the miracles of the kingdom are expressions of grace, freely given.

2. *Confronting a power-oriented society demands power encounter and truth encounter.* In one sense, Philip and Peter outdid the magicians at their own game. They did not shrink back from power encounter because it might not be understood. They healed the sick, cast out demons, and prayed for the fullness of the Holy Spirit. A power-oriented society must be confronted by power.

However, truth encounter is ultimately what distinguishes Satanic power from the Spirit's power.[19] Simon "was more interested in the great acts of power accompanying Philip's preaching than God's reign in his life" (Longenecker 1981:358). As a typical magician, Simon wanted possession of the power without submission to the source of the power. Philip preached the kingdom of God. This message demands submission to the king. It also includes repentance—turning from the kingdom of darkness. Truth encounter and power encounter go hand in hand in extending the kingdom.

3. *Beware of superficial conversion.* We must address motives and stress deep repentance for those from a magical background. Simon had made a profession of faith. However, his actions following his profession reflected a superficial repentance.

---

[19] The Holy Spirit is also called the Spirit of Truth (John 15:26; 16:13).

Acts 13:8-12

The first recorded event of Paul's first missionary journey is a power encounter on the island of Cyprus.[20] Luke's selection and placing of this event as the frontispiece to Paul's missionary career indicates its significance. Moreover, "in narrating the apostles' confrontation with Bar-Jesus, Luke focuses more on the defeat of the magician than on the conversion of the proconsul. Bar-Jesus is introduced before Sergius Paulus and in greater detail. He is the more prominent actor in the narrative as the opponent of Christ's messengers" (Johnson 1997:172-173).

There are also significant contrasts between the magic of Simon and the magic of Bar-Jesus. Whereas Simon astonished the Samaritans with his powerful acts, Bar-Jesus guided the proconsul with his prophetic words. Simon's magic demonstrated supernatural power, while Bar-Jesus' magic stressed supernatural knowledge.

Luke includes a number of important details about this dramatic encounter. First, Bar-Jesus the magician worked closely with Sergius Paulus, a Roman proconsul. Apparently, this magician served in the governor's court[21] as was common in the Mediterranean world.[22]

Second, Bar-Jesus, also called Elymas, is specifically described as a magician (*magos*). *Magos* is a "Persian loan word, which originally referred to one who was a member of a particular kind of priesthood, had come into New Testament

---

[20] "Pliny, *Natural History* 30.11, says that Cyprus had in his times supplanted previous famed centers of magic" (Talbert 1997:127).

[21] His economic livelihood depended on his magical powers.

[22] Talbert thoroughly documents these phenomena (1997:127).

times to mean 'sorcerer,' 'magician,' or even 'swindler' or 'charlatan'" (Newman and Nida 1972:247). Third, Bar-Jesus was also a Jewish false prophet (Acts 13:6), that is, he claimed falsely to be a medium of divine revelation. Fourth, this magician and false prophet tried "to turn the proconsul away from the faith" (Acts 13:8).

Because the magician sought to interfere with the preaching of the gospel, Paul confronted him. However this confrontation was no mere rebuke. After being filled with the Spirit (vs. 9), Paul speaks forth a piercing string of condemnatory charges (vs. 10):

"You are full of all deceit and fraud."
"You son of the devil ..."
"You enemy of all righteousness ..."
"Will you not cease to make crooked the
straight ways of the Lord?"

These spirit-inspired words unmask the magician's diabolical motivations and intentions. Paul's description could not be stronger or more vivid. This magician is not just deceptive or fraudulent, he is *full* of *all* deceit and fraud. He does not just have enemies, but is himself the enemy of *all* righteousness. His crooked ways are contrasted with the straight ways of the Lord and thus Paul calls him the "son of a devil." Next, Paul pronounces a judgment or curse upon the magician. Through Paul's prophetic word God blinds the magician, so that he goes "about seeking those who would lead him by the hand" (vs. 11).

Luke concludes his account by focusing on the response of the proconsul to the encounter. "Then the proconsul believed when he saw what happened, being amazed at the teaching of the Lord" (vs. 12). The teaching of the Lord was confirmed by a sign from the Lord. Again, we see both a truth encounter and a power encounter. The proconsul believed when he saw the encounter and heard the Word. Luke "brings before his readers a dramatic power encounter, in which the Holy Spirit overthrew the evil one, the apostle confounded the sorcerer, and the gospel triumphed over the occult" (Stott 1990:220).

What significance does this encounter with a first century magician have for those of us working in power-oriented societies? At least three principles are worth noting in this account.

1. *The kingdom of darkness stands behind magicians.* While this kingdom's primary orientation is ostensibly power, in reality it is fundamentally moral, or more precisely immoral. An implacably evil spiritual kingdom is seeking to hinder the spread of the gospel. Both the confrontation and the commentary on it underscore the nature of our warfare. This magician was seeking to do in the physical realm what the "god of this world" does in the spiritual realm: "blinding the minds of the unbelieving that they might not see the light of the gospel of the glory of Christ" (2 Cor 4:4). Though at times appearing as an angel of light (2 Cor 11:14), the kingdom of Satan is nevertheless a kingdom of darkness and wickedness (Eph 6:12).

2. *The fullness of the Spirit is key to power encounter.* Paul was "filled with the Holy Spirit" just before his supernatural encounter with the magician who was full of all deceit and fraud. The same was true of Philip. While not directly stated in the story of Philip and Simon, Luke makes it clear that it was a spirit-filled Philip who penetrated Samaria through signs and wonders(Acts 6:3, 5).

3. *Curses or judgments "may" be used in power en-counter.*[23] This passage describes what Paul did, but it does not imply that this is normative for us. We may approach magicians in the same highly confrontational approach, by using a curse, but this is by no means normative. The text allows for it but does not demand it. However, if this apostolic practice is imitated, we had better be filled with the Spirit and led by the Spirit! Anyone experienced in power ministry knows that the Spirit's leading and anointing is crucial to the success of the encounter.[24]

Acts 16:16-18

The third recorded encounter takes place between Paul and a slave girl with a spirit of divination or literally, a python spirit (*pneuma pythona*). This slave-girl was doubly bound—spiritually and economically. Her masters oppressed her physically and made great profit from her spiritually.

---

[23] Curses are found in Paul's letters but they are not pronounced in the context of power encounter or directed against magicians (Gal. 1:8, 9; 1 Cor 5:3-5, 16:22; 1 Tim. 1:20). See Aune 1980:1553-1555.

[24] Peter's words to Simon the magician appear to be a type of curse (Acts 8). However there are other encounters in the Bible with no mention of cursing. For example, Moses' encounter with the magicians of Egypt is neither confrontive like Paul's encounter, nor does he resort to a direct curse upon the Egyptian magicians (Exodus 7-14). Elijah's power encounter with the prophets of Baal is closer to Paul's encounter with Bar-Jesus (1 Kings 18). Elijah uses a highly confrontational approach. Still, he pronounces no direct curse upon the prophets of Baal—although afterward he slays them all! The fortune telling slave girl is not cursed (Acts 16), and there is no mention of cursing in Paul's encounters at Ephesus (Acts 19-20). Hence, while cursing has apostolic precedent, it is not a typical nor normative approach to confronting magic.

The fact that she brought profit to her masters seems to imply that she was controlled by a powerful spirit. C. Peter Wagner observes, "How was it that they could make so much money through this fortune-teller? The obvious answer is that this slave girl was good at fortune telling. She knew the future, and she had built a sound reputation for accuracy. . . . The slave girl had not gained her stature in the occult community by making constant mistakes" (1995:69).

This python spirit originally referred to "a snake, and in particular the snake which guarded the celebrated oracle at Delphi and which was said to have been slain by Apollo" (Marshall 1983:268). According to this mythology, the pythoness was inspired by Apollo to predict the future[25] (Bruce 1975:332; Larkin 1995:237; Stott 1990:264).

During their numerous encounters, the demonized fortuneteller carried out a promotional campaign for Paul's team. She followed them around for many days crying out, "These men are bond-servants of the Most High God, who are proclaiming to you the way of salvation" (vs. 17).

Finally, Paul confronted the slave girl. Why he waited so long to confront the demon is puzzling. We are not told why he waited. We can infer that he was waiting on God's timing and anointing for the encounter.

Paul commanded the python spirit to come out in the name of Jesus. When the slave owners saw their hope of profit gone, they seized Paul and Silas, beat them, and threw them into prison. Power encounter led to persecution; the sign led to suffering. The underlying reason for the persecution was

---

[25] "The implication of the language used by Luke is that the girl spoke as in a trance: she was inspired, like the priestess at Delphi, by Apollo, who was symbolized by a snake" (Dunn 1996:221).

economic. Johnson rightly notes, "The operative motive for the practitioners of divination is neither the quest for truth nor the pursuit of holiness. Rather, profit is their bottom line" (1997:177). Again, Luke mentions the profit motive of magic.

At least three practical implications remain for us today.

1. *We have spiritual authority over the powers of darkness.* Significant differences exit between Jesus' and Paul's exorcisms. Jesus authority is personal and direct; he commands the demons to come out and they obey. People were amazed at His authority to exorcise demons (Luke 4:36). Whereas Jesus authority is personal and direct, Paul's authority is christo-centric and derived. Jesus says merely "Come out," but Paul (and we) must say, "Come out *in Jesus name!*"

The authority of the believer is rooted in Christ. It flows out of relationship (in contrast to ritual) and is based on faith (in contrast to formulas). We have authority because Christ dwells in us, commissions us and accompanies us (Col. 1:27; John 20:21; Mt 28:18-20; Eph 2:6). This principle is foundational to all spiritual warfare (Eph 6:10).

2. *We command demons.* Paul did not ask God to cast out the demon. He commanded the demon to leave. This method of exorcism—what some call the prayer of command—is an apostolic practice based on the biblical principle of Christ's authority. Jesus commanded sick bodies to be healed and demons to leave the demonized (Luke 4:35, 36, 39). This authoritative approach to the demonic realm is unique to the signs and wonders dimension of Scripture and was the practice of the early church (Acts 3:6; 9:34, 40). This is a power ritual.

3. *Magic has economic motives, whereas miracle does not.* All three encounters in Acts between magicians and missionaries underscore the economic motive of the magician

(Acts 8,13,16). Luke repeats this theme to expose these monetary motives and contrast magic with miracle.

Acts 19:11-20

Paul's profound and tireless teaching ministry at Ephesus was complemented by power ministry. In fact, some of the most dramatic miracles of the book of Acts took place in Paul's ministry at Ephesus. Luke says that "God was performing extraordinary miracles by the hands of Paul" (Acts 19:11). The *te-kai* construction in verses 11-12 imply that Luke has in mind two types of extraordinary miracles (Longenecker 1981:496; Haenchen 1971:562). First, miracles were done by the hands of Paul, implying that these miracles took place through the laying on of hands (cf. Mark 6:2; Acts 14:3). Laying on of hands is an important part of apostolic tradition—though there are other models of power ministry in the New Testament (Acts 5:12; 8:17; 9:34, 40; 14:3, 9,10; 16:18). Bruce says, "Not merely Paul's agency but the active use of his hands is implied" (1990a:410). While the laying on of hands is more than a mere ritual, it is at least that. Paul uses a power ritual that was well known among Jews (Twelftree 1993:158) and Hellenistic Greeks (Edelstein 1945, 1:448,456).

In order to open up this new field, the message of the kingdom (Acts 19:8; 20:25) was accompanied by the manifestations of the kingdom: "extraordinary miracles" (Acts 19:11-13). The word "extraordinary" seems odd alongside the word "miracle," for a miracle is by nature "extraordinary." However, in this demon-infested environment, polluted with every type of magical practice, the type of power encounters necessary to bring this city to Christ had to be dramatic. Hence, the miracles described by Luke at Ephesus were different in kind.

Not only did signs and wonders take place directly through the laying on of Paul's hands, but also indirectly: "Handkerchiefs or aprons were even carried from his body to the sick, and the diseases left them and the evil spirits went out" (Acts 19:12). Here is a case were Paul uses *power objects* to heal.[26] This way is not the normal means of power encounter in the New Testament, however.[27] Marshall comments:

> It is undeniably difficult to distinguish what is described here in verse 12 from primitive and crude beliefs in *mana*, i.e., in a quasi-physical power emanating from the healer and infecting his clothes so that these can be the vehicles of supernatural power. It is surprising that Luke, who is so critical of pagan magic, can allow that similar magical beliefs in a Christianized form were effective in the apostolic ministry. Perhaps, we may suggest that God is capable of condescending to the level of men who still think in such crude ways (1980:310).

However, God is not only capable of condescending to communicate to us, he has done so.[28]   For example, besides

---

[26] One of the most frequent ways Sundanese shamans heal the sick is through what could be called "holy water."   The shaman prays over the glass of water and then the patient drinks it.   Sometimes, shamans will merely recite Quranic verses and at other times, they may lay hands on the sick person and pray.

[27] "The skeptic and the mimic will immediately draw the wrong conclusions about these happenings: either they did not occur, or they should be copied. Neither response is the intention of Luke or the rest of the biblical teaching" (Larkin 1995:276).

[28] According to Longenecker,   "It is certainly strange to read of healing occurring through sweat-cloths and work-aprons.   Most commentators are uneasy with the account here and either explain it away as a pious legend or downplay it as verging on the bizarre.   Even when the account is accepted

Paul at Ephesus, God empowered Moses' staff to do miracles in Egypt (Exodus 4),[29] Elisha's bones brought a man back to life (2 Kings 13:21), a woman was healed by touching the hem of Jesus' garment (Mark 5:27-30), Jesus used saliva to heal the sick (Mark 7:33; 8:23),[30] and Peter's mere shadow brought healing (Acts 5:15). While these are not necessarily models to imitate, they do at least indicate that God has indeed condescended in this fashion.[31]

---

as factual, some would prefer to take it as having been done apart from Paul's knowledge and approval. But, Ephesus was the home of all sorts of magic and superstition, and the phrase 'Ephesian writings' (*Ephesia grammata*) was common in antiquity for documents containing spells and magical formulae. . . . So it need not be thought unnatural that just as Paul met his audiences at a point of common ground ideologically in order to lead them on to the Good News of salvation in Christ, so at Ephesus he acted in the way here depicted. The virtue, of course, lay not in the materials themselves but in the power of God and the faith of the recipients" (1981:496).

[29]Although unsuccessful, Elisha attempted to raise a young man from the dead by his staff (2 Kings 4:29-37).

[30] W.L. Lane describes Jesus' method of using saliva as bordering on magic (1974:192). Aune is bolder: "The ideas expressed in the story of the women's healing do not border on magic, they are of the essence of Graeco-Roman magical notions" (1980:1536). Graham H. Twelftree's doctoral studies on this subject support Aune's viewpoint. "There is ample evidence showing the use of spittle was part of the healing technique of the ancient world. It is used, for example, in the Babylonian texts, in the magical papyri and in Pliny. And, importantly, the rabbis prohibit its use" (1993:158).

[31] Oster, however, makes an important distinction between magicians and Paul's use of power objects:

> While it is true that the idea of power reflected in Acts 19:11ff. is similar to that which supported the idea of relics in the popular lore of pagans, Jews, and Christians, there seems to be one point which keeps the two from

Apparently the Ephesian magicians practiced what is known as contagious magic, in contrast to imitative magic. Imitative and contagious magic are terms originally coined by the anthropologist Sir James G. Frazer. Imitative magic refers to formulas that imitate the ends sought by the magician and is based on the law of similarity. Perhaps, the most familiar example of this is when someone wants to injure or destroy an enemy by injuring or destroying an image of that person (Frazer 1963:14).

Contagious magic, on the other hand, assumes that materials or substances once in contact with the intended victim can be used against that person. This method uses "the law of contact," for example, when someone finds a victim's hair or nails and uses them to work his evil purposes on the victim from a distance (Frazer 1963:43).

Luke's account does not make it clear whether these encounters took place because of Paul's initiation or because of God's accommodation. If Paul took the initiative, then he used the methods of the magicians. Dean Gililland exclaims, "What a risk he took! The orthodox would have accused him of syncretism. . . . Paul's method was that of contagious magic alright, but the consequence was healing, demonic confrontation and, 'the name of the Lord was extolled'" (Wagner and Pennoyer 1990:337).

If in fact Paul did use the methods of contagious magic, he does not water down the gospel or compromise truth in adopting these forms. He was contextualizing. Three things kept these (questionable or at least interesting) methods from being syncretistic. First of all, Paul's ministry of signs and wonders was done in the context of a teaching ministry. For

---

being identical. Lk. gives no examples of the *dunamis* of God permanently residing in certain objects (1974:37).

two years he was, "reasoning daily in the school of Tyrannus" (Acts 19:9-10). He was actively teaching the "whole counsel of God" (Acts 19:8; 20:25,27). Paul's ministry at Ephesus was both supernatural and rational. It was Spirit empowered and biblically based. It involved power encounter and truth encounter.

Secondly, Paul's teaching centered around the kingdom of God (Acts 19:18; 20:25). Surely this emphasis on the kingdom would have clarified the differences between the kingdom of God and the kingdom of Satan, thus highlighting the distinction between miracle and magic.

Thirdly, Paul demanded true repentance and faith. In his farewell address to the Ephesian elders, he summarized his message as "repentance toward God and faith in our Lord Jesus Christ" (Acts 20:21). There was a moral and volitional dimension to his message. Because of this emphasis, the Ephesian believers ultimately made a clean break with the occult by renouncing their demonic practices and destroying their charms, amulets, and magical paraphernalia (Acts 19:18-19).

However, Paul may not have been using the methods of the magicians. These encounters could just as easily be understood as taking place outside of Paul's initiative. If this is true, then Luke's account still describes a case of contextualization. Nevertheless, Paul was not contextualizing, God was! God chose to manifest his healing power in ways that those from a magical background could fathom. He met them at their point of need, within their frame of reference.[32]

---

[32] Talbert makes an astute observation about Luke's narration of this incident: "The miraculous power to heal is, as in the case of Peter and Jesus, linked in some way to Paul's body and clothing. Since this has, on first glance in antiquity as well as in modern times, a magical cast to it, it is

However, whether is was Paul's initiation or God's accommodation, teaching about the kingdom of God and repentance insured that these encounters would not be misunderstood. These manifestations of the kingdom pointed to and corroborated the message of the kingdom.

Paul's power encounters at Ephesus resulted not only in fruitful ministry, but also in syncretistic response. True power ministry has Satanic counterfeits. The power demonstrated in Paul's ministry was obviously impressive. It was especially impressive to some Jewish exorcists, *power people*, who wanted to add some Christian tools to their Jewish occultic practices.[33]

The Jewish exorcists (the seven sons of Sceva) wanted to borrow the *power ritual* of Jesus' name to enhance their powers. In a magical worldview, to know the name of someone or something was to ensure ones control over it (cf. Oster 1974:48-53). The superficial resemblance between what they saw and heard Paul doing and their own specialty led them to appropriate this new ritual. This attitude was typical of Jewish *power people* during the New Testament era.[34]

---

followed by a story about Jewish magicians" (1997:175). In this way, Luke ensures that his readers will not confuse Paul's miracles with magic.

[33] A missionary friend in Mali told me a modern example of this. He met a Muslim *marabout* (holy man) who wanted to learn the power verses in the gospel (*Injil*) to enhance his occultic powers.

[34] In fact, the Jews were famous in antiquity for their magic (Alexander 1896:342-379). The book of Acts itself describes two encounters with Jewish magicians (Acts 13:6-12; 19:13-20). There is further historical confirmation in the magical papyri (PGM XXIIb. 1-26) and in the Testament of Solomon (Charlesworth 1983:935-987). Josephus speaks of this phenomena when he describes Solomon's magical prowess:

> God granted him [Solomon] knowledge of the art used against demons for the benefit of healing men. He also composed incantations by which illnesses are relieved,

However, this mechanistic or ritualistic use of the name proved futile. The demon they sought to cast out responded both verbally and physically. First, he questioned the Jewish exorcists. "I recognize Jesus, and I know about Paul, but who are you" (Acts 19:15)?[35]. Second, the demonized man attacked and severely wounded the would-be exorcists.[36]

The name of Jesus was like an unfamiliar weapon that exploded in their hands. Jesus would not let his name be reduced to a magical formula. He is nobody's lackey.

Thus, Luke employs this dramatic encounter as an implicit polemic against magic. Without actually preaching directly to his audience about the folly of magic, he makes his point unmistakably clear (Kurz 1993:146-147).

This failed attempt at power encounter became well known with startling results. First of all, there was a general

---

and left behind forms of exorcisms with which those possessed by demons drive them out, never to return. And this kind of cure is of very great power among us to this day (8:45).

[35] That demons communicate through human vessels is documented throughout the New Testament (Mark 1:24; 5:7-12; Acts 16:16-18)

[36] The New Testament also describes the physical impact of demons on people. During an actual exorcism there are often violent physical manifestations. Jesus commanded demons to come out of a young boy. The response: "After crying out and throwing him into terrible convulsions, it came out; and the boy became so much like a corpse that most of them said, 'He is dead!'" (Mark 9:25-26). Philip's power ministry also encountered disorderly conduct: "In the case of many who had unclean spirits, they were coming out of them shouting with a loud voice" (Acts 8:7). In addition, demons can empower their victims with supernatural strength. The Gerasene Demoniac "had often been bound with shackles and chains, and the chains had been torn apart by him, and the shackles broken in pieces, and no one was strong enough to subdue him" (Mark 5:4).

sense of awe: "Fear fell upon them all" (Acts 19:17). There was the realization that the name of Jesus was not something to be toyed with. Second, the very name that was used as a mantra was now being magnified. Third, those who were involved in the occult began burning their magic books as a sign of repentance.

Luke says that many of those who "had believed" (πεπιστευκοτον) were confessing and disclosing their practices (vs. 18). The use of πεπιστευκοτον, a perfect participle, indicates that Luke has the Ephesian Christians in mind.[37] Paul's ministry, along with this incident, "stirred the saints to confess the hold that the occult had retained on them even after they became believers" (Harrison 1986:312).[38] They made a clean break from their dual allegiance and syncretistic understanding of truth.

Why this dramatic response? "The obvious answer is that in Luke's understanding, the Ephesians perceived the defeat of the seven sons to be a defeat of magic in general: magic has become obsolete (Garrett 1989:95).

Luke's description of the event is enlightening. Since magic is based on secret ritual, the way to break its power over people is through confession and the disclosure of the practices

---

[37] According to Talbert, "This is a power encounter. It is necessary because believers continue to seek spiritual power from sources other than Jesus. . . . They practice a bifurcated religion characterized by dual allegiance and a syncretistic understanding of truth" (1997:177).

[38] Marshall rightly notes regarding the Ephesian believers, "Christians are not fully converted or perfected in an instant, and pagan ways of thinking can persist alongside genuine Christian experience" (1980:312). My personal experience and the experience of missionaries all over the world working in folk Islamic or animistic contexts can testify to the struggle new believers have in these areas. Dual allegiance is an all-too-common problem.

(Acts 19:18). There was also the public destruction of the magical paraphernalia. "They brought their books together and began burning them in the sight of all" (Acts 19:19).[39]

Luke says that fifty thousand Greek drachmas worth of magical books were burned. Commentators differ as to a dollar equivalent. Larkin posits $35,000 worth of books (1995:278), Newman and Nida feel $50,000 is a good estimate (1972:369), while Harrison believes "it is impossible to estimate the amount involved" (1986:313). According to Haenchen, a drachma was the equivalent of a day's wage (1971:567). Thus Wagner concludes, "If each piece of silver represents a day's wage, in today's terms at $10 an hour for eight-hour days, or $80 a day, it would total $4 million. Quite a book burning!" (1995, 3:169). However, whatever the precise equivalent may be, Luke's emphasis is clear. The burning of the magical books was an expensive affair. True repentance can be costly.

Verse 20 functions as a climax and summary for the entire section: "So the word of the Lord was growing mightily and prevailing." Through Paul's ministry of teaching and power encounter, the gospel was advancing and the kingdom of God was being extended. In fact, Paul's ministry at Ephesus "has the characteristics of a people movement, especially

---

[39]The books most likely refer to magical formula and amulets similar to the magical papyri in general (Betz 1992 and Preisendanz, Vol. 1, 1973; Vol. 2, 1974) and the *Ephesia Grammata* (the Ephesian Letters) in particular. These were *power objects*. The *Ephesia Grammata* are described by Chester C. McCown as "the most noted magical formula of antiquity ... the magical formula *par excellence* in the Hellenistic world." (1923:128). These were *power objects* that were used in *power rituals*.

considering the communal decision to burn magical books and other paraphernalia publicly" (Wagner 1996:215).[40]

What is Luke saying to the church about confronting power-oriented societies?

1. *Miracle is based on relationship, whereas magic is based on ritual.* The name of Jesus is not a power ritual that can be used indiscriminately. Talbert explains:

> Since a magician has no personal relationship with the power involved, but simply uses it for his own purposes, these exorcists who are not disciples of Jesus attempt to use the name of Jesus, with whom Paul has the relationship. The Lukan point is that the spiritual power manifest through Jesus' disciples like Paul is not appropriated or dispensed as a commodity (see 8:18-24) but is the result of a personal relationship with the risen Lord (1997:176).

2. *Dual allegiance or syncretism is denounced. Renunciation of the occult and repentance from all ties with magic are demanded.* Luke's polemic against magic climaxes with the burning of the magic paraphernalia. Luke records this

---

[40] Luke's four summaries highlight Paul's success and indicate that a movement was birthed:

> "All who lived in Asia heard the word of the Lord" (Acts 19:10).
>
> "Fear fell upon them all and the name of the Lord Jesus was being magnified" (Acts 19:17).
>
> "So the word of the Lord was growing mightily and pre-vailing" (Acts 19:20).
>
> "Not only in Ephesus, but in almost all of Asia, this Paul has persuaded and turned away a considerable number of people" (Acts 19:26).

act of public repentance to underscore the depth of repentance necessary for true conversion.

The following two tables summarize some of the main themes in each of the four accounts. The first highlights the exegetical details of the four encounters, whereas the second describes the major differences between magic and miracle in Acts.

These four stories in Acts describe some of the most salient aspects of magic. Through the indirect approach of narrative, Luke equipped the early church in their confrontation with power-oriented societies. This same message can equip those of us ministering in similar societies.

Stories like these in Acts, coupled with actual experience ministering to those coming out of a magical background, ultimately led the early church to include exorcism as part of the baptismal process (cf. Arnold 1997:107-112).[41] The following story shows how we integrated this into our ministry to Sundanese folk Muslims.

In April 1995, I had the privilege of participating in a baptism of a folk Muslim convert that included deliverance. The baptism ceremony began with a prayer of renunciation prior to the actual baptism. Everyone being baptized made a public renunciation of any type of magic. They publicly declared, "I renounce every act of seeking power for myself through magic, charms or amulets of any kind."

The pastor then asked each baptismal candidate if he or she had been involved in magic of any kind. Only one man admitted that he had. (In this particular baptism, many of the

---

[41] My point is not that exorcism must be done at baptism, but rather that exorcism should be a part of the churches discipleship program in power-oriented societies.

TABLE 2
COMPARING AND CONTRASTING
LUKE'S FOUR ACCOUNTS OF MAGIC IN ACTS

Text	Acts 8:4-24	Acts 13:4-2	Acts 16:16-18	Acts 19:11-20
The Magician	Simon the magician	Elymas the magician	Slave Girl with a python spirit	Jewish exorcists
The Type of Magic	Power	Divination	Divination	Power
Evangelistic Approach	Power and truth encounter	Power and truth encounter	Power encounter	Power and truth encounter
Role of the Magician(s)	Convert?	Opponent	Bystander	Bystanders and converts

Text	Acts 8:4-24	Acts 13:4-2	Acts 16:16-18	Acts 19:11-20
Weapons of Our Warfare Emphasized	The fullness of the Holy Spirit	The fullness of the Holy Spirit	The name of Jesus (properly used)	The name of Jesus (improperly used)
Errors Exposed	Economic motive, control issue, evil intents of the heart	Economic motive and evil intents of the heart	Economic motive	Control issue & syncretism

TABLE 3
DISCERNING THE DIFFERENCES
BETWEEN MAGIC AND MIRACLE IN ACTS

Differences	Magic	Miracle
Ontological	Source is Satan.	Source is God.
Relational	Focus is on ritual.	Focus is on relationship.
Eschatological	Manifestation of the kingdom of Satan.	Manifestation of the kingdom of God.
Ethical	No ethical orientation.	Ethical orientation.

candidates were teenagers who had not been involved in magic).

Next, the leaders of the church took the man into a different room and ministered deliverance to him. The pastor challenged him to say "Jesus is Lord of my life." The baptismal candidate strained to confess Christ as his Lord. But his words were strangely muffled by an unholy spirit. He looked agitated. His body had become a battlefield. This internal turmoil and inability to express Christ's Lordship persisted. So we rebuked the evil spirits in the name of Jesus, and commanded them to leave. At the same time we continued to encourage the man to submit himself fully to the Lord. The pastor had him verbally renounce evil spirits and every type of occultic practice. After renouncing the forces of darkness, he convulsed. The spirits left and he was set free. He blurted it out with great relief, "Jesus is Lord, Jesus is my Lord!"

References Cited

Alexander, P. S.
    1986   "Incantations and Books of Magic." In *A History of the Jewish People in the Time of Jesus Christ*. Vol. 3. Emil Schurer, (ed.) Pp. 342-379. Edinburgh, Scotland: T. and T. Clark.

Apostolic Fathers
    1985   Vol 1. Kirsopp Lake, trans. Loeb Classical Library. Cambridge, MA: Harvard University Press.

Arnold, Clinton E.

> 1992a *Ephesians: Power and Magic. The Concept of Power in Ephesians in Light of Its Historical Setting.* Grand Rapids, MI: Baker.
>
> 1993 "Magic." In *Dictionary of Paul and His Letters.* Gerald F. Hawthorne, Ralph P. Martin, and Daniel G. Reid, eds. Pp. 580-583. Downers Grove, IL: InterVarsity.
>
> 1997 3 Crucial Questions about Spiritual Warfare. Grand Rapids, MI: Baker.

Aune, David E.

> 1980 "Magic in Early Christianity." In Aufstieg und Niedergang der Romishen Welt 2.23.2:1507-1557. Berlin, Germany: Walter De Gruyter.

Betz, Hans Dieter, (ed.)

> 1992 The Greek Magical Papyri in Translation Including the Demonic Spells. Chicago, IL: University of Chicago.

Bruce, Fredrick F.

> 1988 *The Book of the Acts.* New International Commentary on the New Testament. Revised edition. Grand Rapids, MI: Eerdmans. (1st ed. Eerdmans, 1954.)

Charlesworth, James H.

> 1983 *The Old Testament Pseudipigrapha.* Vol. 1. New York: Doubleday.
>
> 1985a *The Old Testament Pseudipigrapha.* Vol. 2. New York: Doubleday.
>
> 1985b *The Old Testament Pseudipigrapha and the New Testament.* Cambridge, England: Cambridge University Press.

Conzelmann, Hans

> 1987 *Acts.* Philadelphia, PA: Fortress.

Deissmann, Adolf
    1901   *Bible Studies*. Edinburgh, Scotland: T. and T.
          Clark .
    1927   *Light from the Ancient East*. London: Hodder
          and Stoughton.
Dunn, James. D. G.
    1996   *The Acts of the Apostles*. Valley Forge, PA:
          Trinity Press International.
Erdemgil, Selahattin
    1997   *Ephesus: Ruins and Museum*. Istanbul: Net
          Turistik Yayinlar.
Fee, Gordon D., and Douglas Stuart
    1993   *How to Read the Bible for All Its Worth*. Grand
          Rapids, MI: Zondervan.
Frazer, James George
    1963   *The Golden Bough*. Abridged edition. Vol. 1.
          New York: Macmillan Publishing Company.
Garrett, Susan
    1989   *The Demise of the Devil: Magic and the De-
          monic in Luke's Writings*. Minneapolis, MN:
          Fortress.
Greig, Gary S. and Kevin N. Springer
    1993   *The Kingdom and the Power*. Ventura, CA:
          Regal Books.
Gundry, Robert
    1982   *Matthew: A Commentary on His Literary and
          Theological Art*. Grand Rapids: Eerdmans.
Haenchen, Ernst
    1971   *The Acts of the Apostles: A Commentary*.
          Oxford, England: Blackwell/Philadelphia, PA:
          Westminster.

Harrison, Everett F.
   1986   *Interpreting Acts: The Expanding Church.*
          Grand Rapids, MI: Zondervan.
Hiebert, Paul G.
   1989   "Power Encounter and Folk Islam." In *Muslims
          and Christians on the Emmaus Road.* Pp. 45-
          62. Monrovia, CA: MARC.
Hull, John M.
1974   *Hellenistic Magic and the Synoptic Tradition.* SBT
          Vol. 28. Naperville, IL: Allenson.
Johnson, Dennis E.
   1997   *The Message of Acts in the History of
          Redemption.* Phillipsburg, PA: Presbyterian and
          Reformed.
Josephus
   1950   *Jewish Antiquities.* Vol. 5. H. St. J. Thackeray
          and Ralph Marcus, trans. The Loeb Classical
          Library. Cambridge, MA: Harvard University.
Kaiser, Walter C. Jr., and Moises Silva
   1994   *An Introduction to Biblical Hermeneutics.* Grand
          Rapids, MI: Zondervan.
Kallas, James
   1961   *The Significance of the Synoptic Miracles.*
          London: Talbot.
   1966   *The Satanward View: A Study in Pauline
          Theology.* Philadelphia, PA: Westminster.
   1968   *Jesus and the Power of Satan.* Philadelphia,
          PA: Westminster.
Kee, Howard C.
   1983   *Miracle in the Early Christian World.* New
          Haven, CT: Yale University.

1986   *Medicine, Miracle and Magic in New Testament Times.* Cambridge, England: Cambridge University.

Klein, William W., Craig Blomberg, and Robert L. Hubbard
     1993   *Introduction to Biblical Interpretation.* Dallas, TX: Word.

Koester, Helmut
     1995   *Ephesos: Metropolis of Asia.* Harvard Theological Studies. Valley Forge, PA: Trinity.

Kraft, Charles H.
     1989   *Christianity With Power.* Ann Arbor, MI: Vine.
     1992   "What Kind of Encounters Do We Need?" In *Perspectives on the World Christian Movement.* Eds. Ralph D. Winter and Steven C. Hawthorne, pp. 71-78.

Kurz, William S.
     1993   *Reading Luke-Acts: Dynamics of Biblical Narrative.* Louisville, KY: Westminster/John Knox.

Larkin, William J.
     1995   *Acts.* Downers Grove, IL: InterVarsity.

LaSor, William Sanford
     1979   "Artemis." In *The International Standard Bible Encyclopedia.* Geoffrey W. Bromiley, (ed.) Vol. 1, Pp. 306-308. Grand Rapids, MI: Eerdmans.

Lehman, Arthur C., and James E. Myers
     1985   *Magic, Witchcraft, and Religion.* Palo Alto, CA: Mayfield.

Lessa, William, and Evon Z. Vogt
     1972   *Reader in Comparative Religion.* New York: Harper and Row.

LiDonnici, Lynn R.
   1992   "The Images of Artemis Ephesia and Greco-
          Roman Worship: A Reconsideration." *Harvard
          Theological Review* 85(4):389-415.
Liefeld, Walter L.
   1995   *Interpreting the Book of Acts.* Grand Rapids, MI:
          Baker.
Longenecker, Richard N.
   1981   "Acts." In *The Expositor's Bible Commentary.*
          Vol. 9. Grand Rapids, MI: Regency Reference
          Library Zondervan.
Love, Richard Deane, II
   1992   "The Theology of the Kingdom of God: A
          Model for Contextualized and Holistic
          Evangelism among the Sundanese with Special
          Reference to the Spirit Realm." 3 vols. D.Min.
          dissertation, Westminster Theological
          Seminary.
   1995   "A Plea for Missiological Theologians and
          Theological Missiologists." Paper presented at
          the Evangelical Missiological Society West
          Region Meeting, held at The United States
          Center for World Missions, April 7, 1995.
          Pasadena, CA.
   1996   "Power Encounter Among Folk Muslims"
          Frontier Missions. Vol. 14, Num.4. Pp. 193-
          195.
   1998   "Pauline Contextualization at Ephesus: Power
          and Leadership Issues with Special Reference to
          Sundanese Folk Muslims." A Ph.D. dissertation
          at Marshall, I. Howard.
   1978   *Commentary on Luke.* Grand Rapids: Eerdmans.

1983   *The Acts of the Apostles: An Introduction and
        Commentary.* Tyndale New Testament
        Commentary. Leicester, England:
        InterVarsity/Grand Rapids, MI: Eerdmans.

1992   *The Acts of the Apostles.* New Testament
        Guides. Sheffield, England: JSOT Press.

Martin, Hubert M. Jr.

1992   "Artemis." In *The Anchor Bible Dictionary.*
        David Noel Freedman, (ed.) Vol. I. Pp. 464-
        465. New York: Doubleday.

Martin, Ralph P.

1981   *Reconciliation: A Study of Paul's Theology.*
        Atlanta, GA: John Knox Press.

McCown, Chester C.

1923   "The Ephesia Grammata in Popular Belief."
        *Transactions and Proceedings of the American
        Philological Association* 54:128-140.

Metzger, Bruce. M.

1944   "St. Paul and the Magicians." *Princeton
        Seminary Bulletin* 38(1):27-30.

Moulton, James Hope

1930   *A Grammar of New Testament Greek.*
        Edinburgh, Scotland: T. and T. Clark.

Moulton, James Hope and George Milligan

1929   *The Vocabulary of the Greek Testament.* Parts
        1-9. London: Hodder and Stoughton.

Musk, Bill

1989   *The Unseen Face of Islam.* London: MARC.

Mussies, G.

1995   "Artemis." In *Dictionary of Deities and
        Demons in the Bible.* Karel Van der Toorn, Bob

Becking and Pieter W Van der Horst, eds.
Pp.168-180. Leiden, Holland: Brill.

Newman, Barclay M. and Eugene A. Nida
1972 *The Acts of the Apostles.* UBS Handbook
Series. New York: United Bible Societies.

O'Brien, Peter T.
1982 *Colossians, Philemon.* Word Biblical
Commentary. Vol. 44. Waco, TX: Word.
1984 "Principalities and Powers: Opponents of the
Church." In *Biblical Interpretation and the
Church: Text and Context.* D. A. Carson, (ed.)
Pp. 110-150. Exeter, England: Paternoster.

Osborne, Grant R.
1991 *The Hermeneutical Spiral: A Comprehensive
Introduction to Biblical Interpretation.*
Downers Grove, IL: InterVarsity.

Oster, Richard E.
1974 "A Historical Commentary on the Missionary
Success Stories in Acts 19:11-40." Ph.D.
dissertation, Princeton Theological Seminary.
1976 "The Ephesians Artemis as an Opponent of
Early Christianity." In *Jahrbuch fur Antike und
Christentum* 19:24-44. Munster Westfalen.
1990 "Ephesus as a Religious Center under the
Principate, I. Paganism Before Constantine." In
Aufstieg und Niedergang der Romishen Welt
Part II: Principate. 18(3):1662-1728. New
York: Walter De Gruyter.
1992 "Christianity in Asia Minor." In *The Anchor
Bible Dictionary.* Vol. 1. David Noel
Freedman, (ed.) Pp. 938-954. New York:
Doubleday.

Parshall, Phil
    1983   *Bridges to Islam.* Grand Rapids, MI: Baker.
Poythress, Vern Sheridan
    1995   "Territorial Spirits: Some Biblical
            Perspectives." *Urban Mission* 13(2):37-49.
Preisendanz, Karl
    1973   *Papyri Graecae Magicae.* Vol. 1. Stvtgardiae
            in Aedibvs B.G. Tevbneri.
    1974   *Papyri Graecae Magicae.* Vol. 2. Stvtgardiae
            in Aedibvs B.G. Tevbneri.
Ramsay, William M.
    1953   *The Bearing of Recent Discovery on the
            Trustworthiness of the New Testament.* Grand
            Rapids, MI: Baker.
Segal, Alan F.
    1981   "Hellenistic Magic: Some Questions of
            Definition." In *Studies in Gnosticism and
            Hellenistic Religions.* R. van den Brock and M.
            J. Vermaseren, eds. Pp. 349-375. Leiden,
            Holland: Brill.
Steffen, Tom A.
    1993   *Passing the Baton: Church Planting that
            Empowers.* La Habra, CA: Center for
            Organizational and Ministry Development.
    1996   *Reconnecting God's Story to Ministry.* La Habra, CA:
            Center for Organizational and Ministry
            Development (1996)
Stewart, Z., (ed.)
    1972   *Arthur Darby Nock: Essays on Religion and the
            Ancient World.* Vol. 1. Oxford, England:
            Clarendon.

Steyne, Philip M.
    1989   *Gods of Power*. Houston, TX: Touch
            Publications.
Stott, John. R. W.
    1990   *The Message of Acts*. Leicester, England:
            InterVarsity.
Stott, John R.W. and Robert T. Coote, eds.
    1980   *Down to Earth*. Wheaton, IL: Lausanne
            Committee for World Evangelization.
Strelan, Rick
    1996   *Paul, Artemis, and the Jews in Ephesus*. Berlin,
            Germany: Walter De Gruyter.
Talbert, Charles H.
    1997   *Reading Acts: A Literary and Theological
            Commentary on the Acts of the Apostles*. New
            York: Crossroad.
Tannehill, Robert C.
    1994   *The Narrative Unity of Luke-Acts.* Minneapolis,
            MN: Fortress.
Thiselton, Anthony C.
    1980 *The Two Horizons: New Testament
            Hermeneutics and Philosophical Description.*
            Grand Rapids: Eerdmans.
Tippett, Alan
    1987   *Introduction to Missiology*. Pasadena, CA:
            William Carey Library.
Trebilco, Paul
    1994   "Ephesus." In *The Book of Acts in its Graeco-
            Roman Setting*. D. W. J. Gill and C. Gempf,
            eds. Pp. 302-354. Grand Rapids, MI:
            Eerdmans.

Twelftree, Graham H.
1993 *Jesus the Exorcist: A Contribution to the Study of the Historical Jesus.* Peabody, MA: Hendrickson.

Wagner, C. Peter
1988 *How to Have a Healing Ministry without Making Your Church Sick!* Ventura,CA: Regal.
1991 *Territorial Spirits.* Chichester, England: Sovereign World.
1995 *Blazing the Way.* Book 3. Acts of the Holy Spirit Series. Ventura, CA: Regal.
1996 *Confronting the Powers.* The Prayer Warrior Series. Ventura, CA: Regal.

Wagner, C. Peter and F. Douglas Pennoyer, eds.
1990 *Wrestling with Dark Angels.* Ventura, CA: Regal.

Warner, Timothy M.
1991 *Spiritual Warfare.* Wheaton, IL: Crossway.

Wax, Murray and Rosalie
1962 "The Magical World View." *Journal for the Scientific Study of Religion* 1(2):179-188.
1963 "The Notion of Magic." *Current Anthropology* 4(5):495-503.

Williams, David J.
1993 *Acts.* New International Biblical Commentary. Peabody, MA: Hendrickson.

Williams, Don
1989 *Signs, Wonders and the Kingdom of God.* Ann Arbor: Vine Books.

Wimber, John
1986 *Power Evangelism.* San Francisco: Harper and Row.

1987   *Power Healing.* San Francisco, CA: Harper and Row.

Witherington, Ben, III

1994   *Paul's Narrative Thought World.* Louisville, KY: Westminster/John Knox Press.

1998   *The Acts of the Apostles: A Socio-Rhetorical Commentary.* Grand Rapids, MI: Eerdmans.

Woodberry, J. Dudley

1990   "The Relevance of Power Ministries for Folk Muslims." In *Wrestling with Dark Angels.* C. Peter Wagner and F. Douglas Pennoyer, eds. Pp. 311-337. Ventura, CA: Regal.

Yamauchi, Edwin M.

1983   "Magic in the Biblical World." *Tyndale Bulletin* 34:169-200.

University and Church:
Prisoners of Culture or Partners
For the Great Commission?

Sherwood Lingenfelter

Andrew Walls (1996:54) has shown how the history of the church is one of tension between the "indigenizing principle" which pressures churches and peoples into independence, isolation, and conformity to their peculiar cultures, and the "pilgrim principle" which draws the church and its peoples to the universals of the faith, rooted in obedience to Christ and the scriptures. This chapter explores the role of the Christian university as partner and prisoner with the church in its journey of obedience to Christ and in its mission to make disciples of all nations. How are university and church rooted in and prisoners of their culture? How can they sustain the "pilgrimage" of their distinctively Christian mission? What are the respective roles of the church and the university in engaging the cultures in which they are rooted, in making disciples of the children of their culture, and in making disciples of all nations?

In the first 200 years of post-reformation history the universities reflected much of the thinking and life of the

111

church, and together, church and university mirrored the tensions and changes occurring in their respective cultural settings. However, Marsden (1994) notes that in the 19th and 20th centuries the long standing relationship of the university and the church began to fracture and then to disintegrate. As the university became more focused on research related to the sciences, the gulf between them increased. Science replaced theology as the central discipline and methodology of Christian universities, which in turn resulted in the secularization of these institutions.

This chapter begins then with the assumption that the idea of a "Christian" university remains a viable alternative in American public life, and that it can and must partner with the church of Jesus Christ for His mission of world evangelism and making disciples. It will first examine the character of this mission and follow with a brief discussion of the viability of such a partnership and the role of the Christian university in that partnership.

Culture, the Church and Making Disciples

Andrew Walls (1996:52-53) finds the distinction between proselyte and convert helpful in his discussion of what it means to make disciples. The proselyte leaves his culture and religion to fully embrace a new one. A Gentile who became a Jewish proselyte had to be circumcised, keep every aspect of the Jewish law, abandon his Gentile culture, and identify wholly with the Jewish community which he had entered. A convert in contrast accepts a new message, adopts a new faith, but does not adopt another culture. A Christian convert becomes a Christian, but is not particularly identified with a given culture. The convert observes the faith community of the people who bring the message and realizes that some parts of the faith community do not match his or her way of life. So the convert accepts the message, but does not necessarily accept much of the culture of those who brought it.

This contrast is useful in our reflection on the mission of making disciples. The Apostle Paul rejected the notion of proselyte in his ministry to the Gentiles. He articulated his concern to become culturally relevant, all things to all men, to win converts. Moreover, he wholly repudiated the idea of making converts into Jewish Christians. Therefore, in our reflection on the role of the church and the university for making disciples, we, too must reject the notion of proselyte. We begin with the assumption that disciples of Jesus will remain in their cultural communities, and retain ways of life that differ from that of the source community of the Christian message.

Walls provides further help in clarifying our task through his discussion of how the faith message is communicated, received, and transformed into a viable, dynamic local church community. Walls speaks of this process as one involving two potentially contradictory principles, the indigenizing principle and the pilgrim principle.

The "indigenizing principle" addresses the necessity of the local community to bring the Christian message into its own context and to make it relevant to its own way of life. In essence, it is a local vision of the church. When a new disciple receives the gospel, she actually translates it into her local family, community, and way of life. Walls notes how this was exemplified in the early history of the church in the book of Acts. For example, the early Gentile Christians in Acts 11 dared to used the word Kyrios, "Lord" for Jesus instead of "Messiah," which was the proper reference for Jewish believers. Greeks used the word, Κυριος, "Lord" for any cult divinity worshipped in their pagan culture. By using this term, evangelists risked syncretism among new believers. Eating meat offered to idols was another cultural issue for these Gentiles. While the Jews would never have eaten this meat, Paul left the matter to the conscience of individual converts. Although syncretism may indeed have occurred among these Greek converts, the longer-term effect was conversion not only of the persons, but of their thought and their local way of life.

What happens in the conversion process that prevents syncretism? Walls (1996:54) describes this counter process as the "pilgrim principle." While indigenization must occur for persons to become converts, they also are invited to embark on a journey of pilgrimage. Pilgrimage connects a new disciple to the universal vision of the church. New believers gain an identity that comes through their relationship and loyalty to Jesus Christ. They develop an allegiance to the authority of the Word of God and a commitment to obeying that Word. Since the Word of God is not localized in any particular culture, but is written to all people, disciples learn of and experience faith and relationships of a universal faith community. This universal word provides the knowledge foundation upon which the universal church sustains its identity and focuses upon the person and lordship of Jesus Christ. Pilgrimage leads new believers to the practice of discipleship that is transcultural, and transforming to their individual lives and to their cultural communities.

In summary, the indigenizing principle and the pilgrim principle highlight for us the tension that new converts and newly formed churches have experienced throughout church history. From these principles the church must grapple with fundamental questions. Will the church be part of its local culture? Will it engage on a journey that takes it in a new direction that is different from the local culture? And how will that happen? The local expression of the church in any culture cannot be effective unless it participates in both of these processes.

The local church, employing the indigenizing principle, serves to contextualize the message, enabling people to understand it, to receive it, and to become followers of Jesus. Once they have become disciples, they may engage their local language and culture as witnesses, bringing other people to Christ. Within that same context the local community invites new believers to join in an adventure of pilgrimage, which serves to transform these disciples of Jesus Christ into culturally relevant servants of the master. The pilgrimage is one which draws the local community into a relationship with the universal church, and gives local believers a distinctive sense that they are in the world, but they are not of it.

The Church, the University and Culture

Let us return now to the question of partnership between Protestant churches in America and American Christian universities. How can and should these two institutions, united in their commitment to Jesus Christ and to His mission, partner in the task of world Evangelization and church planting? Walls (1996:49-50) has two additional ideas that are intriguing and I think helpful in our discussion. He quotes Jewish Rabbi, Johannan Ben Zakkai, with regard to the subject of training disciples. Zakkai noted a particular contrast between two of the five men who were his disciples. One he described as a "plastered cistern." The modern swimming pool is our closest cultural equivalent. The plastered cistern is designed and carefully plastered so that it will not leak; it will hold every drop of water placed in it. Zakkai describes the disciple who is like a plastered cistern as one who holds on to every word of scripture! He is very reluctant to lose one thought; even the smallest word is important to him. Every aspect of God's word is precious, a treasure to be cherished, preserved, and observed.

Zakkai describes his second disciple as an "ever-flowing spring," running deep from the mountain, becoming a river of sparkling water. This disciple exhibits a vivacious exuberance of God in her life and work. For this disciple, the scripture pervades her personality and is incorporated into every aspect of life. This disciple is dynamic, creative, always thinking about new things; she is never stuck on the past.

Walls (1996:50) concludes that complete discipleship involves a Christian community which nurtures both kinds of people. Some people, like cisterns, hold as precious treasure each and every detail of the Word of God. Others, like gushing mountain springs, allow the deep waters of scripture to flow through them and out into the world around them, bringing renewal and change. The strengths of each combine to form a complete community in which pilgrimage and transformation characterize the lives of its people.

Churches as Plastered Cisterns, Universities as Ever-flowing Springs

Drawing upon these analogies, while recognizing the danger of oversimplification, I suggest that the various expressions of the church in the Reformation tended to place higher value on disciples who are like plastered cisterns. *Sola Scriptura*-the great theme of the Reformation, emphasizes the authority of the Bible and the Bible alone. Kevin Lawson (Lawson 1997:49-64) comments that conservative reformation thinkers restricted their notions of authority to scripture, creeds, and key Reformation preachers like Luther, Calvin, Zwengli, and others. The fundamentalist and evangelical Protestant denominations of this century have emphasized scripture alone as the source of right doctrine and Christian living. Because of their deep distrust of human agency, the fundamentalists in particular have rejected any source of knowledge that is not wholly grounded in the biblical text. As a consequence their powerful thrust for world evangelization in this century was deeply biblical in orientation, but often ethnocentric and culturally imperialistic as they nurtured new churches taking root in non-western cultures.

The universities of the Reformation in contrast placed high value on disciples whose lives were "ever-flowing springs." The ideal of the university was that all truth is God's truth. The disciples in the university committed to a search for knowledge outside of the word of God as well as in it. They sought truth in natural revelation as well as special revelation.

Marsden (1994) in his research on American universities, notes that the great Christian Protestant universities rejected the sectarianism that characterized their founding church communities. They believed that through Christian education they could create a non-sectarian Christian culture. To achieve this goal they sought to exclude the "plastered cisterns" from their faith communities, and they relegated theology, which they judged sectarian, to the periphery of university life. As a consequence the seminaries of Harvard, Yale, and Princeton had faculty, programs, and identities separate from the rest of the university. While university faculty and presidents professed allegiance to Christian faith and living, the pursuit of knowledge became an empirical agenda of science, for which theology had no relevance. Their faith in the possibility in achieving a Christian culture was nevertheless rooted in two specific assumptions of reformed theology–an amillenial interpretation of scripture and a sincere belief that their "Christian" culture was superior and would overcome the secular culture of society.

The fatal theological error that energized this dichotomy between the church and the university was their failure to recognize the indigenizing power of culture. Reformed theologians and church leaders underestimated the powerful force by which culture pressures the church into conformity with the world. Without a continuous and powerful tension in the Christian community toward pilgrimage, stressing the eternal and universal truths of scripture, the drift toward indigenization leads the church into conformity with its culture and in that conformity to its death.

The history of universities and churches in America in the 19th and 20th centuries illustrates what social anthropologists term "cultural drift." The indigenous principle in the life of churches dominated until the tension of pilgrimage weakened to ineffectiveness. The university conformed even more rapidly to the culture, so that its Christian identity was social, rather than a substantive part of its character. The testimony of Biola's first dean, R. A. Torrey, illustrates the tensions in this historical period of change. As a student at Yale, Torrey lived a fairly nominal Christian life, seeking pleasure and scholarly pursuits that were typical of his social class as a banker's son. He then went to Yale Divinity School and became a leader among those students who challenged the authority of scripture and embraced the critical perspective of contemporary theology and biblical studies. In his senior year at Yale (1870), Torrey had an encounter with D. L. Moody. Moody challenged Torrey with the result that Torrey asked Moody to teach him how to lead men to Christ. Torrey's experience of leading a ballroom companion to Christ transformed his attitude toward Christian ministry. Upon graduation from seminary he entered the pastorate for a time and then left for Germany to study at Leipzig and Erlangen, two Lutheran seminaries. During this period in his life he was torn between the scientific critical approach to scripture and the traditional view that God's revelation was infallible and inerrant. Torrey decided to act on the assumption that the Bible was indeed inerrant, and stated "I will follow the Bible wherever it leads me." He returned to the United States and began a life of ministry that led to his appointment as the first dean at the Bible Institute of Los Angeles.

Stagnant Cisterns, Acid Springs

The gradual separation of church and university, the removal of theology from a university education, and the creeping indigenization of the church as a civil religion had the unintended consequence of secularizing both church and university.

The churches, as repositories of theology, tended to become stagnant cisterns. The stagnation of liberalism and the stagnation of fundamentalism are expressions of the church which reflect an internal focus which leads to the reproduction of self. Departing from their mission of making disciples, they have become preoccupied with issues of their own culture, and lost their collective commitment to pilgrimage. This is not to say that nothing good has come of American Protestantism in this century. The mission movement of conservative and fundamentalist Protestant churches in the 20th century is unparalleled in church history. The establishment of Bible Institutes and Bible Colleges all across America have grown out of a renewed interest in the study of scriptures, and a commitment to the mission of making disciples. Yet, within this great movement of the Spirit of God, many local congregations became defensive, inwardly focused, and then stagnant in their life and vision.

The universities, as centers of research and new knowledge apart from theology, have become "acid springs." Like acid rain, they destroy rather than nurture life. The disciple of the university embraced skepticism and relativism. Many scholars argue today that we cannot know any truth. The majority of faculty in most American universities reject the idea that scripture could be authoritative or could have any utility in knowing truth. So the universities and the churches exist in a state of alienation, which is most frequently expressed as cultural wars between conservative Christianity and liberal public culture.

The conservative and fundamentalist Protestant churches turned during this period from universities to Bible Institutes and Bible Colleges to accomplish their mission of training leaders. These schools, like Biola, refocused their mission around *Sola Scriptura*. Their students were to be "plastered cisterns," drinking in every part of the word of God and losing nothing. At the same time they rejected the wider culture, withdrew from it, and failed to engage it in a way that would bring transforming life to it. The anti-intellectualism that followed from this movement has characterized conservative Protestantism in American to this day. I received a letter in February, 1998 from an alumnus of Biola who is deeply concerned that we have lost our way, and that we are trying to follow in the path of Harvard and Yale. The vision of this alumnus is that Biola should produce disciples of Jesus Christ who are only "plastered cisterns." He cannot comprehend the making of disciples who are able to engage the culture with the word of God, as "ever-flowing springs."

Reuniting Church and University Through Mission:
Making Disciples

Is it possible to bring the university and the church back together? Could pastors, lay people and faculty trust one another, and commit time from their ever full agendas to dialogue about issues of mutual importance to them? Could they again engage in substantive conversations about the critical issues? The AD 2000 and Beyond Movement for World Evangelization, has been compelling enough to prompt a few academic leaders to join pastors, mission leaders, and businessmen at an International conference in South Africa in July of 1997. The fact that such a conversation could happen once gives me hope that it could happen again. Yet, the obstacles to this process are great. To overcome them it is helpful to reflect on the issues that divide us, and refocus on a mission of great enough significance to bring us together again.

Reflection: Causes of Division

What are some of the causes of the failure of the reformation partnership? Marsden (1994) documents many reasons in his book, *The Soul Of The American University*, which I will not repeat here. Rather, I will discuss two which I believe have primary significance and application to the question of this paper. First, Reformation leaders of Christian Universities in America had an overly optimistic view of culture. In that optimism, they failed to see what Scripture says about culture as "prisons of disobedience." Summarizing from some of my earlier work (1992; 1996). Peter speaks about culture in his epistle as an empty way of life handed down to us form our ancestors. The Apostle Paul, in documenting the tension between Jews and Gentiles throughout the book of Romans, concludes in Chapter 11:32 that God has given all men over to prisons of disobedience so that He might have mercy on them all. Paul speaks of the futility of the Gentile mind, and of the world pressuring believers to conform to its mold. For Christian leaders swept away by the optimism of modernity, these texts were an anomaly to their world view, and were ignored. Smitten by the seductive power of science and modernity, and confident in their Christian culture, they failed to see Biblical warnings of the power of culture for the indigenization of their faith. In effect, they lost their pilgrimage with Christ, and refocused their faith on an American civil religion.

In a second strategic error, faculty and university leaders embraced logical positivism, the central philosophy of modernity. Logical positivism asserts that one truth exists, and that truth can be discovered through the rigorous application of scientific methodology and rational thought. Scientific naturalism is the religious outcome of logical positivism. People believe that the methods and data of science are more reliable than the Word of God. As scholars and leaders in the universities acclaimed this philosophy they reduced all knowledge to what could be observed in nature. Scripture and theology were thus relegated to the periphery of the university and cultural life. Faculty viewed theology as sectarian, and therefore unacceptable in the university community. Within a very short time Christian pilgrimage was not even a topic for discussion.

The outcome of these choices is self-evident today. The reformed university project of creating a Christian society through education has utterly failed. Further, materialism and scientific naturalism has replaced Christian theism as the dominant religious paradigm. The great Christian universities of the 19th century no longer even aspire to promote Christian culture.

Refocus on Mission

The failure of America's universities to be a Christian force at the end of this century can ultimately be attributed to their loss of mission. While Yale and Princeton focused on Christian culture, they neglected the central Christian mission to make disciples of Jesus Christ. Unless the Christian university holds a very deep commitment to making disciples, it cannot sustain a viable partnership with the churches in its culture. The central mission of the church is to observe the command that Jesus gave us in the gospel of Matthew, to "make disciples of all nations, teaching them to observe all things that I have commanded you." The mission of making disciples is not a parachurch mission. The university cannot accomplish this apart from the church. It is possible, however, to renew the vision of the founders of the reformation, and establish universities that engage in significant partnership with the church for the mission of making disciples.

The strategic role that the university has to play in this mission lies in our potential contribution to sustaining the tension between what Walls has termed the indigenous and the pilgrim principles. The university is a place where we can continue to think about how to make Christianity relevant in our culture. In this regard we are partners in the process of contextualization and indigenization. At the same time the university must be a place were we continue to teach the fundamentals of pilgrimage to the next generation. The faculty of the university must grapple with the character and qualities of a Christian life, and seek to understand how pilgrimage calls us to a life of tension with our culture and a continuous process of renewal and change. The church has already entrusted us with a mission of training church and secular leaders for the next generation. It is our responsibility to assure that the tension of cultural relevance and biblical pilgrimage are sustained in this preparation process, and that we are equipping people to accomplish the mission of Christ in the church and society.

Complementary Roles

From the first emergence of Christian universities in the Reformation, the leaders of the universities recognized their complementary role to the unity and life of the church. Further, the church has priority over the university in this relationship in its ministry as the body of Christ. The church, with its mission to nurture the people of God, must continually focus upon teaching scripture, and nurturing the people of God to become effective disciples of the Lord Jesus Christ. The church also is a primary force for Evangelization in a lost world. Local churches tend to focus on one aspect of this mission at the cost of the other. The recent history of fundamentalism and evangelicalism suggests local churches tend to be more powerful in their role as plastered cisterns, repository and teachers of the Word of God, than they are effective agents of Evangelization in the wider culture.

The university has served traditionally as a place of dynamic reflection, a place where scholars think and research the fundamental questions of their disciplines and of that moment in history. The university acts as a catalyst for innovation and change. Yet the university has also failed to contribute in a substantive way to the mission of Evangelization of the lost. University leaders and faculty have traditionally assigned the responsibility for evangelism to the local church. Substantive research on Evangelization is typically confined to the departments of missions and evangelism in the seminaries that have been a peripheral part of university culture.

In their respective roles in culture the church tends to take the conservative stance and the university tends to take a liberal stance. The conservatism of the church blinds it to the issues of contextualization that are essential for evangelism, and encourages the building of walls to protect its people from the surrounding culture. In this process the church does not recognize that these walls actually promote conformity to a more traditional culture instead of engaging the changing culture to make disciples. The university in contrast tears down the walls of conservatism, seeking to engage the changing culture and discover new knowledge. But the university, too, fails to focus this new knowledge on the task of Christian pilgrimage and world Evangelization.

In the cultural milieu, the church needs a relationship with the university to stimulate reflection that is more open and to enable its people to be an ever-flowing spring of living water to a lost world. Likewise, the university needs the church to stimulate its deeper reflection on the unchanging Word of God, to call it back to the universals of the Christian faith, and to keep the university focused on pilgrimage. The genius of their partnership is that, given a clear focus on their mission of making disciples, they together are much more powerful than either is alone.

The task for university and church, then, is to lead the next generation to conversion and transformation in the Lord Jesus Christ. Conversion occurs when people hear the gospel, understand it, and receive Christ; transformation occurs when people engage the universal Word of God, and follow the Living Word to become like Christ. The church and the university combine unique strengths that are essential to the completion of this mission.

Walls (1996:51) reminds us that every nation has a "pattern of thought and life that is essentially its own." Conversion to Christ does not isolate the convert from his or her community, but rather begins the transformation of the new believer, and then spreads that transformation to the whole community. Transformation involves Christ's entry into the thought and cultural fabric of generations of believers. Walls emphases that "this process is never finished in one generation." Transformation into the likeness of Christ is a never ending process, as generation after generation engage a culture which seeks to squeeze them into its mold, and faces the question of following culture or becoming a disciple of the Lord Jesus Christ.

Reviving the Conversation

Partnership between church and university will not occur unless the participants make a new commitment to revive their conversations on the mission of making disciples of the nations for the Lord Jesus Christ. Such a conversation was initiated by the organizing committee of the AD 2000 Movement in their planning of the Global Conference on World Evangelism 97 in Pretoria, South Africa. For the first time in the history of this movement, Presidents and Academic Deans from Christian educational institutions around the world were invited to join the conversation. One of the positive outcomes of this meeting was the decision on the part of the organizing committee of the AD 2000 movement to make the Presidents and Academic Deans consultation a continuing part of the AD 2000 consultations. In the conference in Pretoria, pastors and mission leaders spoke to the Presidents and Academic Deans who had gathered about the mission of world Evangelization and challenged the colleges and universities to change the way they do business. The conversation was more of a monologue, as Presidents and Academic Deans listened to the concerns of pastors and mission leaders. Following these monologues, Presidents and Academic Deans discussed together how they might respond.

While I am pleased with the beginning dialogue that occurred in Pretoria, the lecture pattern of the conference is typical of the kinds of exchanges that occur between leaders of the church and the university. When church leaders are invited to Christian universities, they too sit and listen to faculty and academic deans, who expect the pastors to respond by changing the way they do business. These types of conversations do not result in substantive change on the part of either party. Further, they highlight issues of difference, but do not lead the participants to a sense of partnership and common mission.

If the church and the university are truly to renew their partnership toward fulfilling the mission of our Lord Jesus Christ, substantive, prolonged conversations are essential to the process. These conversations may take various forms and address a wide range of issues. It is not so important what is discussed as that the discussion begins and continues into the next century. It is through prolonged discussion that church and university leaders build trust with one another, and sharpen one another in their thinking and in their strategic action for the church of the Lord Jesus Christ.

Ralph Winter, founder of the U. S. Center for World Mission and President of William Carey International University, has designed one of the most effective programs for dialogue between the academic community and evangelical churches. Winter and a team of Christian scholars designed a

course on world evangelization entitled Perspectives on the
World Christian Movement. Winter and his colleagues prepared a comprehensive text of articles and exerpts from books
by major church historians, missiologists, anthropologists, and
strategists on the challenge of world evangelism. Then,
working with strategic pastors and churches, first in the Los
Angeles area and then across America, a coordinating team
from the U. S. Center of World Mission facilitated the offering
of a fifteen week courses on the subject matter of world
evangelism. The Perspectives Class has been offered hundreds
of times in the Los Angeles basin and has touched the lives of
tens of thousands of lay people in churches. The courses have
similar impact in major metropolitan centers across the United
States. Out of this class hundreds of men and women have
responded to the call of God to commit their lives to the task of
world evangelism. Other pastors and lay men and women have
experienced a renewal of their vision and a much deeper
understanding of the strategic action that must take place in the
local church to reach a lost world with the gospel. Out of this
course hundreds of churches have begun to focus on unreached
people groups in their prayer and mission strategies. Pastors
and lay men have attended international conferences, they have
visited their missionaries in their respective fields, and they
have gained a renewed vision for how they as a local church
can participate in the task of world evangelism. The genius of
Winter's strategy has been to take the university to the local
church, and through visiting lecturers, excellent materials, and
a vision for a lost world, the academic community has had a
profound impact in the local church for the cause of world
evangelism. This model could be utilized in a number of new
and strategic ways by university faculty and leaders with a
vision to make it happen.

  In the remaining part of this paper I will focus specifically on the distinctive role that I believe a Christian university

like Biola can play in such a conversation. Biola and other Christian universities have a very strategic opportunity and have much to contribute. However, unless the leaders of Biola plan intentionally to engage in conversation with the leaders of the churches who are part of their constituency, the conversation will not occur. For church and university to truly engage in partnership, there must be intentional commitments on the part of both to open dialogue and to sustain that dialogue until each of them have committed to a long term relationship around the central mission of Christ.

The Christian University as "An Ever-flowing Spring"

What is the unique role of the university for engaging the culture in which it is rooted, for making disciples of the children of this culture, and for making disciples of all nations? What contribution can and should the university make to the church for their common mission of making disciples?

Zakkai's analogy of the disciple as an "ever-flowing spring" is a useful one to reconsider our mission as a university. Repeating again Walls (1996:50) definition of such a disciple: scripture pervades the disciples personality and is incorporated into every aspect of his life-dynamic, creative, conceiving of new things, never stuck on the past. If the faculty and leadership of Biola and other Christian universities engage in personal discipleship of this nature, then their pattern of life will flow into their practice of education in the Christian university and will empower the university to play a similar role in the wider society.

Changing our Academic Culture

The first step in the process of becoming "ever-flowing springs" is to re-center our lives and our university education around scripture and theology. We must not make the same mistake that our academic ancestors did in the 19th and early 20th century, relegating theology to a place outside the university curriculum. Our predecessors did this because they feared sectarianism, but in eliminating sectarianism they lost the greater value of Christian pilgrimage. We must bring scripture and theology back to the center of our personal lives and to the center of our university education. The Lordship of Jesus Christ and the normativeness of scripture are keys.

Robert Saucy (1998), a theologian, focuses on the issues of the Lordship of Christ and the normativeness of scripture. Saucy speaks of reshaping the Christian mind and will for service to Christ and the world. Clearly, Saucy's agenda is one that we must accept if we are to accomplish our mission. Saucy challenges us to develop consensus in the academic community on the theological essentials that are needed for the discovery of truth, both in the natural world and in the world of revealed truth. Saucy also calls us to be practicing supernaturalists in a world which questions even the existence of the supernatural. If any university is to partner with the church in the making of disciples, we must challenge the pervading worldview of naturalism and be practicing supernaturalists.

Doug Geivett (1998), a philosopher, raises important concerns about epistemology. Geivett explains that the question of how we know is answered in two very different ways in modern university culture. The post-modern approach is to deny that there is any possibility of knowing truth and the assertion that all knowledge is political and relative to the perspective of the viewer. The other, carried over from the modernist perspective of logical positivism, suggests that understanding truth is possible, but only through empirical and rational methodology. Geivett argues that Christians must contend for the possibility of objective knowledge through both revelation and through empirical observation and research. His conclusion is that questions of knowing are particularly fundamental to Christian witness, Christian research, and cultural transformation. We must not ignore the questions of how we know which are strategic in reaching for Christ the next generation of American students.

We must also address and change what Bloom (Bloom 1998), a physicist, calls the classical dichotomy between church and university—"churches do ministry and the universities do science." Within this scenario, the church typically has ignored what happens in the university about science and faith. And Christian faculty have typically compartmentalized their world view. Faculty go to church on Sunday and do science on Monday and never the twain meet. The church typically accepts cultural solutions to the questions of science instead of solutions that come out of substantive research. The outcome of the dichotomy is that the university rejects the church and the church rejects the university.

Bloom makes two comments that I think are very helpful in addressing this question. Bloom (1998:8) suggests that the gospel prospers when Christians "articulate faith according to the intellectual standards of the day." And, the gospel also prospers when Christians live lives that reflect Christ in His purity, and engage in significant ministry in the culture. Bloom proposes that Christian faculty should engage the intellectual issues of science and faith and communicate in a more effective way with pastors and lay people in churches with regard to these issues. The university should be a source of dynamic, creative new knowledge and insights, an ever-flowing spring with regard to scientific knowledge.

On the same theme of compartmentalization and dichotomy, Roger Feldman (1998), an artist, notes that Christians have retreated from the arts in the earlier part of this century. In the fundamentalist phase of Biola's history, art and popular culture were deemed as secular and corrupting, so that people in the church and in schools like Biola refused to participate in the arts and did not educate students to serve as salt and light in the arts. Feldman suggests that the conse-quences of these choices, a "sensate culture," are seen in the popular culture and media of America today. The sensate culture is committed to the pursuit of pleasures of the body and of life and has rejected anything that has to do with Christian faith. Feldman's vision is for an integration of Christianity and the arts in the university around either the model of Moses or the model of Jesus. Moses took the role of a powerful critic of the cultures of Egypt and of the Israelites, exposing misplaced trust, energizing people for righteousness, and revealing a sovereign God through the arts. The other alternative, the prophetic role that Jesus took, challenges the culture, disman-tles the established order, and energizes a new order through wholeness in the community of the church. Feldman articu-lates a vision for art as being a place where the truth of God might be expressed in a new and unique way in our culture.

J. I. Packer (1998) characterized the Christian educator as men and women of God who are committed to incarnational relationships. The task of Christian education is much more than the communication of fact or the impartation of skills. The Christian educator is engaged in the process of training followers of the Lord Jesus Christ. Packer describes the teacher than as a critical realist, one who has examined care-fully issues of the world and understands the joys, the triumphs, the failures, the disappointments, and despair of living. The teacher engages in piercing communication, communication that catches the attention that motivates the student and challenges them to new and difficult journeys. Perhaps most important, the Christian educator is one who lives a live that is abounding in obedience to and service for the Lord Jesus Christ. As students experience relationships with people who abound in their lives with God, they are encouraged to take the risk of separation from the securities of culture and to embark on the journey of pilgrimage with Jesus Christ.

Changing our Program of Research

One component of Biola University's mission is biblically centered research. If you were to ask a faculty member what this means, you would probably get as many answers as you have faculty. All of us struggle with the question of how biblical truth and the traditional research agendas of our academic disciplines connect with one another. In the disciplines of the natural sciences and professions the connections are often more difficult to make than in the humanities or social sciences where faculty are studying human behavior. But all of us grapple with the question, what does it mean to do biblically centered research.

Returning to Zakkai's analogy of the disciple as a "ever-flowing spring," I suggest that we all need to draw more deeply upon the living water that we find in our relationship with Christ and with His Word in our reflection upon our world and upon our work. To help us in this process I will review briefly the example that Jesus set in his relationship with the Samaritan women. As Jesus and his disciples walked through Samaria it was evident to the local people and to his disciples that they were of different cultures. The Samaritans were ethnically different from the Jews, and the Jews deemed them inferior and heretics. The Samaritans understood the Jewish hatred and perhaps returned the same. Jesus' disciples were not happy about being there, but they had no other choice since they had to pass through Samaria on their way to Galilee.

Jesus, as always, acted in ways that countered the expectations of his own culture. When the woman from Samaria came to the well, he initiated a conversation with her. This act astonished her and his Jewish disciples. In that conversation Jesus did some basic research as part of his ministry.

The first thing he did was to recognize her thirst. In a short conversation he understood that she needed more than water, that there was a deeper thirst in her life that had not been met. The second thing he observed was that she was living a life style that was contrary to her beliefs, and contrary to a way of life that would lead to enduring relationships of joy and peace in God. As Jesus interviewed this woman, it soon became evident that she also did not see eye to eye with him about religion. She told him about how her ancestors worshipped nearby on Mount Garizim, and observed that Jews worshipped in Jerusalem. Finally, he learned from her that she and her fellow townsmen were expecting a Messiah. From this research Jesus was able to meet her needs. He told her about a source of living water from which she could drink that would satisfy her thirst. He challenged her lifestyle, especially the fact that she had no husband and had been married to five. He told her that neither she nor the Jews understood truly what worshipping God was all about. He told her that the time would come when they who worship God would worship Him in spirit and truth. Finally, Jesus revealed himself as the Messiah for whom she was looking, the source of living water.

The research Jesus did in this setting provides a basic outline for us from which we can do research in a Christian university as a foundation for making disciples and reaching a loss world for Jesus Christ. His first observation focused on an understanding of this woman's thirst. What are the profound human needs of the people in our own culture and in the cultures around us? What are the thirsts of the different generations in our culture and in the unreached cultures of the world? Many of the academic disciplines taught at Biola University might explore these questions. The university is an ideal place to conduct the research. We have people, library resources, internet connections to the world, and the methodology and tools to address these questions in a substantive way. Jesus was a master at discerning human need. The Christian university can assist the church in understanding contemporary human need by doing substantive research and communicating the results of this research to the church.

As we research human need, the question will inevitably arise as to the validity of rival claims as to how those needs could be met. Jesus claimed to have living water, and the Samaritan woman challenged him to give it to her. As Christian faculty we claim that obedience to Christ brings deeper joy and fulfillment with regard to the thirst of life. Yet few of us are willing to risk our careers and our research energy on testing the truths of our claims. How do we know that the claims of scripture are true or false? What evidence can we find through our research that what we believe is indeed true in the lives of the people who respond to the gospel? Can we show the world that in fact obedience does bring deeper joy and fulfillment? I don't know of any specific research projects at Biola University that are seeking to address these questions. Perhaps there are, and if not, I hope there will be some.

The second area in which Jesus did significant observation and analysis is in the cultural lifestyle of the Samaritan woman. I do not know exactly what he saw, but it was clear as he engaged this woman in conversation that her lifestyle was keeping her from the living water that she clearly wanted and needed. Once again there are many disciplines in Biola University that might do research on cultural lifestyles. What are the dominant lifestyle themes in American culture? In Japanese culture? And in the cultures of the world? How does a culture promote its agenda, communicate its values, and condition its members to follow its way of life? In his work on Art and Pop Culture in America, Roger Feldman (1998) notes that American culture promotes sensuality and a gratification of material wants. This pattern of communication has developed over more than a century, and has now come to characterize the popular culture of the 1990's. We might ask the question, what are the counter themes in scripture? What are the social, psychological, and spiritual effects of contending lifestyles? Can we show that sexual freedom is any better or worse than abstinence? Do we have research to document that a lifestyle of infidelity has consequences in marriage that are damaging to both partners and to extended family relationships? Can we demonstrate that fidelity in marriage confers more positive outcomes in reference to husband-wife relationships and relationships between parents and children? As Christian scholars are we seeking concrete evidence to show that purity in entertainment and visual stimulation produces different kinds of behavior and quality in relationships than those generated by pornographic stimulation? As Christian scholars it is incumbent upon us not only to proclaim the Christian message, but also to provide an apologetic through our research that demonstrates the practical implications of Christianity and cultural life are superior to the contending lifestyles of the culture.

I am intrigued that Jesus conversation with the Samaritan ultimately led her to a discussion of her religion. Religion always underlies the basic choices that we make concerning our way of life in a culture. We have already observed that faculty in most American universities embrace the faith assumptions of scientific naturalism and exclude the faith assumptions of Christian theism. For all of our academic disciplines then, it is important to ask the question: What is the dominant rival belief system of my academic discipline, and how does it preclude Christianity? Once we understand that there are competing belief systems, then we should ask: "How can we frame new research questions that challenge the faith assumptions of this rival belief system?" For example, in my field of social anthropology I was socialized into the view that culture is neutral and that systems are adaptive. For many years I did not question that viewpoint, but accepted it as the basic paradigm from which I did my research and writing. After some years here at Biola, and substantive conversations with theologians, I have re-examined the scriptures and changed my view of culture. Today I believe that culture is not neutral, it has been skewed by sin, and I believe that systems apart from Jesus Christ all become mal-adaptive systems. Some, of course, have much more damaging effects upon their adherents than others. These two substantive differences in approach to a culture should and must be tested empirically. I should be training students here at Biola to do research which tests the rival claims of these two views of culture and demonstrates that one or the other of them is false.

As I read the promotion applications of the faculty at Biola University each year, I find very few examples of research that addresses these issues. In fact, the only substantive example that I know that does a comparative analysis of a Christian subculture in a dominantly non-Christian setting was not done by a Christian. Elizabeth Brusco (19950, a social anthropologist with a Marxist bent, studied a community of Pentecostal believers in Colombia, with the purpose of comparing the difference in their cultural and social life with a wider community. She found that a community of believers, who were deeply committed to the Bible and to living their lives in accord with its teaching, had experienced fundamental changes in their family relationships. Husbands were reintegrated into the household, the prosperity of individual families increased significantly through the reallocation of resources from alcohol and prostitutes to family purposes, and family and church community experienced significant change through teachings of scripture.

As I reflect upon my own professional research, I am somewhat chagrined to acknowledge that I intentionally omitted doing substantive investigation among the Christian families and in the Christian community of the people in Yap where I did research. I saw them as outside of the focal point of my interest, traditional culture, and neglected to explore any of the questions that I have raised in this paper. My goal then is to encourage Christian faculty members to break out of the research paradigms that we have learned in our graduate programs, and begin to frame our research objectives in more than naturalistic terms. Learning from the example of our Lord Jesus Christ, we might ask questions about the people and the subjects that we research that grow from our theological commitments, our understandings of our human need and the teachings of scripture which address those needs. I believe that such research is possible in every academic discipline that we have within the university. And much that we learn in this research could assist us in the task of world Evangelization.

The goal of research in a Christian university must ultimately be focused on how we can best participate with the church in proclaiming Jesus Christ, the Living Water. If the

Christian university is to be "an ever-flowing spring," we must sink our roots deeply into the source of living water which is Jesus Christ. As Dallas Willard shared in a chapel message during Biola's 90th Anniversary week, Jesus knows more about algebra than any of our math professors and more about physics or accounting or nursing than any of our specialists in those disciplines. This is not to say that we use scripture simplistically in our understanding of complex issues. Rather we must be critical realists, digging deeply into the substance of our research, and understanding the results with reference to the highest intellectual standards of our academic disciplines.

Equipping Disciples for Ministry

Allow me in this conclusion of the paper to reflect upon the church and the university with reference to my own area of specialization, that of culture. If indeed our calling is to make disciples of the generations in our culture and of the nations, then we must understand how our cultures facilitate and constrain this process.

I have stated elsewhere (1998) that our cultures are both our palaces and our prisons. Our culture provides us comfort, tools of relationship, and the meanings within which we live our lives. As such, these palaces become our prisons because they pull us away from the meanings and the relationships that God has intended for us in Jesus Christ. As we grow up in our respective worlds, it is inevitable that we become conformed to our cultures and, in that conformity deterred from the journey of pilgrimage with the Lord Jesus Christ. One role of a Christian university then is to help men and women who are preparing for service to engage the tension between the indigenizing force of culture and the pilgrimage of discipleship with Jesus Christ.

In the Presidents' and Academic Deans' consultation the Global Conference on World Evangelism (PAD) in Pretoria, South Africa in 1997, participants identified seven foundational principles that are essential for equipping people for the ministry of Evangelization in Christian seminaries, universities, and colleges. These principles include:

1. The primacy of missiological concern for world evangelism in the total curriculum;
2. Partnership at all levels and in multiple forms to reach the unreached;
3. Formal, non-formal and relational approaches to learning;
4. The uniqueness of Jesus Christ and the necessity of personal faith in Him as Lord and Savior;
5. Training that produces practicing supernaturalists;
6. Education with a focus on spiritual and character formation in the life of the student;
7. Education that addresses the whole council of God wisely contextualized and sustainable by local and national resources.

In this chapter I have sought to show that the university can be an effective partner with the church in the task of world Evangelization and in making disciples. Further, I have tried to make clear that this agenda is not just a function of the missions department or the school of theology. It is clear from the works of my colleagues in our 90th Anniversary symposium that world Evangelization is central to the humanities, the arts, and the sciences, as well as to the disciplines of the seminary and the missions programs. Further, I believe that a focus on world Evangelization and a partnership with the church will provide a balancing tension for the university that empowers our research and impact upon our culture in every area. I anticipate that the outcome of such a partnership would include profoundly moving works of art, compelling musical dramas, provocative literature, all of which uncover the pain and anguish of the present generation and offer hope through meaning that can be found in Jesus Christ. I see our graduates in the professions engaging the people of their culture and other cultures in the quest of satisfying their thirst, and I see them pointing to living water that can only be found in Jesus Christ. I see the power of our graduates in the media -- writers, producers, technicians -- transforming an industry whose bottom line has been greed, and satisfying the basis desires of human flesh. Unless the whole university joins in the task of world Evangelization, we will not be able to achieve the task given to us by our Lord Jesus Christ. I quote His final words,

> All authority in heaven and on earth has been given to me. Therefore, go and make disciples of all nations, baptizing them in the name of the Father, and of the Son, and of the Holy Spirit, and teaching them to obey everything I have commanded you. And surely I am with you always, to the very end of the age (Mt 28:18-20).

References Cited

Bloom, John
  1998   "After the Divorce: How Can Evangelicals Gain Regain a Voice in the Natural Sciences?" in *The Christian University for The Next Millennium: A Symposium Celebrating Biola University's 90th Anniversary.* February 27-28.

Brusco, Elizabeth
   1995   *The Reformation of Machismo.* Austin:
           University of Texas.

Feldman, Roger
   1998   "Aesthetic Deviation and the Dinghy that Dares:
           Reflections from the Visual Arts on a Christian
           University for the Next Millennium." in *The
           Christian University for The Next Millennium: A
           Symposium Celebrating Biola University's 90th
           Anniversary.* February 27-28.

Geivett, Douglas
   1998   "Christian Intellectualism Within a Rudderless
           Academy: An Epistemological Perspective." in
           *The Christian University for The Next
           Millennium: A Symposium Celebrating Biola
           University's 90th Anniversary.* February 27-28.

Lawson, Kevin
   1997   "Theological Reflection, Theological Method,
           and the Practice of Educational Ministry:
           Exploring the Wesleyan Quadrilateral and
           Stackhouse's Tetralectic." *Christian Education
           Journal*, Vol. 1NS, No. 1, Spring. Pp 49-64.

Lingenfelter, Sherwood G.
   1992   *Transforming Culture: A Challenge for Christian
           Mission.* Grand Rapids, MI Baker Books.
   1996   *Agents of Transformation: A Guide for Effective
           Cross Cultural Ministry.* Grand Rapids, MI
           Baker Books.

Marsden, George
   1994   *The Soul Of The American University: From
           Protestant Establishment To Established Non-
           Belief.* Oxford: Oxford University Press.

1994   *The Soul Of The American University: From Protestant Establishment To Established Non-Belief.* Oxford: Oxford University Press.

1998   "From Bible Institute to Christian University: New Challenges in a New Era." in *The Christian University for The Next Millennium: A Symposium Celebrating Biola University's 90th Anniversary.* February 27-28.

Packer, J. I.

    1998   "Christian Educators for Tomorrow: Prospects and Challenges." in *The Christian University for The Next Millennium: A Symposium Celebrating Biola University's 90th Anniversary.* February 27-28.

Saucy, Robert

    1997   "On Being A 'Single Christian' University: Reflections From a Theologian on the Christian University in the Next Millennium." in *The Christian University for The Next Millennium: A Symposium Celebrating Biola University's 90th Anniversary.* February 27-28.

Walls, Andrew F.

    1996   *The Missionary Movement in Christian History: Studies in the Transmission of Faith.* Maryknoll, NY: Orbus Books.

Willard, Dallas

    1998   "The Redemption of Reason and The University in the Next Millennium." in The Christian University for The Next Millennium: A Symposium Celebrating Biola University's 90th Anniversary. February 27-28.

THE ROLE OF HIGHER EDUCATION IN THE CHRISTIAN WORLD MISSION: PAST, PRESENT, AND FUTURE

Larry Poston

The Influence of Higher Education

This chapter does not engage in the debate about whether the local church, the mission agency, or the theological school is the most important of the institutions associated with the Christian world mission., but rather suggests that Christian higher education is the most influential.

In local churches in the westernized world the paid leaders—pastors, youth pastors, and other administrative officials—almost without exceptions hold at least, a Baccalaureate degree. In the case of the pastorate, only in rare instances will a person without a Master of Divinity or its equivalent be employed. For large churches or churches that serve a higher socio-economic class, a Doctor of Ministry or even a Doctor of Philosophy is becoming an expectation. Thus, virtually all of the most influential persons within a local church structure have passed through at least one, institution of higher learning.

Similarly, the majority of mission agency personnel have college degrees—from the executive officers, who give overall guidance to the organization, to the accountant who keeps track of the individual missionaries' financial support. Finally, virtually every mission organization expects missionary candidates to hold at least a Bachelor's degree in some ministry- or Bible-related field of study. It is increasingly common to see men and women with Masters and even doctoral degrees beginning the process of deputation. Higher education is thus the common denominator in each of these aspects of ministry involvement.

On the other hand, it is possible to become a missionary while bypassing a mission agency entirely. While the corps of "tentmakers" living abroad and engaged in missionary activity has never been large[1], awareness of this group has increased significantly over the last two decades. Some mission organizations have offered services to Christian business people, teachers, engineers, and government workers abroad, providing loose structures of fellowship and accessibility to materials and counsel. However, little direct influence, and even less overt control exists in all but a handful of cases. Nearly all of the independent missionaries, who have heard "a call" and have made their way overseas with no direct connection to a mission agency have been in theological schools of some kind—Bible

---

[1] While for centuries business, professional and military personnel have served as "tentmakers" carrying the gospel abroad and establishing churches, only recently have these kinds of Christian workers been considered as potential candidates for established missions. Relatively speaking, few "tentmaking" missionaries have been sent by churches or mission agencies.

Institutes, Bible colleges, Christian Liberal Arts institutions, seminaries, universities. Even if these alma maters were not specifically "Christian," involvement in parachurch campus groups was often the spur which led to a missions emphasis while on an overseas assignment. Parachurch experiences also make it possible to bypass the local church in one's spiritual development. Campus Crusade for Christ, InterVarsity Christian Fellowship, the Navigators and other similar groups have produced entire generations of Christians with tenuous connections to traditional local church structures. Many students make their way from university undergraduate programs to Evangelical seminaries and thence to mission organizations. Short-term internships in local church situations may—or may not—be required in the course of seminary training. Some students merely continue their parachurch involvement when choosing a practical assignment. Candidates with interdenominational agencies, charged with raising their financial support from whatever sources they are able to discover, are sometimes fortunate enough to establish contacts with local churches seeking to extend their missionary outreach. Many candidates, however, rely almost totally on the support of individuals, and thus the influence of or involvement in the local church in their lives is minimized. Even those candidates whose deputation experiences bring them in contact with church structures often have very little interpersonal contact other than the monthly financial contribution.

For these reasons schools are the linchpins that hold the missionary enterprise together—or weaken it irreparably. The educational institutions and their faculties bear the chief responsibility for the success or failure of the Christian world mission. The questions, therefore, that must be answered include: *Have educational institutions and their faculty members clearly understood their responsibility for Christian missions? Are they taking the steps necessary to carry out this responsibility in an adequate fashion given the current trends which exist both within higher education as well as within the missionary enterprise itself?*

Educating for Ministry--From Yesterday to Today

Currently, Christian institutions of higher learning are being forced to walk an incredibly narrow tightrope bridging between academic integrity and credibility on the one hand and faithfulness to the Bible and the Great Commission on the other.[2] Some schools have seemingly been more successful at walking this rope than others. It does not, for example, appear to have troubled most Roman Catholic institutions. Catholic universities and colleges have maintained at least some semblance of religiosity while attaining enviable academic reputations. Notre Dame, Georgetown, Loyola, Fordham—the list is an impressive one. However, Protestants have not been successful at developing institutions that have stayed the course. The Ivy League universities—nearly all of which were

---

[2] Can an institution have *both* academic integrity/credibility *and* faithfulness? The answer is "yes" —but only from "our" side. From the "secular" side the answer to this question is a resounding "no." Not perhaps so much from the perspective that it is *impossible*, but rather that it is undesirable. Personal faithfulness belongs in one's private life, not in the Academy. From my experience and from the current literature, this attitude is prevalent in academia today. To address this issue Rhodes College, for instance, has convened the "Rhodes Regional Consultations on the Future of the Church-Related College." The project is an ongoing series of discussions about how or if this trend can be reversed. An excellent example also appears in the May, 1999 issue of *Religious Studies News* entitled "Living on the Boundaries: Evangelical Women and the Academy.

founded and sponsored by Protestant denominations—have been sundered from their religious roots and rate only the term "secular" at the present time. Moreover, the Bible Institutes, Bible Colleges, Christian Liberal Arts colleges and seminaries established by conservative Evangelicals have never attained either the academic or societal status that Catholic universities have acquired.[3]

The absence of such status was not a problem in the past. Indeed, one can easily substantiate the claim that a primary reason for the failure of these Christian institutions to attain the heights of academic respectability was simply that they never aspired to do so. Their very establishment was an act of protest against much of what the drive for academic "respectability" had produced; namely, institutions which not only sidelined all attempts to discover aspects of spirituality and the Divine, but which in many cases openly ridiculed such aspects in the context of academic pursuits. For most Evangelicals, acceptance and approval of their own institutions from "Ivy League" schools would have been a mark of failure in that such acceptance would have signaled nothing less than an apostate status.[4]

Therefore, A. B. Simpson's Missionary Training Institute, Jonathan Blanchard's Wheaton College (begun as the Illinois Bible Institute), Lewis Sperry Chafer's Dallas Theological Seminary and other such schools forged new paths of their own. For the majority of these schools, such concepts as "state approval" and "regional accreditation" were of no

---

[3] Some may question the religiosity of Catholic institutions like those mentioned above. For an in-depth analysis of the spiritual state of these schools, see David J. O'Brien (1994) and George Marsden (1997:101-104).

[4] For a detailed examination of the transformation of Christian institutions, see George Marsden (1994) and Mark Noll (1994).

concern for the first several decades of their existence. Students in these institutions were, for the most part, adequately equipped to perform the tasks of evangelism, disciple-making, Christian education and church-planting. Pastors, missionaries, and Christian educators were the products of these institutions. They carried out the Great Commission in accordance with a Pietistic interpretation of the Bible's texts, emphasizing the internal and personal transformation of the individual rather than an external and institutional development of society. This Pietistic emphasis contributed in part to the nearly unanimous adoption of dispensational premillennialism by Evangelicals in the opening years of the Twentieth Century and the concomitant rejection of the amillennial and postmillennial eschatologies of historic Protestantism. Consequently, the focus of the Christian world mission shifted from national and global concerns—such as extending the kingdom of God in a physical sense through expansion of the institutional Church—to a strictly individualist orientation. Dispensational premillennialists had no intention of establishing a worldwide Christian culture—that would have involved a much more holistic approach to the education of converts. Instead, they were primarily concerned with "bringing back the King"—an event which could be hastened by concentrating solely upon the task of "preaching the Gospel to every creature."[5] The establishment of "Christian" political, economic, judicial and other such structures was considered a colossal waste of time. These tasks would require a basic

---

[5] A great deal of A. B. Simpson's missionary motivation arose from his desire to "bring back the King." See Robert Niklaus *et.al.* (1986:73). Hudson Taylor's philosophy of ministry was also a primary example of this type of thinking. Evangelism pure and simple was the goal of the China Inland Mission.

liberal arts education in addition to Bible training. The King would be forced upon His return to dismantle all such earthly structures (including those established by Christians) in order to build His millennial kingdom.

Paradigm Shifts in Evangelical Higher Education

Three major changes occurred after World War II that had the effect of producing a new focus on the part of Christian institutions of higher learning. First, *evangelicalism began to undergo a subtle transformation with regard to its "Christ and Culture" philosophy.* Using H. Richard Niebuhr's paradigm, one can maintain that prior to the War, dispensational premillennialism had placed its adherents either in the "Christ Against Culture" category or the "Christ and Culture in Paradox" position (Niebuhr 1951). Both of these perspectives marginalized Evangelicals not only from the standpoint of secular society, but also from the perspective of a large portion of the mainline Protestant denominations as well. Such marginalization was not problematic for Christians living in the late 1800s and early 1900s. However, the devastation to human civilization wrought by World War II in the 1940s, the crass materialism and rise of Communism in the 1950s, and the political, social, and moral liberalization of the 1960s forced Evangelicals to ask themselves if they had been correct to concentrate so exclusively upon the individual aspects of human life. Perhaps, something needed to be said about external and institutional concerns after all. Nevertheless, it was immediately apparent that the transformation of *cultural institutions* requires a much different form of education than that which existed in conservative Christian colleges. New curricula involving the humanities and the social sciences had to be developed, and the only extant models for such curricula were in the secular colleges and universities. In order to provide this education from a Christian perspective, it was necessary either to draw upon Christians who had earned their degrees from secular institutions, or to send teachers who had gained their credentials exclusively through Christian institutions to acquire further education within the secular university system.

When a person receives an undergraduate education from a Bible Institute or Bible College, proceeds then to a seminary graduate program, gains experience through involvement in a pastorate or missionary context for several years and then returns to a teaching position in a Christian institution, a cycle is formed which permits only a minimum of new ideas to enter a curricular program. In contrast, when men and women are educated from "the outside," (i.e., a secular educational environment), the concepts which then enter the pool of Christian ideas contain drastically different philosophical (not to mention theological) underpinnings. The effect of such ideas upon Bible College and Seminary curricula has been profound, and the consequent effect upon those educated in accordance with such curricula—including missionary candidates and aspiring pastors—has been profound as well. Secularizing worldview influence has brought serious disruptive effects. However, one should not see that "truth" found in "secular" institutions continues to be truth. The problem is often the worldview from which it is interpreted. This set of issues is addressed in more detail below.

A second post-war change concerns *the kind and quality of the education provided by Christian institutions of higher learning.* The expectations of Evangelical Christians regarding what their educational systems should be characterized by have been shaped in recent years by various media.

These media have published comparative data regarding institutions of higher learning in the United States. The availability of such rankings to the Christian public has led many to question why Evangelical institutions--with only a handful of exceptions--never appear in such rankings. The implication, of course, is that the education received at such institutions is of such poor quality that they have been completely excluded from the charts. Not long ago, such neglect by secular rating systems would have been worn as a badge of honor. In addition, the fact that the secular rating systems use somewhat subjective criteria for their assignments should be of significance.[6] However, separatist "badges of honor" are no longer worn by Evangelicals. *Perception*—rather than objective data—has become the order of the day. Therefore, parents who are doling out increasingly higher tuition fees for their sons and daughters to attend Christian institutions of higher learning have begun to conclude that they are not getting sufficient value for their dollars. Consequently, Christian institutions have been faced with two unattractive options. 1) They can adapt their curricular programs and campus environments to compete with the institutions that are ranked at or near the top of the rating systems. These institutions are essentially

---

[6] College rankings are often based on surveys taken of various college presidents as to which institutions they would rank as the highest. Rankings are also based on such items as "selectivity"—a concept which is essentially circular, in the sense that a school which, for whatever reason, suddenly finds itself "popular" or "attractive" and is flooded with applications, which in turn increases its ability to be selective, which in turn establishes the school's reputation as "selective," which increases the number of applications from students (or the parents of students) who desire the prestige of a "selective" college, and so on. See Amy E. Graham and Robert J. Morse (1998:82).

secular in nature. Alternatively, 2) they can look forward to a slow decline in their student populations and eventually close their doors.

The desire of parents to receive more value for their college expenditures is not the only financial pressure brought to bear on Christian institutions, leading to yet a third change in the educational enterprise. *Rising costs have forced an increasing number of schools to seek state and regional accreditation in order to become eligible to receive and award federal and state grants and loans.* Lacking the resources to supply financial aid in significant amounts to students, Christian institutions have been unable to compete with state and private universities that receive heavy subsidies from both government and private agencies. To meet accreditation requirements, certain compromises have often been necessary in the areas of curriculum and institutional ethos. George Marsden, for instance, cites the example of New York State, which has

> withheld aid from religiously affiliated colleges until they furnished satisfactory evidence that religious considerations were secondary to defining the tasks of the college . . . such pressures as well as those growing out of parallel court decisions of the era sped the processes of secularization for many colleges (Marsden 1997:438).

Since, nearly all of the current generation of pastors, youth leaders, missionary candidates, and missionary agency personnel have passed through these institutions, one must conclude that these changes have profoundly affected Christian missions.

The Christian Liberal Arts colleges should be of greatest concern at the present. Bible Institutes, Bible Colleges and seminaries do not stand in nearly as dangerous a position. Why? Most Bible Colleges have acquired state licensure and, in some cases, even regional accreditation. They are generally able to offer Baccalaureate degrees in a very limited number of fields (i.e., Bible and Music). In order to meet accreditation standards, these schools have added a minimal number of liberal arts courses, all of which are taught from an undeniably Christian perspective, most often by professors who have obtained either a "mixed" education (i.e., both "secular" and "sacred") or an exclusively "Christian" one.[7] These liberal arts courses have enhanced the typical Bible College curriculum by injecting elements of the social sciences and humanities. These additions have broadened the horizons of the students in attendance. Bible and Theology courses, however, continue to be the mainstay of the overall course of study, in most cases comprising one-third to one-half of the total number of required credits. Thus, a Bible College graduate comes away with an extensive knowledge of the Bible and Theology. This knowledge will be expanded and sharpened by the seminary experience that most who today plan to enter full-time Christian service eventually obtain. Thus, the traditional criticisms of Bible Institute and Bible College education (i.e., no accreditation and no broad-based general education requirements) have largely been addressed. The Christian Liberal Arts college, however, seeks accreditation for a large number of majors, including subjects in the humanities, social sciences, and scientific or technological fields. The push to

---

[7] Truth may certainly be found in secular institutions. However, even empirical truths at such institutions are almost always wrapped in a non-Christian or anti-Christian philosophy or framework. Unless the Christian learner is very discerning and skilled at unpacking these truths and distinguishing or separating them from their wrappings, the result can be disastrous.

enhance the liberal arts aspects of these schools has in many cases eroded the Bible and Theology content of general education requirements to an absolute minimum.

An evaluation of Evangelical seminaries yields much the same conclusion as was drawn regarding Bible Colleges and Institutes. The purpose of such graduate institutions is to prepare men and women for professional ministerial functions, and therefore most of the curricula offered in these schools are heavily weighted in favor of Bible and Theology courses. This is not always the case, however, and so it would be useful to distinguish between the various categories of entering students and the types of programs available to them at the graduate level, for different combinations of these categories will yield varying products. At least four combinations can be suggested:

Category #1: *The graduate of a Bible College or Institute who prepares for ministry through attainment of a Master of Divinity seminary degree.* Such a combination essentially adds three or four years of Biblical and theological studies to the four years of introductory level courses acquired at the undergraduate level.

Category #2: *The graduate of a Bible College or Institute who prepares for ministry through a Master of Arts seminary degree.* If this graduate level degree is in Old Testament, New Testament, or Systematic Theology, further education in Biblical studies is, of course, forthcoming. A Masters degree in Missions or Christian Education, however, moves the student into a very different set of academic disciplines. For the aspiring missionary, studies in anthropology, linguistics, comparative religions and urban ministry will most likely be the standard bill of fare. Built upon a Bible College or Institute background, these studies have the effect of broadening one's education in directions helpful to one's professional aspirations, although further training in purely Biblical studies will most likely be minimal.

Category #3: *The graduate of a Liberal Arts college or university who prepares for ministry through attainment of a Master of Divinity seminary degree.* In most such cases, the undergraduate degree will be in a field unrelated to Bible or Theology. Thus the seminary program must bear the full responsibility for preparing such a student both in terms of Biblical/ theological knowledge *and* in terms of professional ministerial training. Since statistically speaking this kind of student is the most common type found in Evangelical seminaries, most such institutions have adapted their programs to meet these needs. At the completion of his or her formal training, however, the student in Category 3 will most likely have up to sixty or so credits *less* of Bible and theology instruction than his or her colleague who is in Category 1.

Category #4: *The graduate of a Liberal Arts college or university who prepares for ministry through attainment of a Master of Arts seminary degree.* Again, if this degree is in the area of Old Testament, New Testament, or Systematic Theology, at least some training in Biblical studies is acquired, though not nearly to the extent of one enrolled in a Master of Divinity program, and certainly not to an extent even distantly comparable to the Category 1 student.

The student in this category who chooses to major in Missions (or some other than purely Biblical field) will without a doubt be the "weakest" in terms of overall Bible preparation. As noted above, the courses in this program of study will revolve around anthropology, communications, urban studies and the like. *Some* Bible courses will, of course, be required, but they will be minimal. The question that all mission agencies must ask is whether or not the candidate who is a Category

4 graduate is adequately prepared to be a minister of the Gospel in cross-cultural situations. It may indeed be the case that Category 1 students are, by comparison, "overqualified." However, would it not be that those in Category 4 might be dangerously under qualified to "teach new disciples to obey everything that Jesus taught?"

Some might object that if the Category 4 person were a graduate of a *Christian* Liberal Arts college, the "danger" suggested here might be mitigated. Yet to be frank, this mitigation may not be the case at all. It is even conceivable that a student who has graduated from a fully secular institution might actually be better off concerning Bible and Theology training than one who has attended a Christian liberal arts college. Let me explain.

The Christian liberal arts college is not a new concept; indeed, many of the earliest Protestant institutions of higher learning such as Harvard, Yale, Princeton, Brown and Northwestern could be said to have been Christian Liberal Arts institutions at the time of their inception. The title is now reserved, however, for schools which have banded together around a specific set of criteria, in the main espousing a conservative view of the Bible as the inspired Word of God and a likewise conservative approach to the interpretation and application of the Scriptures within the context of life and society.

James Davison Hunter (1987), professor of sociology at the University of Virginia, has been a leading researcher into trends involving Evangelicals, including Evangelical higher education. His study of nine leading Evangelical liberal arts colleges and seven seminaries noted several disturbing trends in these schools. Stated simply, the educational process of these institutions often serves to *undermine* the religious commitment of students rather than strengthening it. With statistical support, Hunter claims that "the more intent Evangelical higher education is on preserving the integrity of its traditions, the less successful it is. . . . Among Protestant colleges, the more serious a commitment to the task of higher education, the more prevalent the liberalization and seculariza-tion tendencies" (1987:176-177).[8] This last statement could well be interpreted in the following manner: the better the institution is from the standpoint of secular ranking systems— the standards which "count" with contemporary parents and students—the more likely the institution is to "secularize" its students. It would thus be tempting to conclude that the *lower* an Evangelical institution is ranked by such systems, the better an institution it will be from the standpoint of Biblical values. A college or seminary that does not appear at all on these lists could presumably wear this omission as a badge of Biblical integrity. However such conclusions—even if they are warranted—are essentially without value at the current juncture of history for two reasons. First, it would be impossible to convince the parents of college-age young people of the truth of such logic, for the plausibility structure of our time disallows the separatist notions that accompanied the establishment of the early Bible Institutes. The argument that

---

[8]One notable flaw in Hunter's study is that when he speaks of "Evangelical higher education" he does not include either Bible Institutes or Bible Colleges (Hunter 1987:176-177). Whether this omission is due to the fact that none of these institutions has ever come close to appearing in the rankings of, say, *U.S. News and World Report*'s annual college edition, or whether Hunter himself does not consider the academic process at these institutions to be worthy of the term "higher education" is not forthcoming. He does explain that "the limitations of time and expense prohibited their inclusion in the sample," but this is rather unconvincing. Washington Bible College, Philadelphia College of the Bible, Lancaster Bible College, and even Columbia Bible College are all an easy drive from Charlottesville, Virginia.

approval by a secularist ranking system is indicative of spiritual decline might conceivably have succeeded in the last quarter of the nineteenth century, but not during the corresponding period in the twentieth. Secondly, it would be even more difficult to convince the faculties and administrative personnel of the Evangelical institutions which are now beginning to appear on the lists of "quality" schools that all of the striving they have undergone to attain academic respectability has actually resulted in a decline in their spirituality. Suggesting that they should seek a *lower* position in ranking systems would be considered ludicrous in the extreme. Given the current cultural context, these problems must be attacked in another way.

Implications of Current Trends in Education
For the Christian World Mission

If, institutions of higher learning are significant clearinghouses for church leadership, mission agency leadership and missionary personnel, then trends in education will eventually make their presence known within both church and mission contexts. Christian denominations and mission agencies must keep their fingers on the pulse of the schools from which their personnel are drawn. Meanwhile, the schools must assume responsibility for the physical, intellectual, and spiritual development of the men and women who enter their halls and engage in the pursuit of truth. Part of this responsibility involves an awareness of the constantly changing profile of today's students.

The following are some of the more significant trends:

1. *Older Students.* Demographically, the pool of students in the traditional college age range of 18-22 years has declined significantly during the last three decades. This

change may be difficult to observe at first, since a much larger *proportion* of persons in this age range attend college now than was true in previous generations. Many begin college programs—and so the numbers look good. However, a large percentage of these persons are not adequately gifted or prepared to withstand the rigors of a college education, and so less than half of those who begin actually complete a four-year degree.[9] Thus the generation of 18-22 year olds can no longer be expected to supply the recruiting needs of tuition-driven institutions, and therefore other markets are being tapped.

A result of this change in demographics is the growing popularity of Degree Completion Programs, designed specifically for persons who began a college career, but who for one reason or another never completed their program. These persons re-enter the academic environment at a (usually) much older age. Often, they plan to use their degree to facilitate a career change. Sometimes, the change is to a ministry-related field. The person has experienced the new birth, developed a desire to be involved in pastoral or missionary ministry, learned that a certain amount of education is required, and, because of a "late start" attitude, seeks to complete this academic training in as rapid a manner as possible.

Most undergraduate degree completion programs require one or two years. Seminary or graduate school training—almost universally required in older denominations for the pastorate and increasingly necessary for missionary service—adds another two to four years. Acquisition of the requisite educational credentials can thus take from three to six years. For a person who begins in their late 20s, 30s, or 40s, time spent in the classroom can easily boost the age at which

---

[9] According to research reported by the Council for Christian Colleges and Universities, the actual figure is 47%. See Christine J. Gardner (1998:34).

they assume full-time ministerial responsibilities into the next decade of their life. In addition candidates with faith mission agencies can look forward to up to a three year support-raising period after their completion of educational requirements. Since the pool of college and seminary graduates is likely to increase in its median age, maximum age requirements imposed by some mission agencies may have to be waived.

2. *Dysfunctional Family Backgrounds.* As the rates of divorce and remarriage continue to hover at approximately 50% of all marital relationships, the familial experiences of students entering Christian institutions of higher learning are, in perhaps a majority of cases, very different from the situations of previous generations. Effects include either a profound distrust of and skepticism regarding the institution of marriage in general, or an overly eager desire to find a marriage partner and "succeed" where one's parents failed. The first attitude produces a delay in entering into serious relationships until the late 20s or even beyond, which from the standpoint of personal spiritual formation may be good (in that more time is devoted to undistracted physical, intellectual, and spiritual development) or bad (when the temptations of the profoundly immoral modern world beset the single Christian). The second attitude may produce a motivation strong enough to make a marriage succeed at any cost, or it may result in ideals and expectations which are so unreasonable that the union is destined to fail before it even begins, thus renewing the cycle of divorce and remarriage. Students arrive at institutions of higher education with a host of family-oriented problems which can manifest themselves in ministerial situations long after the educational process is completed. Clearly, the stresses of cross-cultural adjustment may exacerbate these problems to the point where new missionary candidates will break down under the strain.

Mission agencies and churches that insist upon appointing or employing only "well-adjusted" individuals without such backgrounds are most likely already feeling the strain of a vastly decreased pool of qualified candidates. To fill the constant— and in many cases increasing—number of available positions, denominations and independent missions agencies are often forced to choose persons who are a "risk." This change is necessitating the establishment of counseling programs for those who, under normal circumstances, would be expected to be spiritual counselors themselves.

3. *"Short-Term Commitments."* Many young people today are characterized by an inability to fix their minds and wills upon a single task until completion. Educators recognize this cultural pattern as a "sign of the times" which spans the entire spectrum of student cohorts and carries over into one's work and career. The trend manifests itself at the college level in the number of changes that students make in their choice of academic majors within a single school or transfers between two or more schools. It appears in an employment history in the multiple career changes that have become the subject of a variety of studies. This unsettledness is in large part a legacy of our national commitment to pluralistic democracy and the individual liberation brought about by modern industrialization and the technology of rapid transportation. Automatic inheritance of the occupation of one's parent and residence in close proximity to one's relatives are now so rare as to be anomalous at this juncture of history. The "global village" beckons and the adventurousness glamorized by the media "Indiana Joneses" both mirrors and influences contemporary social trends.

Affordable semester-abroad programs and summer missions trips have also contributed to the mobile orientation of young people—and the consequences for schools, churches, and mission agencies are profound. The phenomenon manifests itself most noticeably in brief tenures at local churches and in "short-term" missionary stints. Concerning the latter, rhetoric is now regularly heard from the standpoint of the champions of "life-long" and "career missionary" service which is either subtly or blatantly patronizing of young people who cannot "stay the course." The implication is that the "older" missionaries were (or are) "tougher" and "more enduring," but such attitudes are misguided and will eventually prove to be counterproductive. Like it or not, "short-term" missions are the future of the missionary enterprise, and as some of the more innovative missions thinkers are beginning to write, such strategies can be seen as a return to the pattern established by Paul, who, when all is said and done, spent no longer than three years in any one place, and according to the reckoning of certain commentators, dedicated no more than a total of nine years to cross-cultural ministry.[10] While it is true that Paul did not have to spend time in language acquisition—an important distinction between his experience and that of present-day missionary personnel—there is still room for a great deal of innovative thinking with regard to efficient and effective short-term missionary involvement.

4. *Undisciplined Lifestyles.* The peoples of North America and Northern Europe have been historically characterized by a work ethic and view of the concept of "progress" that were in many ways unique in the history of humanity. To a great degree, these characteristics were a legacy of the influence of Christianity in a generic sense (Weber 1958). Other contributions of this generalized religious sociology were a linear view of history and a sense of "mission" which impelled Westerners to the "cutting edge" of scientific and

---

[10] See, for instance, Scott Bessenecker (1997:326ff)

technological achievement, resulting in improved health and hygiene, lengthened life spans and increased leisure time for pursuits other than physical survival. The "double filtration" undergone by American immigrants produced highly moti- vated, disciplined, and entrepreneurial men and women.[11] The rigor of the requirements of general college curricula in bygone years testifies to the kinds of students that were produced by the set of conditions described above.[12]

Since the 1950s, however, the profile of the "typical American" has changed. Contemporary studies speak of a "culture of narcissism" and "a culture of disbelief" (Lasch 1991 and Carter 1993) having replaced traditional American values. The increase in leisure time coupled with the development of work- and time-saving technological advancements have led to a "flabbiness" in the American psyche which was not present in previous generations. Gone is the "ruggedness" that accompa- nied the pioneer spirit of early Americans. Now instead we find an addiction to modern amenities which weaken the body and stifle the mind. The "Protestant work ethic" has given way to a demand for extended vacations and "flex-time," and the

---

[11] The "double filtration" spoken of here involves first the filtration of those who dared to step onto a boat sailing across the Atlantic to begin with. Generally speaking, only the bravest, the hardiest, the most stubborn or the most desperate were willing to risk the dangers of ocean travel at that time. The second filtration occurred when those who arrived on the shores of America then found it necessary to survive in an undeveloped country. Those who were able to get through the winters were the bravest of the brave, the hardiest of the hardy, the most stubborn of the stubborn, and the most desperate of the desperate. The result of this two-stage filtering has produced a pool of citizens unique in the world's history.

[12] In his book *In Defense of Elitism*, William A. Henry III cites the work of Cornell University professor Donald Hayes, which reveals that prior to World War II, general eighth grade textbooks were of the same level of rigor as senior-level honors textbooks today (1994:42).

former preoccupation with "the great outdoors" and sportsmanship has evolved into a lounge-chair-by-the-pool lifestyle with a portable television tuned to a baseball game.

This lack of discipline has carried over as well into the realm of morality and ethics. Increases in sexual promiscuity, marital infidelity, divorce, and open homosexuality have been paralleled by demands for abortion rights, the legalization of marijuana, voluntary euthanasia, and the protection of pornography under the U.S. Constitution's First Amendment. The ready availability of the latter via cable television, video, and the Internet has produced an unparalleled access to visual experiences which in the past were reserved only for the most depraved elements of society.

All of the above have combined to change the general profile of today's college students—Christian as well as non-Christian—into something quite different from previous generations. The men and women who walk the halls of our Bible Institutes, Christian Liberal Arts colleges and seminaries are as likely as not to be the products of broken marriages. Often, they have been exposed to an environment in which little or no discipline has been exercised with regard to interpersonal relationships inside—or outside—of marriage. These students have viewed thousands of hours of television and motion pictures, the overwhelming majority of which have glorified immoral, gluttonous, and materialistic lifestyles which are a mockery of the entire concept of a disciplined life. As a result, study skills are often undeveloped; reading and writing competencies verge in many cases on functional illiteracy. And, the real tragedy, of course, is that the persons who have met the requirements for matriculation in institutions of higher learning are among the "brightest and best" that America is currently producing. Most of the students who remain in a program eventually acquire enough of the skills and discipline necessary for completion of a college degree. Some graduates who present themselves as candidates for employment to mission agencies and church denominations have shed very little of the psychological and emotional baggage they brought from their home life. The camaraderie and supportive environment of dormitory life along with a busy academic schedule can serve to submerge some of the wounds for a time, but many wounds may reappear later. To have such scars re-opened in the midst of cross-cultural—or congregational—adjustment can be a horrific ordeal indeed.

5. *Shallow worldviews.* Ours is an age of "nowness;" often with little—if any—sense of the past. Radio and television commentators speak in terms of "the worst storm since 1987" or "the best cost of living index since 1992" as though these statements have actual historical significance. "Tradition" is a concept that is openly denigrated by persons from both secular and "Christian" society.

For Christians, such a lack of perspective isolates each individual in a niche so tiny and insignificant that any sense of "mission" is lost completely. Communicating to students that they are participants in a Divine "search and rescue operation" that has been ongoing since the dawn of Earth's existence evokes nothing more than a vacant stare. Somehow the idea does not sound nearly as exciting as becoming a "Raider of the Lost Ark."

One might be tempted to see the beginnings of a correction to this state of affairs in the recent return of some conservative Protestant Christians to denominations and rites which are much more deeply rooted in history than the newer "low-church movements." In keeping with this trend, Evangelicals are showing a renewed interest in both the Roman

Catholic and Eastern Orthodox churches.[13] However, serious questions remain as to whether this trend should be viewed as a true reformation (or counter-reformation, as the case may be). The majority of participants are able to explore such alternatives only at the expense of biblically-based theological reflection. In many—perhaps most—cases, the exotic character of the experience attracts rather than a true sense of tradition, and thus shallowness continues, albeit in a new form.

For people who have not found this trend attractive, the lack of "rootedness" which accompanies a shallow worldview manifests itself in several ways. In the schools, it appears in the readiness of students to change majors and/or institutions with no thought given to the historical background of the institutions that are chosen. Issues of geographic location and financial aid have replaced such items as denominational or theological loyalty. A shallow worldview ultimately results in an insecurebase of operations, and therefore one lacks the "sense of self" so necessary to be able to adapt to a congregation or a culture.[14]

6. *Global naiveté.* With the advent of satellite relay systems, the human race has never been so aware of its various ethnic and cultural components as it is today. Comparatively inexpensive air travel has made overseas summer "missions" trips possible for church youth groups, college students, and other laypersons in general. As with many trends, this phe-

---

[13] Richard Mouw notes this trend, along with some of its implications for Evangelical higher education, in a chapter entitled "Challenge of Evangelical Theological Education" (1996:287).

[14] According to John 13:3, Jesus was able to wash the feet of His disciples because He knew where He was, where He had been, and where He was going. Those who do not possess such knowledge will be unable to serve effectively in any context.

nomenon is two-edged. Such short-term exposure to foreign missions contexts can be—and in many cases has been—extremely positive. Mission agencies in particular note that a significant percentage of young people who participate in summer missions programs return later as career missionaries. Another positive aspect is that some young people discover that cross-cultural adjustment is not a part of their personal gifted-ness, and they consequently eliminate direct missionary involvement from their future plans. Such a filtration process can save a great deal of anguish and embarrassment at a later time.

The downside, however, is that some young people gain an unrealistic perspective on the nature of missionary activity. The period of time spent in a foreign context is either too short or too sheltered—or both—to allow the participants to experience the vicissitudes of "culture shock." They return with a sense of "That was easy!" or "That was fun!" whereas long term evangelism, disciple making and church planting are far from easy and are rarely characterized by those who are most closely involved as "fun."

For others, the experience is one of adventure—the thrill of visiting exotic locations with opportunities for photography and the acquisition of artifacts with which one's bedroom or dormitory room can be decorated. For this group, the spiritual or theological elements regarding the communication of the Gospel in order to elicit decisions for Christ and thus procure eternal life for lost men and women are often given strictly secondary or even tertiary priority. The "adventure" is the thing. Yet a third group may take the attitude that their international ministry involvement is now accomplished. They have functioned as "missionaries" and in so doing have "conquered" that bit of life and are thus now ready to move on to whatever is next on the list of "things to experience."

These observations are by no means intended to disparage the continuation of summer or other short-term programs. However, mission agencies and churches should be cautious regarding the format of such ventures. Unless they are carefully planned and staffed by the proper personnel and include time for special de-briefing at their conclusion, they may produce the exact opposite of what is intended.

A Vision for the Future

Other trends could be discussed,[15] but the ones above are the most significant. In a sense, students with the above characteristics represent the "raw materials" that enter our Christian institutions of higher learning. Schools may mold this "material" into new forms, but with all of the above-mentioned "impurities" still present in their alumni. Such impurities are in actuality structural weaknesses which under stressful conditions may fail at critical junctures. Thus it becomes the responsibility of our educational institutions to do much more than merely produce *educated* older students from broken families with short-term mentalities who are undisciplined, shallow, and naive with regard to international issues. The "raw material" must be re-shaped and these impurities either removed or reduced to insignificant proportions. How might such an effect be produced?

The very first adaptation which today's institutions of higher learning must undergo is to *come to terms with the "raw*

---

[15] For a very fine perspective on the conditions existing within today's student population, see Ken Baker (1997:70ff).

material" educators are being given to work with. Many faculty members bemoan that the time is seemingly gone forever when entering freshmen had a modicum of preparation: they could read, write, pay attention, take notes, fulfill the requisite assignments and enter into stable career tracks. However, little is to be gained by yearning for "the good old days."[16] Educators must rise to the challenge of a generation of students with new characteristics calling for revisions in traditional educational programs. The following are some suggestions regarding a new paradigm for Christian higher education.

1. *Welcome and utilize the special qualities of older students.* Their experience and (hopefully) their maturity should be celebrated. Presumably, their motivation level is high, particularly those who are in the midst of career changes. For the schools, the following innovations are suggested. The experience of older students should be incorporated into the learning experiences. Application to real life settings should be included. Learning experiences should be designed so that several "options" are presented to address the needs of both younger, inexperienced students as well as older, more seasoned veterans.

Older *married* students should be tracked into a Degree Completion Program with all possible haste, and from there into a seminary or graduate school. My reasons for this suggestion are multiple. First, at nearly every undergraduate institution, the relatively small cadre of married students is an anomaly that few schools have been able to fit into their overall environment. In most cases, such persons live off campus, are

---

[16] Not only is such thinking futile; it also violates a clear Biblical precept. Ecclesiastes 7:10 states: *"Do not say, 'Why were the old days better than these?' For it is not wise to ask such questions."*

employed off campus at (usually) odd hours, and often celebrate their independence as non-residential students. Their ties with professors outside of the classroom are tenuous at best. The creation of programs to "fold them into" the school at large generally fail. However, a well-structured degree completion program builds these students into cohorts that function as support groups in ways that traditional undergraduate programs never do for married students. Secondly, these curricula are usually *accelerated* programs that also award credit for "life experiences" These two factors save the student both time and money, which are important considerations when one is older and has a family. Thirdly, these programs generally meet only one night per week, leaving opportunity for employment and the attendance of family responsibilities. For all but a few married students, these characteristics are ideal.

Arguments against older missionary candidates have traditionally included issues of language acquisition and family concerns. These aspects can be addressed by our Christian schools—both undergraduate and graduate—if they are willing to step out of traditional molds. Regarding language study, a different paradigm and higher standards for foreign languages must be introduced for personnel who intend ministry among peoples of other cultures and languages. This upgrading should begin at the undergraduate level and make use of techniques that are much more focused on oral ability. Educational institutions—both undergraduate and graduate—which have required New Testament Greek as part of their Bible or ministry curriculum should seriously consider allowing more flexibility for students intending overseas or inner city ministries. [17] Studies in Spanish, Portuguese, French, Swahili,

---

[17] Ironically, the same Protestants who have railed against Roman Catholic conservatism with regard to the use of Latin in the Mass have for all

Arabic, Russian, Chinese, and Japanese should be supported and staffed. Every effort should be made to utilize—or create—language programs which produce students who are fluent communicators in major foreign languages while still in the United States.

For their part, mission agencies must begin to re-think their age limitations. Cut-off points such as the early 30s will need to be moved upwards or made more flexible. Historically, nearly all of the earliest missionaries to foreign lands (i.e., Patrick, Columba, Columban, Boniface, etc.) were in their forties or beyond when they began their ministries. They went in a day when the life expectancy was considerably shorter than the present. With life expectancies currently reaching into the 80s, and with projections of the 90s and 100s in the near future, there is no reason why "older" missionaries cannot be expected to have ministries equally as fruitful as younger candidates .[18]

2. *Give serious consideration to the ideas of celibacy or limited family size.* I am aware of how "touchy" such topics can be, especially in an age of Evangelical "focus on the family." While family values have been a popular issue since the 1970s, and marriage and child-rearing remain "sacred" and "inviolable" traditions among contemporary conservative Christians, We as Evangelicals must seriously consider developing a corps of men and women who have discerned in themselves a gift of celibacy for several reasons.

First and foremost, the apostle Paul—often held to be the "prototypical missionary"—recommends the non-married

---

practical intents and purposes created the same aura for Greek within Protestant circles. Greek should continue to be an option for students intending ministry. It should not, however, be required, but rather made one alternative among many.

[18] For more on this subject, see Ken Dychtwald and Joe Flower (1990).

state, particularly in conjunction with "crisis" situations (see 1 Cor 7:26). While such a description would perhaps not be appropriate for a large part of today's world, the fact that between two-thirds and three-quarters of the global population is currently unreachable by "traditional" missionaries presents a situation calling for what may be considered "extreme" measures. Single missionaries are both physically and psychologically less encumbered than married missionaries. They are consequently freer to risk clandestine entry into "closed" countries for involvement in cutting-edge evangelism, disciplemaking and church planting. As an earlier mission agency motto put it: "There are no 'closed' countries—as long as you are not worried about coming back." Only singles truly have this kind of freedom.

Secondly, this recommendation deals in a non-traditional way with the characteristic of "broken families." Evangelicals often fail to admit that for many of our young men and women the emotional and even physical scarring of a shattered family background has made the "ideal" of the "Biblical family model" either undesirable or unattainable. Unfortunately, these same institutions often derided the alternative of celibacy as "anomalous" or "medieval," whereas biblically speaking it is neither of these. Voluntary celibacy may actually become a haven of healing and a source for dynamic Christian ministry (Clapp 1988:20). Undistracted devotion to the Lord and undivided commitment to a life of ministerial service could very well become a welcome option to many of today's students. Faculty members, counselors, pastors and mission agencies alike should embrace and even in certain circumstances recommend this institution.

Among Evangelicals, children are held to be a "heritage from the Lord." Even the suggestion that one might choose to have no children or limit one's family size to one or two children for the sake of ministry draws fire from a number of Evangelicals.[19] Many missionaries take pains to show that their offspring greatly enhance their ability to identify with the adherents of specific cultures. While true in some cases, it is also undeniable that the testimony of the historical record does not bear out the claim that couples with children are more effective or productive in their ministries. Again, from the standpoint of freedom and flexibility, single missionaries or childless couples are able to devote much more time and energy to ministry endeavors. A childless couple is able to function as an undivided team. The wife does not feel separated from the ministry, does not miss out on language study, and is not closed off from the culture as sometimes happens in the midst of child-rearing. The problems associated with schooling—either those involving the separation of parents and children through boarding schools or those involved in the placement of children within foreign public or private schools—are eliminated entirely, as is the risk of the psychological malformation.

One of the darker secrets of the modern missionary movement (as well as the pastorate) is the number of broken families and damaged children that have resulted from the inability of a large number of ministers to maintain a proper balance between family and ministry (Tucker 1989:17:ff). Thus, the options of celibacy or limited family size should be made available to today's ministry aspirants. It is within the

---

[19] Phil Parshall in a well reasoned and carefully balanced article advocated limitation of family size by missionary couples to a maximum of two children. Responsive letters to the editor which appeared in future volumes, however, were in most cases passionate denunciations of the very idea, and were neither well-reasoned nor balanced (1977:20ff).

context of our educational institutions—through chapel sessions, courses on contemporary issues, and carefully chosen conference speakers—that such seeds can be sown.

3. *Develop short-term, "strike force" mentalities and the concept of "seasonal" approaches to career missions.* Rather than continuing to castigate today's young people for their lack of long-term commitment, we must capitalize on their shorter bursts of energy. Such adaptation may take two forms. The first would be an expansion and refinement of the already-existing and explosively expanding phenomenon of short-term missions.[20] The Christian and Missionary Alliance has, for instance, developed the concept of a "mobile strike force" consisting of missionaries who already reside and minister in various countries around the world. They are "on call" and ready to move to any location where God has pre-pared a receptive and productive setting. The CoMission cooperative effort has provided another example. When it became apparent that the former Soviet Union was undergoing a state of dissolution and that a window of opportunity was opening for Christian missionary activity, a number of mission agencies pulled seasoned veterans from fields where work was well-developed and moved them to Russia.

A second approach would involve a more deliberate utilization of the current pattern of alternating periods of overseas ministry and "home service." Each overseas term and home assignment could be cast as completely independent

---

[20] The 1997 edition of the *Mission Handbook* notes that while the number of long term missionaries increased by 1.3% between 1992 and 1996, the number of short termers increased by 28.2%. And while in 1992 38,968 persons were involved in terms of service ranging from two weeks to one year, by 1996 that number had swelled to 63,995. See John Siewert and Edna Valdez (1997: 74).

segments of missionaries' lives. Each of these time periods would thus become in effect a "short-term" assignment, with clear goals and objectives partitioned off by a starting date and an ending date. Some missionaries might need to be moved around within a single country or even within a specific geographic area in order to curb the restlessness that appears to infect a large number of today's young people. If not the geographic location, then perhaps the specific ministry or work assignment could be changed on a regular basis. For a number of "baby boomers" and "busters," a variety of experiences is considered necessary to develop one's "self" or "full potential." This is not necessarily a "New Age" concept as some have categorized it, for the Bible indicates that we are all being "transformed into his likeness with ever increasing glory" (2 Cor 3:18), implying a process of development toward maturity. To provide such means of self-fulfillment for missionaries and pastors can be made an integral part of both mission and denominational planning processes.

Here, of course, our educational institutions will need to partner with mission agencies and local churches to introduce and cultivate the concept of "short-term" or "seasonal" involvement while playing on the same "team" for life. "Team loyalty" is certainly understood within the context of athletics. The same mindset must be created in today's students with regard to a mission organization or denomination. We must encourage our young people to choose a team--carefully and with much consideration--and then stick with that team for life.

4. *Cultivate an elitist mentality.* Perhaps, the greatest service our Christian schools can render to individuals is the inculcation of an "elitist" mentality in them. Unfortunately, the recent trend has been to reduce Christians to a level of "humility" that is more culturally defined than biblically prescribed.

Actually, the Bible abounds with images of the people of God as an elite group. The children of Israel were a "holy, called-out and elect people"—the "apple of God's eye." The New Testament saints are "the Bride of Christ" and *"a chosen people, a royal priesthood, a holy nation, a people belonging to God"* (1 Pe 2:9). Christians are the sons and daughters of God, princes and princesses in the Kingdom of Heaven, citizens and ambassadors of that kingdom, living on Earth to fulfill a special commission at the completion of which they will obtain specially prepared dwelling places in a City built for them by God Himself. The New Testament writers consistently call all readers to ponder and apply such concepts of identity; Paul urges each of the Galatians, for instance, to *"test his own actions; then he can take pride in himself, without comparing himself to somebody else"* (Gal 6:4). In the fullness of confidence born of our understanding of who we are in Christ, we are to acknowledge our highborn position and giftedness and from that secure base serve humankind in a number of ways.

Throughout history, an appeal to elitism has shown its worth time and time again. The sense of "self" and of "mission" coupled with the discipline required both to attain and maintain elite status has set the adherents of elite groups in a far different class from that of the masses. While the context has usually been military—the Green Berets, the Army Rangers, the Navy SEALs—occasionally the phenomenon has appeared in the history of the Church. The Society of Jesus, for instance, was able to capitalize on the *mystique* of elitism, producing in the process one of the most highly educated and skillful groups of people in the history of the planet.[21]

---

[21] See, for instance, Douglas Letson and Michael Higgens (1995).

However, Evangelicals appear to be so afraid of arousing "pride" that educational curricula are reduced to a set of "general requirements" which are applied to all alike. The diversity of giftedness seems to be ignored. While one may have little hope in doing away with general education curricula, corrective measures may be instituted. Through "honors" courses—classes that require a minimum grade point average, for instance—crafting may take place in ways which are not practicable in most general classes.

Intellectual giftedness should not be the only criteria for an "elite" designation, particularly as applied within Christian contexts. Therefore, steps must be taken within the contexts of general education classes and faculty advisement to help students who are not as gifted intellectually to discern their giftedness. Attention should be given to design the best ways to develop each individual's sense of being part of God's "elite." Every instructor should be equipped to give holistic guidance to each student. The grade point average need not be the sole criteria for inclusion in an "honors" course.

Students who have determined their major specific career goal should be banded together to form a close community. They must be *carefully* and *individually* educated and trained. Each individual should be "stretched" to attain his or her own *maximum* potential. Finally, each must be endued with a sense of *mission.* The undisciplined must be equipped with a ruthless discipline in every area of life—spiritual, mental, moral, and physical. They must be honed and sharpened until they become instruments of effectiveness, motivated to exercise their knowledge and skills in whatever situations the course of life places them. As Paul reminds Timothy, the Christian revelation is designed to *"equip persons thoroughly for every good work"* (2 Ti 3:17).

Most young people today lack a sense of tradition or heritage. Consequently, studies in history are needed to form a consistent part of their education. However, to be meaningful, these studies must be a *contextual* history, emphasizing aspects of the past which link directly to the mission that students are preparing for today. Students need a Biblical view of history in which they see the sovereignty of God forming the foundation upon which all subsequent aspects of learning are built. Students who aim at the pastorate or the mission field must come to understand that they are participants in a cosmic "search and rescue" operation which was begun in Genesis 3 and which will not end until Revelation 20. In addition, the Bible must be taught as it was meant to be taught: from a missiological perspective. A hermeneutical system which gives pre-eminence to any theological topic other than missiology is a system which is essentially erroneous in its approach to the Word of God. Our theology, Christology, pneumatology, soteriology, ecclesiology and eschatology are all rooted in missiology; otherwise, they are hopelessly skewed.

5. *Generate programs which produce specific identity constructs.* The characteristics of Biblical apostolicity (cf. 1 Cor 9) and of Biblical elder- and deaconship (cf. 1 Ti 3:1-13) must become the core around which the curricula of Bible Institutes, Bible colleges, Christian liberal arts institutions and seminaries are formed. Biblical apostolicity consists of the abilities to gather Christians into a definable church structure (1 Cor 9:1-2), to be a wise steward of finances (3-15), to preach the gospel with passion (16-18), to adapt oneself to various cultures, races, and social classes (19-23), and to exercise a ruthless self-discipline (24-27). The qualities characterizing an elder and deacon must be clearly addressed in some way in *every* ministry-oriented course that a student takes. Further-

more, the *life principles, values and skills* that underlie all of these abilities or states must appear in "liberal arts" courses as well. Such principles, values and skills need not be overtly "Biblical". However, the knowledge that one's students are required to be participants in ministry no matter what occupation or career they choose should shape the content of every course that is offered.

Courses are not just "taught"—they are taught by *people*. Great care is necessary not only in the selection of our educational curricula, but of our educators as well. The faculty members should ideally reflect education and experience on both the "secular" and "sacred" sides of academia and culture in general. In recruiting professors in liberal arts fields, Evangelical institutions should insist upon a significant amount of Christian education and/or ministry experience.

Conclusion

Christians who have chosen a life of service within Christian institutions of higher learning occupy a position of influence that has the potential of transforming the lives of literally millions of people. The pastoral and missionary candidates along with students studying business, education, health care, counseling and other professions will contact hundreds of persons in the course of their lives, who will in turn contact hundreds of other persons, and so on. Knowledge of the mechanics of exponential multiplication should cause the heart of every teacher to pound with excitement upon entering a classroom for any given lecture period. Such knowledge should also sober each instructor during his or her hours of preparation, knowing that errors or areas of neglect could be multiplied a thousandfold. It is no wonder James included the solemn warning in his letter that *"not many of you should presume to be teachers, my brothers, because you know that we who teach will be judged more strictly"* (Jas 3:1).

While this sober statement should remain constantly in the mind of every teacher, a better point to ponder is the more positive theme found in Acts 19. Here, Paul's two year "Bible Institute," housed in the lecture hall of Tyrannus, produced men and women who were so well-equipped and so fired with enthusiasm for mission that *"all the Jews and Greeks who lived in the province of Asia heard the Word of the Lord."* May such a saturation of entire geographical areas become the goal—and the product—of our educational institutions today.

Bibliography

Baker, Ken
  1997   " Boomers, Busters, and Missions: Things Are
         Different Now," *Evangelical Missions
         Quarterly*. January, pp.70ff.
Bessenecker, Scott
  1997   "Paul's Short-term Church Planting: Can It
         Happen Again?" *Evangelical Missions
         Quarterly*. July, 326ff

Carter, Stephen
    1993   *The Culture of Disbelief.* New York: Basic Books.

Clapp, Rodney
    1988   "Remonking the Church" in *Christianity Today.* August 12, 1988, p. 20.

Dychtwald, Ken and Joe Flower
    1990   *The Age Wave.* New York: Bantam Books.

Gardner, Christine J.
    1998   "Keeping Students in School," *Christianity Today.* September 7, 34.

Graham, Amy E. and Robert J. Morse
    1998   "Our Method Explained, " *U.S. News and World Report.* August 3, 1 82.

Hart D.G. and R. Albert Mohler, Jr. (eds)
    1996   *Theological Education in the Evangelical Tradition* Grand Rapids, MI: Baker Books.

Henry ,William A. III
    1994   *In Defense of Elitism.* New York: Anchor Books.

Hunter, James Davison
    1987   *Evangelicalism: The Coming Generation* Chicago: The University of Chicago Press.

Lasch, Christopher
    1991   *The Culture of Narcissism.* New York: W. W. Norton and Company.

Letson, Douglas and Michael Higgens
    1995   *The Jesuit Mystique.* Chicago: Loyola Press.

Marsden, George
    1994   The Soul of the American University: From
            Protestant Establishment to Established
            Nonbelief. New York: Oxford University Press.
    1997   The Outrageous Idea of Christian Scholarship
            New York: Oxford University Press.

Mouw, Richard
    1996   "Challenge of Evangelical Theological
            Education," in *Theological Education in the*
            Evangelical Tradition, (eds). D. G. Hart and R.
            Albert Mohler, Jr. Grand Rapids, MI: Baker
            Books, p. 287.

Niebuhr, H. Richard
    1951   *Christ and Culture.* New York: Harper.

Niklaus, Robert *et.al.*
    1986   *All for Jesus.* Camp Hill, PA: Christian
            Publications.

Noll, Mark
    1994   The Scandal of the Evangelical Mind. Grand
            Rapids, MI: Eerdmans.

O'Brien, David J.
    1994   *From the Heart of* the *American Church:*
            Catholic Higher Education and American
            Culture. Maryknoll, NY: Orbis Books.

Parshall, Phil
    1977   "A Small Family is a Happy Family,"
            Evangelical Missions Quarterly. October, 207ff

Siewert, John and Edna Valdez (eds.)
    1997   *The Mission Handbook* (17th Edition) Pasadena,
            CA: MARC.

Tucker, Ruth A.
>1989   "Growing Up A World Away," *Christianity Today*. February 17, 17ff.

Weber, Max
>1958   *The Protestant Ethic and the Spirit of Capitalism.* New York: Charles Scribner's Sons.

Mission in Postmodern Contexts:
A Journey of Deconstruction and Discovery in Life Community — Los Angeles, California

Jonathan Campbell

We are living in a *post*-modern era. Reality and perceptions about reality are changing. Postmodernity challenges *all* of our assumptions. Everything, old *and* new, is being questioned. Insecurity and skepticism plague the global scene. We are a culture in crisis.

Having been shaped in *and* by modernity, the church has been marginalized by modern culture, and is now further put aside by postmodernity. In an age that values "tolerance," postmodern is with little or no tolerance for institutionalized religion. Postmodernity presents a formidable threat to church as we know it.

Postmodernity forces many questions about the nature of church and the nature of missionary encounter in post-Christian cultures. The challenge facing the church today is to see through the modern-postmodern crisis in order to see the many opportunities for sharing the gospel and being a missionary community in postmodern cultures.

Engaging Postmodern Cultures

Do you not say, " Four months more and then the harvest"? I tell you, open your eyes and look at the [postmodern] *fields! They are ripe for harvest* (John 4:35).

Over the past four years, we have been gathering people's perceptions of church. We have asked countless people, "What's your idea of church?" or "Why don't you go to church?" We have heard numerous reasons, ranging from rational objections to religious hypocrisy, judgmentalism, instititutionalism and simple irrelevance. These feelings are expressed in a diversity of ways. Here are just a few:

"I can stay home and watch someone preach at me on TV. . . . but I don't want to." – Kathy (32), administrative nurse, married mother of one.

"I'm not religious." – Amy (29), reads Buddhist writings, dabbles in Judaism and regularly visits psychics.

"Life is just not as simple as the church makes it out to be." – Dave (33), landscaper, former homosexual now married with children.

"I just don't fit in. . . . These people are cultural misfits . . . . I don't want to become like them" – Jennifer (29), Mother of two, raised in southern California megachurch.

"It's easy for pastors to ask people to put time in at church . . . . They get paid to be there. I have to carve out time from my schedule" – Ray (29), CDF fire engineer, father of two.

"I hurt. My husband told me to visit the priest, but I didn't want to. All he will have me do is say 'Hail Mary' many times—that doesn't do anything." – Gladys (28), Catholic from Casa Blanca, CA.

"I can't trust the leaders. It's like they are paid to be nice. They don't know me. They don't want to know me." – Brian (21), student, raised in church.

"I don't have to go to church to believe in God. . . . I love God, but I hate the church" – Melissa (20), daughter of missionaries.

"The church has been bastardized.[1] All it's about is money and politics. . . . There's little resemblance between the church of today and the life of Jesus." – Dee (35), Ex-Catholic mother of two.

These perceptions, as well as media portrayals, reflect a growing discontent with institutionalized religion. At best, the church is seen as archaic religious structures that exist to conserve and control for the sake of itself and, at worst, a mean-spirited, intolerant political group. For most postmoderns, church has become something to avoid—even oppose.

---

[1] The word, *bastard* is used to designate "something that is spurious, irregular, inferior, or of questionable origin" or that which is substandard or "lacking genuineness or authority."

Today's postmodern ambivalence toward (and sometimes outright attack upon) the contemporary church begins to look very much like Christ's attack on the religious institutions of the first century.[2] Postmoderns see the lack of integrity in the church—something is not right. Modern cultures may have been "Christianized" or "Christened" by the religious structures of Christendom, but a majority of people remains unaffected by the authentic, life-transforming gospel of Jesus. Postmoderns do not reject God so much as religion— human systems and philosophical traditions that try to contain God and control people.

Postmoderns are intrigued with spirituality more than the generations before them though they are reluctant to commit to any one religious tradition. In simple terms, postmoderns are anti-religious and anti-institutional spiritual seekers.

Beginnings of Our Journey

Blessed are those whose strength is in You,
who have set their hearts on pilgrimage.
(Psalm 84:5)

This chapter shares part of our journey as a fellowship of churches that live in postmodern contexts. Like many postmoderns, we have been rethinking religion and spirituality. Our journey has been one of both deconstruction and discovery: deconstruction of our modern concepts of church and mission that hindered effective engagement of postmoderns and the rediscovery of the missional nature of

---

[2] See Jesus' condemnation of religious pride and institutionalism in Matthew 15:1-20; 23:1-39; Mark 7:1-23 and Luke 11:37-53.

church. Though most of us had never heard of "postmodernity," we have been wrestling with our culture and what it means to be a follower of Jesus in post-modern contexts since our beginnings in the fall of 1992.

The purpose of this narrative is to share our struggle in making disciples of postmoderns.[3] Our primary objective is to live the Way of Jesus in our ever-changing world. We have been and are continuing on a journey of translating the gospel and community in and beyond postmodern cultures. Our story is still being written.

Being Church in Our Community

As we began envisioning a new church start, we prayed with a focus not on church growth, but on mission. We sought to disciple those who would never go to church otherwise. We asked, "How will we bring the gospel and church to the unchurched? We were motivated out of seeing a world that needed Jesus but wanted nothing to do with church. They had lost any confidence in the institution of church, saw the credibility of pastors crumble and had no interest in packing church activities in an already busy, overworked schedule.

In the midst of wrestling with models and strategies, I was praying for God to show us the model he wanted us to

---

[3] I am indebted to Paul and Jenny Ingram, Ben and Debbie Stewart, Hsieh and Theresa Sun, Jeff and Beth Kurtz, Michael and Shannon O'Shields, John and Vondella McCombs, James and Laura Russell, Chris and Tess Berry, Earl Anderson, Cameron Stratton and George Patterson who have have been partners in the journey to love Jesus and follow his ways wherever he may lead. We do not pretend to have all the answers, but we do have a lot of questions. We are simply trying to be faithful to the life and teachings of Jesus Christ and his Word.

follow. God's clear answer was "if I show you a model, you will follow it. You will seek to perfect it with the best of intentions . . . . Do you want me or a model? Follow me. I am the Way." So from the start, we began to learn to trust Jesus at his word. As Jesus promised, "on this rock I will build my church, and the gates of Hell will not overcome it" (Mt 16:18). The question for us became, "How then do we let Jesus build his church?" Jesus did not need us to start more churches, but he did desire us to join him. It was (and still is) all about love and obedience to him as our guide and compass of our journey.

Life Community began in January, 1993 as a cell church. Though we started the church without a specific model in mind, we had been influenced by cell church strategies. We liked cell church because of its value on community and relational evangelism. Nine months later, Life Community was operating with three strong cell groups meeting in homes, five evangelistic Bible studies and a weekly celebration in a Karate studio. We began with a strong desire to multiply not only cells, but also churches. For this reason, the teaching at the Sunday celebrations was shared among five people.

A major shift of direction occurred during a leadership meeting in September 1993. In deciding what should be studied in the cells, the group came to the conclusion, "If these cells are basic Christian communities, who are we to decide what they study? Let's let them be basic Christian communities (i.e., practicing the "one anothers" of Scripture) under the headship of Jesus Christ, founded on God's Word and empowered by the Holy Spirit. . . . If these believers are functioning as churches then who are we to tell them what they can and cannot do." The issue was not of whether we could trust the people, but rather could we trust the Holy Spirit to guide a group of believers in community with one another. If they are functioning as churches, why not let them be churches? This realization was the "Ah Ha" moment that began the shift from being a cell church to becoming a community of churches.

The transition to a community of churches was a significant, but very natural shift. The issue here was really about control. The controlling structures of cell church are systemically the same as "traditional" church. Like any other institutional forms of church, cell church structure is dependent on highly skilled leaders, organizational charts and top-down controls. They also need significant resources to pay for professional salaries, buildings and equipment—all of which are irrelevant to most postmoderns. As we studied the New Testament, we realized that the first century church was not a cell church as many cell church leaders advocate, but was rather churches that met in homes throughout a city.

Our changing understanding of leadership also influenced our transition. A few months after beginning to empower the cells as churches, we experienced a radical "pruning" among our leaders. Hidden agendas began to surface that were contrary to our common values. Three of our most experienced Christian leaders had different primary objectives: 1) to build specialized programs along with the building to match, 2) to be paid for ministry as a church administrator, and 3) to be ordained as "pastor." Programs, pay and position were contrary to the direction we were being led. We lost our three most "qualified" leaders and all but died, only to be reborn as a humbled community striving to know what it means to be a living expression of the Body of Christ. From this very difficult time we also learned that the qualifications for being a leader was a desperate dependency upon Jesus expressed in genuine humility toward one another. Soon, God raised up an entirely new group of leaders.

Another reason we moved away from cell church structure was that meeting together as churches every Sunday took emphasis off the churches that met during the week. It seemed strange to us to leave our neighborhoods on the very day people who did not know Jesus were most likely to be home. At the same time we recognized the need to meet together for worship, connection, encouragement, and accountability among the churches. We transitioned into meeting as churches during the week and coming together as a community of churches once a month. This freeing change, put the emphasis on the churches that met throughout the week and increased the mission focus of these churches. From here we saw the churches become established, new people reached and new churches started.

Our Struggle with Church and Culture

In our struggle to be church in such a changing culture our problems are deeper than they seem. The real issues are not methodological or structural; they are theological and deeply spiritual. The modern-postmodern shift is exposing the modern enculturation of the church. Postmodernity threatens church as we know it because it rejects the modern cultural forces that have shaped the church.

We questioned the institutional paradigm which had defined church for the last 1500 years. This Christendom paradigm was initiated by Constantine, affirmed by the Protestant Reformation, and fueled by the culture of modernity. Church as a missional movement with a distinct lifestyle was sacrificed on the foundation of institutionalism. The marks of the modern church are perversions of the simple patterns of

Jesus and the early church: the foundation of the resurrected Christ, the cornerstone, was institutionalized (Eph 2:20; I Pet 2:6), individualism replaced mutual community (Mt 18:20), gnosticism replaced teaching for obedience (Mt 28:19-20), pragmatism replaced faithfulness (Rom 12:1-2; Col 2:8), and clericalism (a limited priesthood) replaced the priesthood of all believers (I Pet 2:1-10). All these led to a syncretistic mix.

Although many churches are making strong efforts to respond to the postmodern shift, the changes are primarily cosmetic. The basic modern perceptions of church remain unaltered. Church is still described in institutional terms—a "worship service" whereby passive laity sit listening to a didactic monologue from a professional cleric. The differences among today's churches are found primarily in the superficialities of "style"—music style, clothing style, program style and architectural style. Styles may change, but the systemic structure is still entirely modern. In spite of being well intentioned, creative, entrepreneurial and purpose-driven, the church and mission remain slaves to modern ecclesial tradition.

We are not suggesting the contemporary church does not care for postmoderns. On the contrary, churches are increasing desiring and attempting to "reach" postmoderns and even start "postmodern" churches. Although they may well be contemporary, they can hardly be described as indigenous or biblically authentic. At best, most attempts are superficially postmodern. They remain systemically modern (perhaps even hyper-modern). While the style of ministry may be creatively relevant to the culture, modernity's influence on the values, structures, and leadership remain for the most part unchallenged. None of them is fundamentally culturally translatable.[4]

---

[4] Even the most celebrated churches of the day are a lot more modern than they realize. The so-called "contemporary," "innovative," or "seeker"

New Wineskins for a New (Postmodern) World

No one pours new wine into old wineskins. If he does, the new wine will burst the skins, the wine will run out and the wineskins will be ruined. No, new wine must be poured into new wineskins. And no one after drinking old wine wants the new, for he says, "The old is better" (Luke 5:37-39).

The radical nature of postmodernity has forced us back to what the New Testament reveals. And the more we wrestled with both the Scriptures and our culture, we realized that if we hope to bring postmoderns (and other unreached peoples) to faith, we must have new wineskins. The modern wineskins are not sufficiently supple to be changed. Jesus warned against trying to re-use the old. We were faced with three choices: 1) Maintain the modern church, "The old is good enough"; 2) Change the Modern Church, "Pour new wine into old wineskins"; or 3) Start radically new churches, "New Wineskins." Renewal is not enough. *For the church to recover her missional integrity in any culture will require nothing less than a radical transformation.*

Through our journey, we have come to realize that the Way of Jesus *is* the wineskin. In him we experience new wine and new wineskins. Jesus is the way to life and the way of life. Jesus never wrote a book, nor built a building nor initiated an institution, but he did gather a new community of believers and

---

churches in the line of Willowcreek, Calvary Chapel, Vineyard, and Saddleback are products of modernity. These churches may not have stained glass windows, large pulpits, robed choirs, but they may have theatre seating, Plexiglas pulpits with PowerPoint, and rock ensembles. They are not radical, but rather modifications of the Reformed Christendom tradition. These represent the new-and-improved modern church.

lived with them. He left nothing else and nothing less. The greatest challenge facing the church in the postmodern era is to rediscover what it means to live the Way of Jesus in community (*ekklesia*) and on mission (*apostolos*) in the world.

The greatest hindrance to the expansion of the church in postmodern contexts is the heaviness of modern structures and methods. We now question everything. Anything that distracts from Jesus and being simple followers of the Way must be removed: modern structures, buildings, hierarchical leaders, and any other institutional expectations. The new focus of church must be on discipling people to become faithful followers of Jesus without having to become "modern" Christians or be initiated into modern religious institutions.

James said, "It is my judgment, therefore, that we should not make it difficult for the Gentiles who are turning to God" (Acts 15:19). In the same way, we should not make it difficult for *postmoderns* (or any other group) who are turning to God. Table 1 sketches the overall thrust of a paradigm shift that we trust will lead toward genuine people movements across cultures.

Jesus is not modern or postmodern. His body (the church) is neither modern nor postmodern. His community is a *way of life*. Postmodernity calls the church to undergo a systemic paradigm shift that goes to the root of ecclesiology— one that questions all the assumptions of the Christendom model. The church should be nothing less or more than what the Word of God makes it. The church must be de-modernized. The church should stay clear of anything that hinders the body from functioning and reproducing (cf. I Cor 6:12; 8:13; 10:23-33; Heb 12:1-3).

TABLE 4

MODERN / POST MODERN CHURCH CONTRASTS

The Establishment Culturally-Specific (Modern) Christendom Institution	*The Way* Culturally-Translatable Missional Community
From . . .	*To . . .*
Organization & Institution	Organism & Movement
Church is Building, Institution or Event	Church is People and Relationships – *Where two or more*
Structure and Programs	Community and Way of Life
Excellence / Performance	Authenticity / Realness
Pragmatism (Creativity)	Patterns (Obedience Christ)
Growth by Addition	Addition *and* Reproduction
Buildings, Budgets, Bodies	Disciples, Churches, Movement
Control, Uniformity, Conformity	Freedom, Unity, Diversity
Evangelism as Event or Program	Evangelism as Way of Life
Colonize Christians	Evangelize Persons of Peace
Didactic Monologue	Narrative Dialogue
Expository	Participatory
Apologetics / Confrontation	Revelation / Community
Attraction: "Come to us" (Centripetal)	Permeation: "Go to them" (Centrifugal)
Ministry Place & Pulpit	Marketplace & Home
Ordain a Few (Clericalism)	Commission All
Seminary Trained	Field Apprenticed
Imported Professionals	Indigenous Believers
Centralized and Top-Down (Hierarchy)	Decentralized and Horizontal (Lowerarchy)
Senior Pastor (CEO/Executive)	Servant Team (Jesus as Head)
Subsidized Clergy	Tentmaker / Bivocational

Christian Community:
Answering the Cry of the Postmodern World

Relationships create reality for postmoderns. With the widespread distrust of established solutions and institutions, many postmoderns are daring Christians to show them the authentic gospel lived in community. Contrary to a modern understanding of spirituality, the most profound spiritual experience we can have is not in isolation but in community (Mt 18:19-20). Mission to postmodern contexts means disciple making in community contexts. *We make disciples in* and *by community.*

The purpose of the church grows out of the relational heart of God. We are the living Body of Christ where people are drawn into right relationship with God and into right relationship with one another. Thus, churches are personal, intimate, committed and small enough to facilitate healthy relationships. In the early church, the mutual nature of the community was like a healthy family whose members are committed to each other because of their common life in Jesus.

The gospel can break through any and all social barriers needed for true reconciliation and peace. Jesus strikes at the root of those influences that tear at peace and justice. Whether male or female, black or white, Bosnian or Serb, old or young, Baptist or Pentecostal, rich or poor, Jesus is the unifying factor. The individual's differences rather than similarities enable them to contribute significantly to both the church and the world. Not only does the message include community; the community is also a living witness to the world. *In and through community relationships are built through which the gospel spreads freely.*

To know Jesus is to be in community. Jesus and his community are not an ideology to be argued, but rather a reality to be experienced. And the gospel is only fully realized in *and* through community. We cannot prove God. We cannot reason God. He has revealed himself. Christian community is the postmodern apologetic. Jesus Himself declared, "A new command I give you: Love one another. As I have loved you, so you must love one another. By this all men will know that you are my disciples, if you love one another" (John 13:34-35).

The church provides a tangible expression of God's love. In the Body of Christ, the Word is "made flesh." Before postmoderns will consider the truths of Jesus, they must see *and* feel (both spiritually and physically) these truths. The church "proves" the gospel by her very existence. Paul Ingram, a church planter in Seattle explains, "A postmodern will only have as much faith in God as they have in you." This statement reflects the promise in Luke 10 where Jesus says, "He who listens to you listens to me; he who rejects you rejects me; but he who rejects me rejects him who sent me" (10:16).

Living in the Way of Jesus

I am the way and the truth and the life.
No one comes to the Father except through me
(John 14:6).

Jesus is good news for postmoderns. The gospel is not an abstract idea or an institutional structure. The gospel is living. The way Jesus lived his life and the words he spoke were his message. [5] If one is absent, a different gospel is represented. His life now continues in a Spirit-empowered community. Jesus is the *Way*, the *Truth* and the *Life*.

Like the word "Christian," the "Way" was a term of derision borne with pride by the followers of Jesus. They perceived themselves as the authentic continuation of the Way of Jesus. They lived with the reality that in Jesus is found not only the Way of eternal life, but also the Way of life itself. They had been commissioned to continue what he had begun. Jesus is both the way *to* life and the way *of* life. The same ministry Jesus began with his twelve disciples is to be continued now in the power of the Holy Spirit. Jesus is still incarnate through his community of followers—the "Body of Christ." The church, is simply to continue to live out the way of Jesus.

The lifestyle of the church is characterized by obedience to Jesus Christ. As Jesus said, "If you love me, you will obey what I command" (John 14:15). To be the people of God is to live in obedience to Christ. Just as Jesus fully obeyed his Father's commands (John 5:19-20, 30; 15:10), so we, his church, are to obey his commands (Mt 28:18-20; 15:14). We are the people of God to the extent that we live as the people of God. In Acts 11:26 we read that in Antioch the disciples were first called Christians. To be a Christian is to be a disciple—a follower of Jesus. All that sustains us as believers and as a church is faithfulness to the simple truths of Jesus Christ. Therefore, the goal of the church's teaching is not knowledge, but obedience to the commands of Jesus. As we examine the gospels, we find at least eight primary commands of Christ:

---

[5] cf. Acts 2:38-39; 4:12,33; 5:17,42; 8:5, 25, 35; 9:20-22; 10:34-43; 12:16-40; 17; 18:5; Romans 10:9-10.

1. Repent and believe in Jesus Christ (Mark 1:15; Mt 21:32; Acts 20:21)
2. Be baptized (Mt 28:18-20; cf. Acts 2:38-40; Rom 6:1-4)
3. Love God, one another and the world (Mt 22:37-40; Luke 10:25-37; John 13:34-35)[6]
4. Make disciples of all peoples (Mt 28:18-20; Luke 24:46-48; cf. II Tim 2:2)
5. Celebrate Lord's Supper (Mt 26:26-28; Luke 22:1-23; II Cor 11:23-25)
6. Pray regularly (Mt 6:5-13; Luke 11:1-13; John 15:7, 16; 16:24)
7. Give freely as faithful stewards (Mt 6:5-13; Luke 6:38)

Our commitments, knowledge and intentions mean very little unless we are abiding in Jesus. And, to obey for any other reason than love is legalism, which God condemns (Rom 13:8-10; I Cor 13:1-3). Through His love and grace God brings transformation in our lives (Rom 2:4; Heb 12:5-14; Hos 2:14-16; 11:1-4; Jer 31:1-3 1).

How We Discover the Way of Jesus Today

In Jesus we discover not only what to believe, but also how to live—to know him and follow his Way of life. In the Bible we see patterns emerge that are rooted in the life of Jesus, are manifest throughout the New Testament record and can be lived out in a variety of cultural (and historical) contexts. Therefore, three basic criteria exist for determining patterns:

---

[6] It is from love that we *forgive one another* (Matt 6:14-15; Mark 11:25-26 and Luke 6:37-42; 17:3-4) and practice all the other "one anothers."

1. *Jesus*:   Are the patterns seen in the life and teachings of Jesus Christ?
2. *Early Church*: Are the patterns seen in the New Testament church?
3. *Culture*: Are the patterns seen throughout a variety of cultural-historical contexts?

The strength and effectiveness of patterns rest in their inherent simplicity and cultural flexibility. They may be expressed in countless cultural contexts. They were so plain that Paul could simply tell his readers to remember how he lived and what he taught (I Cor 4:16-17; 11:1-2; Phil 3:16-17; I Thess 1:4-7).[7] The guiding question for our pilgrimage has been, "How can we pass on the Way of Jesus in a way that will lead to a movement of indigenous churches?"

One of our biggest challenges is to connect with culture without becoming captive to the culture. The reproduction of indigenous churches is the fruit of faithfully translating the gospel message and community. After years of struggle, we now believe the nature of the gospel calls for one Way of being church (i.e. the Way of Jesus), but this Way has the inherent ability to be embodied in a countless number of cultures (one Way, many expressions). The missional question that shapes us is, "Do we have a vision of church that can be translated to any culture?"[8]

---

[7] He also warned churches from straying from these simple patterns and from their devotion to Christ (cf. Rom 12:1-2; II Cor 11:3; Col 2:6-10; Gal 1:6-9; see also Deut 8:6; II Kings 17:13; Isa 42:24; Ezek 33:11).

[8] Here is a simple exercise: Take a blank sheet of paper and fold it down the middle. On one side put the heading, "Essentials for Church." Name the other column "Non-essentials for Church." See what you come up with. There are actually very few essentials and many non-essentials.

Only an indigenous church is capable of ongoing adaptation to a changing environment and for ongoing reproduction. The objective of our mission in any context is to plant the simple seed of the gospel so that it will take root, grow and reproduce throughout new fields. The very nature of the church as a living system calls us to plant the seed (the essential DNA)—nothing more and nothing less. Then let the seed grow! Put no structural expectations based on modern values (i.e. greatness of buildings, size of budgets or number of bodies)—only organic expectations that it be healthy, growing, bearing fruit and reproducing in the soil of the culture.

Church is now a way of life for us. Our hope is that the life of the church reflects the life of Jesus Christ while being embodied in the local culture. We continually wrestle with how to be the Body of Christ in the world—both biblically authoritative and culturally translatable. The ongoing process of translation can be summarized by the following questions:

1. How have we been shaped by our culture(s)?
2. What is the Way of Jesus?
3. How will we live this Way in new cultures?

This journey has not been easy for most of us. As we have exegeted our culture and the Scriptures, we have realized that we are a lot more worldly (i.e., modern) than we thought (cf. Rom 12:1-2). We must continue to critically determine what traditions have evolved during modernity and what it means to be a Christian community in a pluralistic world without compromising the simple gospel.

How We Live As Communities of The Way

The churches of Life Community are committed to facilitating a movement of reproducing churches and to be the

Body of Christ *in* the world. We embrace the relational nature of the New Testament church—the living Body of Christ through which lives are transformed and relationships reconciled. We do not go to church with a focus on receiving, but rather giving to others. The primary question is "How does Jesus wish to use me to edify others?" or "How can I find, or deepen, the experience of Christ which the New Testament offers, and how can I pass it on to others?" The church exists to bring people into right relationship with God and into right relationship with one another. We are continually amazed to see how the Holy Spirit orchestrates our gatherings as everyone comes prepared to not only receive, but to give to one another.

Teams are an integral part of how we reproduce churches across cultures. We advocate teamship in every sphere of leadership—both in the local churches and for church planting. A church planting team is a group of two or more believers who join together in making disciples and reproducing disciple making communities. Teams hold no authority over churches, nor do churches hold authority over other teams. However, churches and teams work together for movement. Church starting is not affected by the common limitations of buildings, money or seminary graduates. They can meet anywhere (homes, apartments, businesses, community centers, public places, etc.) and can be started by any group of people God calls and the church sends to make disciples.

The good news of Jesus was validated by the lifestyle of the church. The church is a living sign of the powerful reality of the risen Jesus. The New Testament reveals patterns that sustained the movement of the gospel throughout the first century. These patterns reflect and reinforce the essential nature of the church as a missional community (Eph 1:5-6, 11-12; 14, 3:21; II Thess 2:12). When these patterns are compromised, we impede the gospel from spreading unhindered to the ends of the earth.

1. **Community** – We experience the power and presence of Jesus Christ in covenanted fellowships that meet from house to house (Acts 2; 16:29-34, 20:20; Rom 16:23; I Cor 12-14; 16:15-19).

2. **Permeation** –We intentionally share the Gospel and establish disciple-making communities in the midst of unreached and/or undiscipled people groups (Mt 28:18-20; Acts 1:8; Rom 15:14).

3. **Incarnation** – We seek group conversions (*oikos* evangelism) by sharing the gospel in and through relational networks and cultural systems (Luke 10; Acts 16: I Cor 9:19-23).

4. **Reproduction** – We reproduce the character and Way of Jesus in every sphere of church life: disciples, leaders, churches and teams (Mt 28:19-20; John 15; II Tim 2:2; Titus 2:3-8).

5. **Teamship** – We identify, equip and empower indigenous leaders to partner together in serving the church and starting new churches (I Tim 3; Acts 4:13; 6:3-7; 13:1-3; 14:23).

6. **Interdependence** – We partner with churches, teams and groups of like faith and mission for mutual edification and mission (John 13:34-35; 17:20-23; Acts 13:1-4; 14:26-28; Phil 2:1-5).

7. **Family** – We uphold the family as the primary context for the spiritual nurture, discipleship and leadership development (Eph 5:22-6:4; Titus 2:1-8).

8. **Tentmaking** – We affirm tentmaking as the primary pattern for supporting pastors and missionaries (Luke 10:1-8; Acts 18:2-4; I Cor 4:12; 9:1-18; II Cor 2:17; I

Thess 2:9; 5:12; II Thess 3:7-13). No one is on salary, though some money is pooled to help send teams overseas.

9. **Open Ministry** – We affirm the priesthood of all believers and empower every believer (regardless of culture, age, education or gender) to actively participate in fulfilling Christ's mission for his church in the world (Acts 2; I Cor 12; Col 4:17; Eph 4; I Pet 2).

10. **Holy Spirit** – We listen and obey as the Spirit leads us in fulfilling his mission (Zech 4: 6; John 5:19-20; Acts 1:8; Rom 15:13-19; Gal 3:3; Eph 3:16-21; I Thess 1:5; II Tim 1:7).

Beginnings of a Global Movement
Fulfilling The Mission of Our Lord Jesus

Our purpose is to fulfill the mission of our Lord Jesus by living the Way of Jesus in today's mission contexts. We encourage and equip churches and teams to start and grow New Testament churches that will reproduce disciples and churches worldwide (cf. Mt 28:19-20; Luke 24:45-49; John 20:21-23; Acts 1:4-8). We believe church growth and reproduction is primarily built upon loving obedience to Jesus Christ. Developing an effective mission strategy involves catching a glimpse of where God is leading and how we can follow him. Our challenge is to discover how to translate the gospel message and church into new cultural contexts.

We live and reproduce communities of churches—clusters of Christ centered, relationally-based and mission-focused churches. Each church represents usually ten to twenty adults and a varying number of children. While each church is autonomous, they covenant together as a community of churches for mission. The churches gather on a monthly basis for fellowship, singing, prayer and testimonies. Currently, three networks of churches in greater Los Angeles share a common mission to make disciples and start churches among the undiscipled. These networks of churches represent about twelve churches, four church planting teams and some ten evangelistic studies. These churches in the Los Angeles area encourage one another to live and reproduce an apostolic lifestyle through churches, community gatherings, team meetings and networks:

- *Churches* – focus on families and neighborhoods (throughout the week)
- *Community Gatherings* – focus on churches (flocks) and cities (fields) (once a month)
- *Team Meetings* – train and reproduce servant leaders (once a month)
- *Baton Networks* – our global connection to encourage apostolic movement worldwide

Though we have clearly shifted away from the modern church, we do not advocate starting "postmodern churches."[9] Trying to be postmodern is sure to be self-defeating. The idea of a "postmodern church" is no better than the "modern church." What we really need are communities living in the Way of Jesus that are culturally-translatable and are self-renewing. Our call is to be the church *in* postmodern culture without being *of* postmodern culture—to "be in the world, but not of the world."

---

[9] We should not start "postmodern" churches any more than we should start "black" churches, "Vietnamese" churches, "Anglo" churches, "Gen X" churches or "house" churches. We start churches. Our identity is first in Jesus, not in our ethnicity or culture or generation or style (cf. Gal 3:28).

Lifecycle of a Movement

We see church reproduction as a natural process of healthy church life. Local churches send teams with the purpose of evangelizing and starting a cluster of indigenous churches that will continue the process of reproduction. This lifecycle is not so much a rigid sequence, but rather an organic rhythm seen throughout the book of Acts (Acts 13:1-14:26). Like any living organism, churches go through identifiable phases of maturation. Though the process has an obvious beginning, it does not really have an ending.

1. **Send . . .** *Apostolic Team(s)* The team works to build relationships in the community. In a context of prayer, the team begins to make contact in the community through a variety of means to discover spiritually receptive people and those who will open their homes for discovery Bible studies.

2. **Gather . . .** *New Disciples* We gather seekers and new believers on their "turf" with their family and friends to hear the gospel (Acts 16). We pray for a relational network of people who will put their faith in Jesus, be baptized and become a church.

3. **Covenant . . .** *Churches* As new believers are being discipled, we seek to develop a disciple making community. A group of believers is a church when they commit (or covenant) to relate to one another and to the world as a church—the Body of Christ in that community.

4. **Reproduce . . .** *A Movement of Churches* Ongoing movement results from living a simple missional lifestyle in community. We regularly pray for unreached peoples and equip the church to regularly send out teams who will reproduce disciples and disciplemaking communities.

Where We are Moving

This very simple experience of the Body of Christ has spread through relationships into the greater Los Angeles area, across the country and overseas as well. While a young movement, the fourth generation of disciple-making communities is present across a diversity of cultures and locations.

- **Within North America** – Riverside, Los Angeles, Santa Cruz, San Diego, San Jose, San Francisco, Mill Valley, Auburn, Nevada City, Portland, Seattle and Orlando.

- **Across Cultures** – Diverse people groups in the United States are being discipled in the Way of Jesus including African immigrants, Latinos, Eastern Europeans, Arabs, Anglos, universities to the homeless, low income to white collar, postmoderns and various alternative subcultures.

- **Globally** – Teams/churches are currently ministering in Mongolia, Belize and the Philippines. Teams are currently preparing for China, Romania, Mexico, East Africa and the 10/40 Window.

We are just at the genesis of a lifetime journey. We are still struggling with what it means to live in the Way of Jesus. Many questions remain unanswered—certainly more than at the beginning of our journey. We have no hope of perfection until Jesus comes (Phil 1:6). We still need to learn much. Some present challenges include:

1. How can we make disciples and create community among people who long for relationships, but also cannot trust anyone?

2. How can we better engage and empower the poor and marginalized of society?
3. How do we equip and reproduce indigenous leaders who will continue to train others in the Way of Jesus?
4. What do we do with those people who embrace community, but do not see the need for embracing Jesus?
5. How do we respond to people who embrace Jesus but don't want to change their lifestyle?
6. How can we help established churches to better engage postmoderns?

Conclusion: A Call to Courage

Peace be with you! As the Father has sent me,
I am sending you into the [postmodern] *world*
(John 20:21).

Jesus still wishes to incarnate himself in the world through his body—the church. In a world where people feel more alienated from the environment, the spiritual and the relational realms of life, there is a growing hunger among postmoderns for that which is genuine and satisfying. The church in any age must recover what it means to be a missionary community on move in the world. This presents a two-part challenge: to be faithful to Jesus in the midst of a culture antagonistic toward modern religion and to translate the radix gospel and community of Christ into increasingly postmodern cultures. The love of Jesus and the needs of our world demand that we translate the gospel and community for postmoderns.[10]

---

[10] The apostle Paul was motivated out of such a love (cf. I Cor 5:14; 9:19).

The important thing is not what is *on* these pages, but the life of Jesus *lived out* in community. This description is just a sketch of our pilgrimage. We cannot fully understand this way of life outside of experience. It is more than doctrine—it is inherently spiritual and relational. It is spiritual in that Jesus is the head of the church. The Spirit gives life to the church. It is relational because the reality and fullness of Jesus Christ can only be experienced in community, not individually.

We hope the missional value of our journey offers direction for other cultures around the world where modernity has shaped the church and where the search for a renewed vision of church is already underway. Only as we return to the organic nature of church will we be prepared to faithfully translate the gospel *and* community among postmodern cultures. And only an organic paradigm of church will enable movements among *all* peoples of the world.

To harvest the fruit that the Holy Spirit is producing, we must recapture a biblical vision of the fundamental nature of the church. To live in the Way of Jesus—nothing could be more simple. Nothing could be more difficult. Nothing could bring more pain. Nothing could bring more joy. Nothing could be more *real*. And nothing could appeal more to the social and spiritual longings inherent in our world.

"Making Disciples Through Teaching Obedience Among Generation X"

Rick Sessoms

To introduce this case study of mission mobilizing from Simpson College entitled, "Making Disciples through Teaching Obedience Among Generation X" two comments are in order. First, the information presented herein is not a new program. Tom Phillips, president of International Students Inc. recently stated, "We are on the verge of the greatest student movement the world has ever seen." Certainly, God is moving at Simpson College in similar fashion to His recent work on many of our campuses. He is choosing to pour out His Spirit among us in fresh ways.

Second, this information is not complex. What I have to present is quite unadorned and practical. My purpose is not to suggest sweeping solutions to the challenges we face with today's collegians, but to help articulate a couple of the key questions we face and present what Simpson College is doing to address those questions.

Simpson College is similar to many of the Christian Coalition colleges across America. We offer degrees in professional studies and the liberal arts. We have been in existence for seventy-five years, first in Seattle, then in San Francisco, and since 1989 in Redding, California. We have approximately eight hundred traditional undergraduate students and are one of four colleges in the United States associated with the Christian and Missionary Alliance. C&MA priorities for Simpson College include preparing vocational church leaders and preparing church planting missionaries. The question before us is "How do we motivate and mobilize today's generation to participate in this Great Commission enterprise?"

"Generation X": Descriptions

One day last spring, Sally (not her real name) showed up at my office to talk. She came wanting to pursue her relationship with Christ, but she was filled with anger at God, her parents, and especially the church. She said, "I love Jesus, but I hate the church." During the next 1½ hours, she related her story to me.

When she was very young, her parents divorced. Sally went to live with her mother, who was soon remarried. Her stepfather sexually abused her intermittently as she grew up. Sally's mother and stepfather took her to church regularly; her stepfather was an active leader in the congregation. Sally described the evangelical church they attended as a good church: a nice youth program, a good music program, good teaching, and a nice building.

However, in her perception, the church was either un-willing or powerless to deliver God's mercy to her in her area of deepest need. Even when she reached out for help, it seemed unavailable to her. Externally, the church appeared successful, but behind the veneer, the lives of spiritual leaders were seriously wrong. This contradiction created distrust in

Sally for the church that has been a source of struggle for years. Sally's story is rather common among our students of this generation. They have witnessed the acute dysfunction of many leaders in the church.

These collegians have been labeled "Generation X." Though opinion varies regarding boundary dates, I employ the label to designate those born 1964-1981. The term refers generally to those living in the western world or those directly affected by western thought and social structures.

Current western society is popularly described as post-Christian. Generally, those born within the past thirty-five years are the first westerners that possess no primary recollection of a cultural milieu in which the Judeo-Christian perspective is popularly normative. This phenomenon, along with the impact of the information explosion of our age, has significantly altered their worldview, their collective identity, their confidence in authority, and their beliefs about the future.

Our personal observations of current students who attend colleges like Simpson suggest that they express significant interest in spirituality. When I attended college twenty-five years ago, students on our Christian campus generally did not consider being overtly spiritual a "popular" character trait. Today, spirituality is a topic of intense conversation.

We also note that our students demonstrate a quiet cynicism toward established institutions, including the church. As in Sally's case, many students today are aware of dysfunction in their homes; consequently, they are proficient in detecting dysfunction within institutions. They observe the flashy churches of baby boomers and are not impressed. Unlike their generation's predecessors, our students do not oppose the church aggressively; they simply disappear from its ranks. In other words, they are not anti-institutional; they could be more accurately described as a-institutional.

Furthermore, we have observed that this generation values teamwork. They express low motivation to pioneer alone; however, motivation to pursue ministry/mission in teams is high. While "Generation X" is popularly described as unmotivated, we have found that our students often feel stymied by feelings of hopelessness. They sense that the current ills of humankind are too vast and unconquerable. For these and other reasons, they do not tend to desire to tackle mission alone. On the other hand, they love to minister with one another in the context of trusting relationships.

On a similar note, our students will choose radical obedience when they are confident that mentor(s) are committed to them. Many of our students need someone to believe in them. They express the need for role models that speak truth graciously into their lives. With good mentoring in place, they have demonstrated a willingness to follow Christ's Great Commission mandate into the most difficult of places and situations.

Cooperating with God: Our Model

What kind of approach would facilitate the mobilization of these students for short-term missions? When Jesus healed the invalid by the Pool of Bethesda, some Jews complained that carrying one's bedroll on the Sabbath was against the rules. When challenged for performing this miracle on the "wrong" day, Jesus defended himself saying, "My Father is working straight through, even on the Sabbath. So am I."

As the religious people persisted in their criticism, Jesus explained himself more precisely, "I'm telling you this straight. The Son can't independently do a thing, only what he sees the Father doing. What the Father does, the Son does. The Father loves the Son and includes him in everything he is doing." (John 5:16-20: *The Message*) Assuming that Jesus' ministry was a model for our own, we take seriously our responsibility to cooperate with the work God is already doing in ourselves and in others. Strategically, we understand Jesus' model to imply that our ministry to students is to respond intentionally to God's initiative so that they are facilitated to make Christ the authentic center of their lives.

In 1993, Simpson College had no active missions emphasis by/for students. In the spring of that year, a student named Jim Bailey with several other students made an appointment with the new president, Dr. Jim Grant. They asked with timidity if the school would be willing to sponsor a team of students for a ministry trip employing drama and music to several churches and camps in the northwestern United States. Grant challenged the students when he responded, "Have you ever dreamed of taking your ministry to another country?" This was the moment for which Jim and his friends had been praying and waiting. They were encouraged to pursue the dreams God had deposited in their lives. That summer several students traveled to Hong Kong.

The next year I assumed the role of facilitating spiritual formation on the campus. One of the initial steps in that effort was to employ Jim Bailey immediately after he graduated to become our first Coordinator of Student Ministries.

For these past five years, God has been doing a new work at Simpson College. Many of the processes we followed are much clearer in hindsight; we have had numerous delightful serendipitous moments along the way.

Developing Leaders: Our Focus

From the beginning of this endeavor, two motivating values have guided us:

1. Student vision: We regularly ask students, "What are your dreams?" We do not begin with a preset program; rather, we embark on each year's summer ministry preparation with student-driven vision. We desire to cooperate with the work God is already doing in students' lives.

2. Student passion: We regularly ask students, "For what are you willing to suffer?" We have observed that students who pursue their own dreams for mission typically express a deeper level of commitment to quality preparation, integrity in ministry, and level of sacrifice.

Life on Life: Our Process

The following chronological preparation process has evolved through trial and error:

1. Students express mission vision to Student Ministries staff.
2. Students (leaders) apply and are selected.
3. Selected student leaders recruit their respective student teams.
4. Student team members apply; Student Ministries staff approves.
5. Student ministries staff networks to arrange mission host and location that matches student vision.
6. Student leaders recruit faculty/staff team sponsor(s) who partner with Student Ministries staff in mentoring responsibilities.
7. Student team raises funds with Student Ministries staff guidance.
8. Student leaders meet weekly (beginning in October prior to travel) with Student Ministries staff.

9. Team leaders meet weekly (beginning in January prior to travel) with respective team leaders.
10. Student leaders complete six-day Wilderness Trek where issues of integrity, trust, relationship to God and others are addressed.
11. Team members complete ten-day Training Week where issues of cross-cultural sensitivity, teamwork, trust, ministry preparation, integrity, relationship to God and others are addressed.
12. Student Ministries staff, team leaders, and sponsor(s) coordinate travel arrangements.
13. After the ministry experience, a thorough debriefing process is completed with student team leaders, hosts, and sponsor(s).

Long-term Church Planters: Our Goal

We believe that exposure to another culture provides a necessary sensitizing experience for students about spiritual needs throughout the world. Though the vast majority of these students will not become career missionaries, our desire is to provide this opportunity for all students in order that their worldview is affected. Hopefully, most will become more responsible to influence their own culture for world mission; more have expressed intention to participate directly in establishing Christ's church in another culture. We employ the "Missions Funnel" (see Figure One) in our understanding of this process.

Level 1 Challenge & Exposure
Who's involved: All daytime undergraduate students, staff and
    faculty of Simpson College
Examples: All that the Missions Task Force does, chapels, Global
    Impact Week
Person responsible: Missions Task Force Chairperson

Level 2 Involvement & Experience
Who's involved: Task force members, summer team
    members
Examples: Urbana, short-term trips
Person responsible: Coordinator of Student Minis-
    tries

Level 3 Mentoring
Who's involved: Mostly students in lead-
    ership positions who have a passion
    for missions
Examples: RA's small group leaders,
    team leaders, worship leaders
Person responsible: MIR/ Coordinator of
    Student Ministries

Level 4 Career Placement
Who's involved: Potential career mis-
    sionaries
Examples: Help in finding an appropri-
    ate organization, walking through their
    selection process
Person responsible: MIR

Goal: To produce vocational, cross-
cultural ministers of the Gospel

Figure 1
Missions Funnel

The statistics below reflect our five-year results:

Participation:
Summer '94 – 3 teams (35 students/faculty/staff)
Summer '95 – 2 teams (21 students/faculty/staff)
Summer '96 – 12 teams (100 students/faculty/staff)
Summer '97 – 16 teams (140 students/faculty/staff)
Summer '98 – 19 teams (165 students/faculty/staff)
Summer '99 (projected) – 21 teams (200+ students/faculty/staff)

Total teams: (as of Summer '99) – 73
Total participants: (as of Summer '99) – approx. 660

Missions Majors/Minors:
Total in 1993 – 4
Total Current – 40

Conclusion

What is the future? We are committed to stir up continually with sensitivity and courage what God is doing within our campus community. We are deeply grateful that God has decided to visit us in such an obvious and profound way. To Him be the glory!

The Limu Valley Project --A Case Study

Abdellah Usman Muktar

Introduction[1]

Ethiopia has a very long and distinguished history. The establishment of its royal dynasty has significant connections to Jewish Israel. About nine hundred years before Christ, the Queen of Sheba of Ethiopia heard great things about King Solomon, his wisdom and his power. Sheba went to visit him with handful of gifts. The Queen fell in love with King Solomon and upon her return she gave a birth to her first son, Menelik.

Tradition says the imperial dynasty of Ethiopia originated from Menelik I. Thus, the Ethiopian dynasty is presumed

---

[1] The, the place, and the name of the NGO have been changed to avoid strained relationships for the parties involved. If you, the reader, wish to have more information, please contact the editor.

to have exercised sovereign power in the line of Judah, and anointed by God. Ethiopia's long Christian heritage and old religious formation has a significant relationship to Jerusalem and later on to Alexandria, Egypt. Ethiopia claims to be the oldest Christian nation with Christianity being the predominant religion in the country. The Christian faith can be traced with a continuous history from 325 AD.

With the rise of Islam in Arabia some early persecution of Muslims led to their fleeing to Ethiopia. While the Ethiopian government was "Christian," the early Muslim refugees were received and cared for. This early welcome led to the emergence of Islam in Ethiopia at an early date as well. And, it led to a different kind of relationship between the Ethiopian Orthodox Church and Islam than began to emerge in other regions of North Africa and the Middle East. The attitude of mutual tolerance emerged without the crusading of one against the other.

Background

Drought has been a never-ending phenomenon for the last three decades in Ethiopia. The growing severity of the Ethiopian droughts and resulting famine(s) forced the government to call for outside support. Non-governmental Organizations (NGOs) have worked in relief and development in Ethiopia since before World War II. However, in 1984 due to massive famine outbreak in the country, the focus for NGOs shifted from development to famine relief. This case study depicts one of these NGO efforts. The place and name of the NGO are not presented in this chapter to avoid local complications. For the purpose of this chapter the name of the NGO will be called "United Aid." The name of the region for the purpose of this chapter will be called "Limu Valley." (For more information please contact the editor of this book.) During this famine period United Aid set up ten feeding shelters in different parts throughout the country to combat the famine.

Limu Valley is situated 350 kms south of the capital city. The drought badly affected this area. During one period of time more than twenty people were dying every day. Countless children under ten, mothers and elderly people were on the ground crying out for assistance. United Aid launched its life saving relief operation in the valley at this crucial time.

The Limu Valley is lies within the Great Rift Valley that runs from northeast to southwest across Ethiopia. The valley is normally in a semi-arid area, but has been seriously overgrazed leading to ecological degradation.

The majority of the people in the valley are engaged with mixed farming and livestock husbandry. The farming depends on rainfall.

The use of irrigation and improved farming systems are alien to this part of the country. Types of crops grown in this area include: *teff*, which is made into *Injera* (local bread) the main staple food of Ethiopia, coffee, sorghum, lentils, barley, beans and peas. The type of soil in this Valley is a rich alluvial soil that was washed down from nearby hills and mountains. The valley floor holds the water when it rains in ways that are conducive for mosquito breading.

The two major ethnic groups in the area are the Amhara and the Oromo constituting 60% and 40% respectively. The Amharas are typically Ethiopian Orthodox while the majority of the Oromos are Muslims.

When the life saving relief program receded, United Aid set a long-term Community-Centered Development program.

What Happened in Limu?

The drought of 1984/85 devastated the Limu Valley. The entire valley was full of dried bones and human skeletons.. Limu was a dust bowl. The people lost their self-respect and dignity. There was no hope for restoration of life in the valley. Many families disintegrated; many lost their loved ones; and others ended up being separated missing each other.

The relief operation was the only means to save the lives of thousands of people. Through the relief operations people regained the energy to resume their normal way of life. The major challenge was what would happen after the relief era.

The trend from relief to rehabilitation to community-centered development was a long process. The relief phase was simple, but demanded a huge effort to help the famine victims survive. The entire community was starving to death. The situation was gravely threatening. The victims had no hope, and no way to think what would happen tomorrow and beyond. The impact was devastating both in the lives of the communities and on the environment. The mode of the relief operation began with free food handouts in order to save lives.

The shift to the rehabilitation phase was also difficult. The people were sent back to their respective areas with three months food ration, supplies of seed and agricultural tools. The rehabilitation phase was putting the people back to their normal livelihood. However, the risk of their falling back into the same predicament remained. The people could very easily in the same environment and being exposed to the same problem experience a recurrence of the famine unless the rehabilitation were followed with long lasting development strategy.

In the case of Limu Valley, the long-term strategy, which was very well designed at the on set of the program, played a major role to bring about transformational development in the valley?

Approach

In attempting to intervene the ever-increasing problems of the community, the approach one can use must be appropriate and locally sound. Luke 4:18 explains how over all dimensions of the human needs can be satisfied. United Aid as a Christian humanitarian organization sought to apply Luke 4:18 to address the complex problem of the poor community.

To be effective and successful, it is best to begin with the people. Beginning with the people allows one to engage the local community and both their diagnostic skills. This kind of beginning launches one toward a solution. The approach must take the following steps:

- Identify the community where one is to work.
- Learn their cultural norms, beliefs, and social values
- Continue to listen, look, learn from the society
- Identify key/potential leaders (who are the most influential/heard locally)
- Team Building, develop sense of trust and confidence, establish relationship, let the community feel that you are part of their community, let them recognize you belong to the society.
- Give them liberty to speak out and express their feelings/ideas
- Identify development constraints

- Our purpose must indicate Christian love and compassion while meeting their needs
- They should see that there is no separation between material life and spiritual life.

Processes

United Aid believed that lasting changes can only be achieved when the local community fully participates at various levels of development process.

In the case of Limu Valley the process United Aid wanted to follow was the process called "Community Based Technical Program" (CBTP). The emphasis in the process of CBTP is the facilitation techniques that help the community to open up and express their feelings. The facilitation process is that:

- Encourages the indigenous community to participate and get involved in problem identification, and seriously think/reflect and determine the course of their future
- Enables community to reflect on the past and learn from it
- Enables community to choose and search for alternatives
- Gives an opportunity for the local community to address their life experience
- Focuses on the people not the program
- Enables people to reach their God given potentials

Major Development Components

The major ministry components in Limu include: agricultural development, reforestation (tree planting) and soil conservation, health/nutrition, training/education, development of infrastructure, gender development, and Christian witness.

Methodology Applied

The methodology applied in the process of community centered development program is integration of development interventions. The over all ministry intervention was integrated as one package and implemented. The sector program integration also called for the integration of multidisciplinary technical expertise. The emphasis was to bring committed technical team and together go to where the members of the community live and being identified with them.

The people according to their own context and realty must be involved in the process of problem identification, prioritization, designing/planning, implementation, and decision making.

The methodology further leads the community to project ownership, accountability, and attain reciprocal responsibility. The involvement and maximum participation of the community from the initial stage further helped the technical team to understand and appreciate the cultural norms, beliefs and values of the society.

Resource Identification

The identification of resources can be put into two categories:

1. Human Resource
   - Skilled manpower
   - Local Care takers
   - Leadership potential/capability/Influential leaders
   - Elders
2. Natural Resource
   - Rivers
   - Springs/Streams
   - Minerals
   - Forests/sands
   - Roads
   - Animals

Conversion

The conversion of many nominal Ethiopian Orthodox and Muslims took place as the community noticed the following characteristics of the people working in development:

- The passion and great concern demonstrated in considering their social, physical economic needs. We felt our social responsibility.
- Trust/confidence building.
- Establishing quality friendships through time.
- Listening to the local people and appreciating their culture, values and recognition given to the community with opportunities for learning in their own setting.
- Loving and caring hands, humility and our daily practical application of the word of God not verbally but in deeds. Living Christ-like lifestyles

- Our Christian stewardship spoke to each individual person and created a provoking question that led the society to visualize a new spiritual dimension.
- The community saw that the development staff was not as outsiders or strangers, but part of their society. We belonged to them.

We were convinced ourselves that a biblical based integrated development was a pivotal part in the process of transformation, local development and conversion. The teaching of obedience was a central part of the instructional process.

We believed that if the teaching of obedience is successful, it will model what Paul instructed Timothy in II Timothy 2:2 i.e., passing on what he had learned to reliable ones who would also teach others. Thus, we started hunting for community caretakers, leaders who were most influential in the society.

The society saw our attempts to expose every area of our development efforts to the power of the gospel. The respective communities saw our servant leadership. They were much inspired to change their attitudes thus opening the way for community transformation.

The community realized that conversion to the Christian faith would have a profound impact in both the lives of individuals and of their families. Converts have seen significant and enduring improvement in the healing of their social lives and economy. Conversion again brought a significant transformation in the society.

The holistic community development process came to reality after a tremendous conversion started under going.

Training/Local leadership Development

The training program was a major developmental component. It not only gave technical training about how to improve their agricultural products, but also to impart skills that could help the community to build up their leadership capacity and ultimately gain control over their resources.

The kind of the training if given to the community must aim to bring changes in the attitude and behavior of the community.

The training program was given before executing development interventions. The training was implemented in three categories:

TABLE 5
DEVELOPMENT TRAINING CATEGORIES

Inputs	Through Put	Output
Training of new innovations	Regular follow up	Livelihood improved
Provision of improved seeds/farm tools	Individual efforts	Transferability
-Imparting skills/ know-how	Time spent with Attention given/ coping with it	Adaptability acceptability / replicability
Demonstration of	Individual exercise/	Transformation = socially
New Ideas	Care given to what has been demonstrated	Economically, spiritually
Personal life sharing	Regular visits / follow up	Attitude/Behaviors changed on individual basis / Discipleship Empowerment assuming accountability

These inputs, through puts and outputs do not seem relevant to many development practitioners, but in the case of Limu they served to bring self-respect, restore individual dignity, self-recognition and ultimately created awareness.

After the community had regained its self-identity, we started discussing development intervention. Our initial strategy was not to list what our agency might do, but to hear them share their ideas and what they anticipate to see five/ten years down the road. In doing this they built trust and confidence in us and felt that we were no more outsiders/strangers, but part of their respective community members. A sense of belonging was established.

The inputs as stated above were engaged in Limu Valley to attain sustainable holistic transformational development. Different kinds of development variables are mentioned later in this chapter. Variables like project ownership, sustainability, maximizing local resources both human and natural, changes that could improve their quality of life, gender issues (the involvement of women in development process), and taking responsibility of leadership roles. All these development variables ought to be within the context of what the indigenous community understands. The respective community started realizing the importance of building up their society in harmony with their environment.

We recognized that training must focus not just on the learning of information, but on a broader scale development in which one is transformed, informed and equipped to function. Elliston stated, "Training must not occur in a once-for-all training program, but rather is seen a lifetime development process" (1992:50). The longer I spend time with the trainees, the more they adapt and develop confidence to go on their own and stand on their foot.

The types of development intervention focused on the attainment of basic needs. The community identified the basic needs they wanted to attain. These are as follows: social needs, justice issues, leadership capacity building, material/physical needs, economic development, improving quality of their

ivelihood, enhancing local potentials, access to local resources
and assuming full control over the resources.

Sector Development Objectives

Agriculture

- Train farmers about improved agricultural techniques to increase productivity.
- Provide early maturing and drought resistant crop varieties.
- Promote irrigation schemes.

Environmental Rehabilitation

- Reinstate the ecosystem through environmental rehabilitation.
- Train farmers to care for soil and water conservation.
- Promote agro-forestry.

Health Care

- Improve the quality of health services to control contagious diseases.
- Enhance immunization program.
- Raise the level of community's awareness on environmental sanitation.

Infrastructure

- Promote appropriate technology.
- Improve status of education and related social services like potable water supply system, establishment of clinics, road networks.

Gender Development
- Promote the involvement of women in development.
- Promote income generation to supplement household income.
- Work towards bringing life transformation.
- Involve local influential people or key prominent leaders.
- To bring sustainable changes emphasize on grass-root participation.

Spiritual Development
- Discipleship
- Build trust and trustworthiness
- Keep integrity
- Share the truth with the other
- Spiritual formation
- Individual counseling.
- What ever is done must be done in the name of the Lord Jesus.

Throughout the development process attention was given to instruction that facilitated the releasing of existing capacities beginning from what the people already knew. The teaching was to be people-centered and focus on bringing empowerment.

Holistic transformation is concerned about gender balance. It includes both men and women in the process of integrated development. In holistic development men and women celebrate together. Synergy generates (win/win) situations.

Transformation

The real transformation starts from within. The Apostle Paul wrote, "Do not be conformed any longer to the pattern of this world, but be transformed by the renewing of your mind" (Romans 12:2). After conversion, this transformation leads away from one's old lifestyle to new way of thinking both individually and in the community. The society starts feeling the dynamism happening in individuals' lives. The by-products of the transformation begin with self-empowerment, then other changes follow in the life of the community.

- The social life of the community is changed and takes on developing leadership capacity.
- Worldview changes.
- The economic setting will improve
- People start caring and rehabilitating their environment.
- They develop a sense of ownership and responsibility.
- People start exercising the three kinds of power (physical, social, and spiritual) (Elliston 1992:50).

We learned in this situation that the whole transformation process must focus on healing the degraded physical environment, and holistic life change of the society. We saw the degraded physical environment must be rehabilitated through planting trees and soil/water conservation mechanisms. The holistic life change of the community members sensitized them to realize the importance of ecology and their relationship to the whole creation. and the care it deserves.

Matthew 28:20

The task of Great Commission to make disciples in Matthew 28:20 is a primary goal Jesus modeled and then gave his disciples. Jesus set this standard for the disciples to promote His Kingdom. The making of disciples is a primary mandate for Christians to participate in the mission of our Lord Jesus Christ. It complements the cultural mandate to care for the social and physical environments.

When Jesus Christ commissioned his disciples, he said, "I will be with you always to the very end of the age." We have this assurance that teaching and making discipleship is an ongoing process.

Jesus Spoke To The Needs Of The Disciples

Early in the morning Jesus stood on the shore, but the disciples did not realize that it was Jesus. . . . He said, throw your net on the right side of the boat and you will find some. When they did, they were unable to haul the net in because of the large number of fish" (John 21:4-14).

It was early in the morning—a time of need. Jesus saw to their need: a) The disciples were physically tired/exhausted; b) They did need to catch the fish not only to eat but to support themselves, but had nothing so far. At this point Jesus appeared to them with the remedy for their problem. However, Jesus did not take action to do it for them, rather instructed them to take action on their own.

Jesus is our model and we need to look up to him for instruction and guidance to do effective ministry. Teaching starts from creating awareness, leading the people to realize their past history, reflecting and learning from their past.

Teaching starts from understanding the context. In the case of Jesus, he understood the real problem of the disciples and accordingly responded. Jesus helped them identify their resources and also how they maximally utilize them.

Obedience also comes from teaching in the context. It demands careful listening when Jesus told the disciples to throw their nets, there is a sense of listening to what Jesus said and from that, we can see the expression of obedience in this passage. Jesus by doing that helped them built trust and confidence in him. Jesus fulfilled his evangelistic mandate and social responsibility.

In the same way in order for our message to get across:

- Start with building trust, we need to gain trust of the people so that they could accept our messages.

- Individual testimonies (life sharing, and controlled lifestyles)

- Appreciate their society, encourage them to move towards their unmet needs.

- Ask some questions whether the people understand the dynamic of the teaching?

The Implications/Final Intended Outcomes

The whole efforts of attaining sustainable holistic trans-formational development are stated as follows.

- The hopeless, isolated, powerless and calamity vulnerable communities and any time vulnerable to any calamity have been empowered. They started deciding for themselves, sharing responsibility, administering themselves, developed a sense of accountability, integrity, and stewardship. They established networking with others, and social services like education for their children. Their local health services reduced infant mortality and death of thousands of mothers during child birth. They piped pure water to the village. This pure water helped them greatly contributing to the general health of the community. They set up grinding mills to reduce the labor intensity for the mothers, and gained control over their local resources. The communities have been legally institutionalized.

- The degraded physical environment was rehabilitated through the effort of tree planting. The results included: erosion was controlled, dried streams and rivers were rejuvenated, wild animals returned, the depleted soil nutrients were replenished, pest control mechanisms were established through intensive farmers training, agricultural products increased by twenty-five percent, and livestock diseases controlled.

- Community participation increased empowerment, program ownership, and the sustainability of development interventions secured, networking and partnership strengthened, societal development redefined.

Church Planting

Our presence in the society must not be manipulating the society, however, it should provoke questions in the about why we are present. In the case of Limu, several times members of the community have came to us asking what compelled us to engage in their lives without compromising our faith.

The society has seen a unique characteristic and sense of obedience in us while responding to their needs. They recognized our team members are different from many people who have been working in their society over the years.

The planting of a church brought great satisfaction to us. A new evangelical community is growing and being led by local leaders. It has contributed towards the success of our ministry in other aspects of development.

The success of the over all program increased our reputation and credibility opening a wide door for our future mission. Our sharing of Jesus Christ within the community became a reality. True love was demonstrated though the expression of a humble approach.

The Church was not there before now came into existence. The local people decided they must plant a church and legally institutionalize. The Church was planted. It was no longer underground. The lives of many people were touched and changed and continue being changed. The training and teaching of local leaders helped them to assume leadership roles, administering their church, taking charge of spreading the Gospel of Jesus to their neighboring districts.

The young adults who were in the feeding centers crying for the food are now church leaders, evangelists moving across the valley spreading the Good News. These people do challenge injustice. They are more respected in the society and have been asked to take some positions in their respective villages. Their reputation and credibility in the society is growing. At every outreach area, they establish a site for future contact.

The Limu Valley stands out to be a model for sustainable holistic development program. It is holistic for it dealt with the physical needs, social issues, and spiritual dimensions. It is holistic for it also dealt with human aspect in relation the social environment. The community, which was once poor and at the verge of death, has now developed self-worth and dignity, self-esteem. The people have all the necessary potential to take charge of their situation. The worldview of the community has been changed. The degraded environment has been rehabilitated to the extent of harvesting trees for sale. The community of Limu Valley now understands that development is the notion of integrated process by which people holistically gain full control over their life in order to realize environment as they attempt to reach their God-given potentials. The holistic transformation has taken place both in the life of the respective communities and on the physical environment.

The teaching, developing, equipping, and building of the capacity of the local young leaders ensured the continuity of the holistic development programs.

Most importantly, the transformation taking place in Limu Valley has been multiplying and replicating the ideas in different parts in the country. Many organizations have been challenged and proactively brought paradigm shift in their development approach.

Lessons Learned

Teaching to make disciple is the expression of the care rendered to one regardless of circumstances. It is self-giving through humility by maintaining consistency. It requires that we know and become known in the community. We further learned never to offer solution for any problem the society may have unless it has been reflected on and tackled locally.

The obedience to take up and assume all responsibility follows as the result of changes in attitude and behaviors. Obedience is the expression of accountability.

The sustainability of holistic development program is the result of obedience and willingness created over a long period. Thus, staying close to the community, living with the lifestyles they live and building relationship is inevitable process that must be followed to bring the disciple making into concrete obedience.

Conclusions

In the process of making disciples we need to understand the challenges of teaching by asking questions like does it apply to their context? How do the people tolerate it? Do I have stated teaching strategy quite well? These questions and several others contributed a lot towards individual empowerment.

The path was very rough, difficult, and challenging however, as Kingdom people we felt that we were called to approach the problem of the human beings in a holistic way satisfying both physical and spiritual needs.

The community of Limu Valley has been transformed and fully assumed the responsibility of their social and evangelistic mandates. Their conversion has helped to keep the continuity of development program and spreading of the gospel through making disciples. The conversion of many members of the community has contributed to the improvement of the quality of life. The members of the society who have been converted took the charge of their community.

Bibliography

Elliston, Edgar J. (ed.)
    1992   *Christian Relief and Development.* Waco, TX: Word.

Moving Forward In Missiological Education

Edgar J. Elliston

Proposition: The future of effective missiological education depends on careful attention both to the foundational issues and appropriate delivery approaches.

Introduction

Both the missiological chapters and case studies presented in this volume stimulate us to consider our own situations as we carry out our mandate to make disciples of all nations and to teach them to be obedient in all matters Jesus commanded. We are keenly aware of inexorable cultural trends that continue to challenge and perplex us. If asked, most of us could provide a broad list of the kinds of competencies that are required for cross-cultural ministries in terms of knowledge, skills and formation.[1]

The range of required competencies required for effective missional service continue to challenge us. Yet in the midst of the complexities, John Pipers' exhortation to bring people to know God and in knowing him to praise and joyfully obey him provides a clear unequivocal goal in our training and discipling mandate.

As we have looked at the theme for the larger Evangelical Theological Society conference for 1998, we have noted the tension between the "teaching of all things" and the "teaching of obedience in all things" Jesus commanded. Our task is not just theological education, but the equipping of people in and for the discipling of the nations. Many seminaries seem to miss the issue of obedience while focusing primarily on the "teaching all things." One denomination, for example, sees the purpose of theological education as preparing "faithful leaders." However, it defines that preparation in knowledge terms using such verbs as to "foster faithful and informed discourse," to "know and believe the Gospel," to "reflect theologically on the mission of God's people," to understand and creatively appropriate the various expressions of the Gospel. . . "(Evangelical Lutheran Church 1996:6). The bringing of people under the discipline of Christ to obey all he commanded seems to be lost somewhere in a theological shuffle.

---

[1] The World Evangelical Fellowship has sponsored a series of conferences and consultations in which the primary focus has been competencies. The U.S. Department of Education is bringing a strong emphasis on outcomes (competencies) and enforcing that emphasis through both regional and professional accrediting agencies. Emerging higher education institutions such as the Western Governors' University base their philosophy of education on around the issue of competencies.

When considering a training ministry, most trainers will not be starting something entirely new. Rather, we will be thinking about what we can and should do to improve our mission mobilizing or how we can improve our training program. Questions for improvement apply whether the program is in a local church or an agency and lasts only a few days, weeks or months, or whether it is in higher education where the programs may last anywhere from a few weeks to a several years. How can we provide the kind of equipping that will reach across generational lines, cultural barriers and the other complexities of our communities? How can we provide the quality desired with the available resources and remain focused missionally? Our task is not one of starting fresh with no history of a mobilization, orientation, or training program. We need to look at how we can change what is already under-way to bring it in line with the mandate Jesus gave us and to communicate effectively in the communities where we serve.

In a time of liminality when worldview perspectives and cultures are undergoing radical change, the rules are changing about what works, what is considered appropriate and what is possible. We could cite a long litany of change that is affecting missions whether in missions support, missions sending patterns, missions training, sending church/mission relations, receiving church/ mission relations, communication, approaches to non-believing peoples, mission structures, receiving community/mission relations. We could point to technologies, economics, politics, and other kinds of cultural change. Jonathan Campbell points to some of this kind of change as it relates to church structures and nature of the church. The rate of change has not subsided and to either ignore it or fail to understand it will leave us inexorably on the path to ineffective irrelevance.

Unless your situation is highly unusual, the inertia of tradition and the patterns of your organizational / learning culture have been well established in your agency or institution. They will likely continue to press you to work toward the familiar. Perspectives have been set, assumptions have been made and buried into the policies, procedures and structures within which you work. Recruitment is already underway, budgets have been planned and future goals already set. Your colleagues do not expect nor desire radical changes. They only expect you to initiate innocuous updates that will not upset the way things are nor challenge the present paradigms of missional education.

We are, however, in a time of liminal change. We are on the threshold of new ways of equipping leaders when many of our comfortably held assumptions will not serve us well. Resource intensive, long cycle, institutionalized, modern, theory focused approaches while appearing ideal to many of us, are being supplanted by the repetitive, short term, functionally focused, community based, change oriented workshops, seminars or short courses. What was teacher focused and institutionally directed is now often collaboratively developed using new technologies. Often mission equipping is occurring in church contexts and mission contexts. We see dissimilar agencies cooperating in educational enterprises not only in mission, but in secular education as well. The Western Governors' University is only a well-known case in point. The for-profit University of Phoenix is not only accredited, but is among the fastest growing higher education institutions in the USA. The threat of the UOP has not gone unnoticed in every WASC (Western Association of Schools and Colleges) meeting over the past five years.

Anthony G. Oettinger of Harvard wrote back in 1993,
The potential widespread availability of faster, smaller, and cheaper means for creating open-ended structures as you go along and interacting with and controlling information calls for a reex-

amination of all prior investment in literacy, nu-
meracy, and artistic sensibility (Oettinger 1993).

With the changes in the world Christian movement, the
political and economic arenas, educational technologies,
organizational structures missiological education is facing
serious challenges for change.

In this chapter I want to give attention to some basic
action steps to implement what we are coming to recognize.
By giving some attention to these basic action steps you may
implement the ideas that emerged in the 1998 ETS/EMS
conference in the context of the profound changes you are
experiencing. I am encouraging you to implement these new
ideas in ways that are both consistent with Scripture and
culturally appropriate. In the midst of our planning we must be
aware of two realities for which I was ill equipped, namely,
tension and paradox. Beginning with our theology of the
kingdom we are faced with present and future tensions and a
host of paradoxes. These paradoxes often appear to be oxymo-
rons such as the idea of a "servant leader." A tension we face
is the knowing-doing-being tension. None is adequate by
itself, but each one contributes to the other two.

This chapter lists several things you can do to initiate
changes that suggested in the other chapters in this text. To
help you remember these steps I have organized my comments
around the word, "*ACTION*." Please note that tensions emerge
within and among each of these steps. These tensions require
constant vigilance to provide a balance among the local concerns and the biblical mandate(s).

A -- Attend to the Basics
C -- Challenge the Present
T -- Trust Others
I -- Intercede
O -- Opt for Opportunities
N -- Notice Others' Contributions

A--Attend to the Basics

In this set of basic issues each variable stands in a dynamic tension with all of the others. When any one is modified, even minimally, the changes amplify through all of the others.

The basic command we are seeking to obey is the command to disciple all the nations. The primary concern for us and the ones we teach is obedience, not just the mastery of a body of knowledge, skills or attitudes. The biblical mandate to disciple all nations remains in effect so our task is clearly to equip men and women to incarnate the good news of God's reign in ways that will form reproducing disciples in multiplying churches who continue to learn to be obedient to all that Jesus commanded. Our task involves the learner who comes to understand the Word in the context of the world where the Word will be applied in the community of the church.

To set the stage for equipping / training / missiological education foundational value questions must be re-addressed:

Why?

The purpose of missiological education is to present workers who are thoroughly equipped to carry out the *missio*

Dei. We are required to be obedient recognizing that people without Christ have no hope for eternal life.

The purpose or mission is the first question to be answered. The answer to the question of "why?" then becomes the principal guiding value along the way. If the purpose for missiological education is something other than the equipping of workers for the *missio Dei*, it will miss the point.

The "why" of the Great Commission clearly reflects the missional nature of God. Even as humankind has been and is disobedient, God has continued to take initiatives to draw all people back to Himself. One can trace the covenant relationships with Abraham, Isaac, and Jacob. One can see the deliverance through the Exodus. The message of the prophets and the sending of Jesus all demonstrate God's missional initiatives to love, redeem and reconcile.

What?

The content of what we teach is the whole gospel and the obedience it requires. The content of the whole gospel certainly requires our finest attention to every level of theological reflection and education. We begin with the first commandment, "To love God with all of our heart, soul, mind and strength." In today's missiological and theological education the focus sometimes misses this primary issue both for the Christian worker and the communities where the work is to be done. We continue to recognize the tension between the commands to "love one's neighbor" and to "disciple the nations." However, to fully obey either is to accomplish both. While the individual activities supporting either may cause tension for the other.

What is to be learned is not only the content and the skills to propagate the gospel, but the development of a relationship with God that will sustain the person through a life of obedience and provide a basis for reproduction. The primary obedience is to know God and to praise him. This knowledge is not a knowledge "about," but rather a knowledge "of" that grows out of personal obedience and a study of God's Word.

Wilkins' explanations of "disciple," "discipling," and "discipleship" elsewhere in this book provides a firm base for both the process and expected outcome of this education. He writes,

> as Jesus called men and women to Him, and as He sent His disciples out to make other disciples, He was calling men and women into a saving relationship with himself which would make a difference in the new disciple's life. Therefore, Jesus' purpose in the Great Commission included both conversion and growth; i.e., "making disciples" meant that one became a disciple at the moment of conversion and that growth in discipleship was the natural result of the new disciple's life. As Jesus sent the disciples out to make converts, the demands for discipleship made by Jesus in His teaching were directed not only to His first followers, but to all true believers.

The "what" should be focused on the long term effectiveness of the person who is serving rather than just a short term engagement. Taylor suggests seven issues that are needed to prevent unnecessary attrition, including: spiritual formation, development of relational skills, ministry skills, specific training for one's missional assignment, regular church involvement, on the field care for the person and his/her family, and regular evaluation (Taylor 1997:358-359).

Who?

Who should teach? Who should learn? Who is the subject of the learning? Who is the object of the learning? A central tension is that the teacher should also be a practicing-learner. The person who is the object should soon become the subject and then the teacher. Another question of "who" is "Who should be in control or making the decisions?" With whom should we partner or network to accomplish our mission?

The questions, " Who should teach? Who should learn?" ultimately reach to every person. Every person is to be discipled as part of the "all nations." Every person is to be taught to obey all that Jesus Christ commanded. Hence, in each subsequent generation the command is inclusive.

The answer to the question, "Who is the subject of the learning?" clearly focuses on the person of Jesus Christ. He is the one with all authority (*exousia*) and the one who promised to be "with you until the end of the age" (Mt 28:18, 20).

The discipled are to be discipling. The discipling of others aids in one's own development. The learner is also the teacher and the teacher remains a learner--another kingdom paradox. In this process one's experience and character are critical. Jesus' statement, " A student is not above his teacher, but everyone who is fully trained will be like his teacher (Luke 6:40) remains true. Harley's admonition to choose the right people with experience and commitment (disciples) to teach remains a clear inescapable concern for mission trainers (Harley 1996:47-57).

Partnering was done and expected to cross both geographical and cultural lines in the early church. To see a church in Antioch of Syria started by Africans from Cyrene and Cypriot Jewish believers and then taught in part by a young Greek speaking Jewish Pharisee candidate shows the diverse partnering even in the early church. Paul's collection of funds in Europe for suffering believers in Jerusalem demonstrates the early "connectedness."

While a consistent concern through the Old Testament is carried on into the New Testament about the care for and instruction of children, one does not find children being selected for leadership development, leadership status or roles. In modern western culture the training of people to become leaders is often focused on the young, inexperienced, uncommitted and untried person. When the question of "who" is raised about the selection and equipping of leaders, while the immature may be brought into mentoring relationships, ones who are expected to lead are expected to be mature and above reproach in their communities (cf. Ac 6:3-4; 1 Tim 3:1-13; Titus 1:6-8). Harley writes, "The selection of suitable students is one of the most important and yet one of the most difficult tasks for those running a missionary training centre." (Harley 1996:59).

When?

When should one learn in terms of one's life or career cycle? When should one learn in a annual, monthly, weekly or daily schedule? How long should the training last? How should it relate to the issue of competence? How long should it be as it relates to one's learning style, the material to be treated, and the resources available? How long should one remain in training before beginning to apply what is being learned?

Modern practices have distorted the apostolic intentions demonstrated both by Jesus and his disciples as well as what was written by these same men. Clearly, as one came to know Christ, the intention was to learn then and to share the good news about him then. Both the learning and application were expected to be continuous and "mastery" was expected. While schools were common and Jesus himself had likely been to a synagogue school, Jesus chose to provide instruction in non-formal and informal ways to his disciples. He deliberately sought to teach some issues along the way in structured out-of-school ways (nonformal). At other times he used the occasions and his relationship to initiate instruction (informal). He blended these two educational approaches to teach in contrast with the formal (schooling) to produce well-informed, competent, changed and committed disciples.

The formal education of the Apostle Paul was put to a very good use for the strengthening of the church. One should not, therefore, totally decry formal education. Sherwood Lingenfelter suggests a way to return the university to the service of the church and the kingdom. Formal education has too long been captive to the Enlightenment in which the empirical and pragmatic has replaced the theological and spiritual. On the other hand, one should be careful not to rule out the nonformal and the informal. Both the nonformal and informal bring strengths in coping with change and relationship building respectively. Jesus provided instruction for his disciples and then sent them out to try out what they had learned (Luke 10). They learned by doing.

Where?

Where should the learning take place? To what extent should the distance between the learner and the primary formational context be minimized? Should the distance between the learner and the applicational context be minimized? Should the learning take place in a legitimizing community? Where should the learner be in reference to learning resources such as printed materials, personal relationships and mentoring?

The "where" should serve the purpose of the "why" as the "what" is being facilitated. Modern education has brought a heavy focus on extended schooling. Formal education risks separating the learners from the community where they are to serve in several critical ways--

Questions about what learning is needed are raised only by the institutional faculty not by the learner from community experience

Questions about how to apply the learning rests on projections from the faculty of the institution rather than the learners as they try to apply the learning in the community

The community to be influenced is typically not the one where the learner is learning how to influence so the transactional and transformational potentials of acting with the community are delayed with the schooling

The potential formational influence of the community is often delayed (or denied) to the emerging leaders during their formative times.

On the other hand, formal education can provide a rich resource intensive context where experienced faculty and students can engage in synergistic ways to employ a wide variety of learning resources that may not be available elsewhere. Formal education does not have to be centralized as seen in the explosion of both accredited and unaccredited distance learning programs.

One must be careful about sharp dichotomies that limit and stereotype. Elizabeth Patterson writes for example,

While distance educators tend to view themselves as delivering on the Great Commission, theological educators have more often understood their role to be the shaping of the few who will carry that Commission responsibly. Further, that training has been understood to involve a formational component that seems antithetical to education at a distance (Patterson 1996:59-74).

The responsible carrying of the Great Commission must include the discipling of the nations by those whose relationship with God forms them into the kind of obedient servants He desires who can and will think well about their task whether done in a centralized formal setting or away from a formal institution.

How?

How should the learning be delivered or facilitated? Here the tensions may cloud our vision. Should we just let it happen "informally" in the context of facilitated relationships where observation and modeling may occur? To do so makes the measurement of competencies difficult and may stretch out time, but the outcomes last a lifetime and are likely to fit the local culture well. Virtually anything can be learned by personal observation and participation. Experiential learning supported by appropriate relational encouragement provides a powerful way to learn.

Should we plan "out-of-school" learning to bring about change and initiate structure into the learning process? To work only nonformally may lead to a lack of an understanding of how things work or skills in designing for new or different situations. A focus only on skills or nonformal approaches may produce outcomes that lack the ability to treat synthesis or evaluative functions of cognitive learning.

Should we plan for more "formal" education or "schooling" and focus on the theoretical? To do so often leads to ineffectual elitism. The risk of learning from the distilled experience of others may leave the affective or skill dimensions under developed. Clearly, a balanced approach using all three modes must be considered for optimal learning.

Should we bring on the technological answers? Appropriate technologies may help enormously, but misapplied technology may discourage learners and even defeat the original purpose of the training program.

We will come back to the "How?" later.

How Much?

When is enough enough? What are the minimal competencies? When does one stop "sharpening the ax" and begin cutting wood? Can we learn from the methods depicted in the New Testament as well as the content of the text? Is one's equipping ever completed?

The tension between the desire to continue to learn and learning as one continues requires our attention in equipping men and women missionally. I have a friend who completed a masters degree in missions, and is now working on a doctoral program related to missions. He has never worked in a mission, but is teaching missions. He has continued to learn (formally), but demonstrates a tension we face in theological and missiological education--a tension between advanced learning and its application.

As we think back through these basic issues, tensions begin to emerge among these issues. However, as you and I return to our places of ministry, these basic issues will continue to require our attention.

Just as a successful basketball or soccer player continues to focus on the basics of ball handling and shooting, the missiological educator must continue to give attention to these basics. Just as a concern violinist or pianist will continue to practice scales, missiological educator will continue to address these foundational issues even as they address the more difficult questions out of the perspective of experience.

Remember the tensions, as our response to any of these foundational variables shifts, the whole changes. The tension is dynamic. What we must come to see is that in our educational settings we are facing changes in all of these variables simultaneously.

C--Challenge the Present

Present assumptions about the church being the center of the culture, teacher-centered institution-based learning, learning styles, idealized delivery systems (formal / nonformal / informal) are all facing serious threats or could be described as threats to appropriate missiological education. We are being called to challenge the present views commonly held in our culture and churches--religious relativity, universalism, self-centeredness, racism, Biblical illiteracy, and pluralism. The current expression, "whatever," requires a challenge! The tension is between continuity with the past and change into the future. We are indeed on the threshold of the new.

While we should not be enamored with change for the sake of change, clearly, we have recognized that the status quo leads to decline, stagnation, and falling short of our mandate to disciple the nations. As obedient believers, we are called to challenge the present with the good news of the Kingdom. The gospel is still good news today.

The prevailing cultural views in modern culture about politically correct pluralism, religious relativity, situational ethics, universalism, self-centeredness, and racism all contribute to the ongoing marginalization of the church in our culture. While I am not interested in media bashing, nor a commentary on our present political system, one does not have to read far into a daily newspaper or watch long into a television newscast to see these values at work. One does not have to see many movies to see the culturally accepted movement of the church to the periphery of both modern and post-modern culture.

I have been both amazed and appalled at the growing rate of biblical illiteracy among seminary students and applicants for mission service. This lack of Bible knowledge simply reflects what is more widely true in churches across this country. In one Bible College I asked a question in a class of about 50 freshmen: "If a person had never heard the gospel, would God save him anyway?" A majority of the class said, "Yes, God would not let that person be condemned because it would no be fair." I went on to ask, "If that same person had heard the gospel and then said, 'No,' what would his eternal destiny be?" Without any hesitation this class all agreed, that to refuse the gospel would leave a person without hope for eternity. The logic then is clear. . . . Do not send missionaries. Do not spread the good news of Jesus Christ because people may after hearing it, reject it.

We must challenge this post-modern "Star Trek" perspective in which we explore new worlds, but do not interfere or bring change. The mandate is the discipling of the nations, not their exploration. The mandate is the teaching of obedience in all things, not the affirmation of all things.

The present assumptions about teacher centered learning are coming under pressure in our institutions today as the average age of our students is on the rise. We are in an age when the "Finishers' Movement" is on the rise. They will not tolerate the failure to recognize their experience. In a time when the number of new people looking for instruction on the web is multiplying weekly, the old ways will simply not suffice.

Now is the time to challenge the present assumptions.

- Formation occurs primarily in a school
- Learning occurs primarily when directed by a teacher
- The teacher and student must be together physically for the student to learn
- Other people prefer to learn as "I" have learned

- Our teaching styles will match the other person's learning style

Can we continue to hold to this paradigm with the growing number present stress indicators?

Many churches and para-church agencies have their own in-house training programs and criticize seminaries for being "out of touch."

A high percentage of seminary graduates have disengaged from seminaries, but are continuing to learn in other structured ways.

Many church leaders (perhaps, the majority) who need training do not have access to advanced leadership training because of venue, timing or cost issues.

A very high rate of attrition exists between enrolling in seminary programs and finishing well in one's ministry (cf Clinton 1995).

Many "church leaders" are not leading effectively, but are dysfunctional as tyrants (Ward 1996:27-32) or ineffectual "wimps", visionless "fad-followers" or on ego-trips that put them out of touch.

A growing focus again in higher education is on outcomes rather than inputs or processes. The question is "can and are the graduates doing the tasks for which institutions claim they were prepared?"

Many seminaries are experiencing a significant decline in enrollments.

The multiplication of nonformal church leadership training institutes, networks, and local educational consortia suggest that the present . . . paradigm is not meeting the leadership equipping needs of the church (Elliston 1997:6). Now is the time to challenge the present. We recognize the tension between continuity with the past and the change into the future. However, to fail to challenge the present in our theological and missiological education is to abdicate to the cultural pressures about us.

T--Trust Others

Empower, entrust, expect, collaborate rather than compete. Trust others in the evangelical community, trust others from different ethnic backgrounds! Again, a tension emerges, we must trust and entrust, but we are also called to be stewards of the gospel. We ask the question with our actions, "dare we trust?" or must we act ourselves?

As one reads through the New Testament, the entrusting of the stewardship of the gospel is a recurring theme. We see Jesus entrusting the good news of the Kingdom to his disciples with the mandate to make the good news known. It was more than just making the good news known, it was a mandate to enlist, empower and entrust. Jesus continued to affirm cooperation and collaboration rather than competition. The apostle Paul entrusted significant missions into the hands of Timothy, Titus, Philemon and others.

The question of trust continues to arise in the arena of missiological education. Can we trust our fellow believers on the other side of the border or on the other side of a language barrier to make wise decisions about training? In one evangelical school that I know there was some conversation about the equipping of leaders in the Hispanic community. However, it was done without existing leaders from that community.

Trusting and entrusting is essential to empowerment, and collaboration. However, trust brings tension. We "know" we could do it better, but can we? When people are trusted, we will see the Myth of Pygmalion lived out--people will meet expectations.

I--Intercede

We are called to intercede both with God and with others on behalf of the learners you seek to influence. Intercession releases God's power in the situation. Serve as interceding mentors who bridge from the past to the future. Again, a tension--even as we are called to intercede, we are called to lead

The prophet Samuel, Jesus, and the apostle Paul shared a common practice. They both prayed for others. They prayed for the people they sought to equip as leaders.

Intercession will help offset a common problem found across educational circles. Many believe if they can have control of a person's time and attention for a given length of time, they can provide the learning experiences and guidance that will form that person into a fully competent Christian leader. This assumption of taking a few hours or in the cases of a college, university, or seminary two to six or more years is displayed the promotional materials of many educational institutions. Many Christian institutions have essentially "open" enrollment practices that will admit anyone who can meet the financial obligations and a minimal faith statement or even no Christian faith commitment. The promotional materials promise that the institution will in the time allotted, make that person into a Christian leader--a pastor, a missionary, a Christian counselor, or a Christian business leader.

Intercession is often a missing ingredient both in the selection and equipping process. Intercession in addition to releasing God's power in the situation may also help us realize that the formation of the character of a person is the work of the Spirit and not just the employment of our well designed curriculum. We have a priestly duty to intercede to release God's power in a situation.

O-- Opt for Opportunities

Educational technologies have never presented more options and opportunities for effective instruction or distracting, wasteful, drivel. The opportunities for multiplying church leaders worldwide has never been as great. More churches have emerged in more places with more opportunities to grow than ever in history. One tension that grips us is that of focus. One can not chase every opportunity nor can one be faithful by just being satisfied with the way things are.

The opportunities / needs facing us are unmatched in history. We have access the whole world's population through mass media. One single network of Christian broadcasters can reach virtually the whole population of the earth in locally known languages. Print media, television, and films continue to impact the world. More and more the internet and its complex linkages via broadband phone lines, satellite links and local radio systems is becoming accessible to large segments of the world's population. MAF can now deliver email access to anyone in the world who lives within 1000 miles of a phone. Phone links with fax capabilities are now possible virtually anywhere on earth.

We could also speak of our contact with peoples world wide through educational resources, economic activities and political interactions. Even in the urban areas where we now live we can set up networks for ministry around the globe.

The available educational technologies have never had such a broad range of possibilities for effective instruction or distracting wasteful drivel. If we become entangled in the race to be fully up to date in our educational technology, we may miss well the point of what we are to do.

N--Notice Others' Contributions

People in other places are often using means to effectively facilitate learning in ways that could serve as models for in the pre-modern, modern and post-modern settings where we are called to serve. For example, an Indian guru spends twelve years providing a relationship where the learner focuses on learning attitudes, obedience, skills and then knowledge. In the Maasai age grade system in Kenya--cross-generational mentoring is brought into focus for both the individual and community. Instructional relationships are set for a lifetime. Sister institutions (missions and educational institutions often have thought through similar issues to what we are facing or about to face. Noticing others not only improves our own perspective, but motivates others to do better.

One key element resulting from noticing what others are doing is networking in cooperative ways to address common missional goals. I am working with a church-planting mission that illustrates in a small way what I mean. This mission looks to MTI for equipping people with language learning skills; it is partnering with established churches to initiate a new church planting thrust in one urban area; it has assembled an association of business people to help establish for-profit businesses to work in some limited access countries to allow both entry and support for church planters; it partners with some training institutions for the advanced training of its staff and missionaries.

At Hope International University we also have partnerships with schools out of the country, mission agencies, community counseling clinics, and local churches for a host of different activities that relate to the accomplishment of our mission. What we are doing is no different from other educational institutions and missions are doing around the globe.

Noticing others' contributions not only allows one to benefit from them but serves to motivate and empower us all to accomplish our mission.

Here again a tension arises. One can have so many partnerships that the mission is lost. Nevertheless, to try to accomplish our mission without recognition across the community leaves one like Elijah in the cave feeling like he was the only one left.

Pride serves well to isolate individuals, institutions and cultures. One often becomes proud of the way things are done locally or in our own institutions. This local affirmation while not wrong in itself may serve to blind us to the offerings / insights others may have about the same issues.

As we take note of what others are doing, we may stimulate their motivation to excel further. We may also find ways to improve our own approaches in addressing the theme before us and shed some of the paternalism that grows well in both successful and plateaued communities.

If we are to disciple the nations and teach them to be obedient in all that Jesus commanded, we will need to recognize the range of learners that are to be equipped. I fully support the equipping men and women who will do the research and provide the development of both the missiological and theological underpinnings for mission. However, the number of these important leaders in the cause is a miniscule percentage compared to the numbers of leaders needed at the local level. This issue has been mentioned in the literature before, but bears mentioning again here.[2]

---

[2] See Donald A. McGavran (1969) or Lois McKinney (1980:171-191). For a more contemporary and extended description see, Edgar J. Elliston (1992:25-35) or (1996:238-240).

Who to Prepare (types)

- The face-to-face squad or small team leader -- small group leader (1 for 5-10)
- The platoon or multiple squad leader -- the elder or department head (1 for 20-50)
- The company leader -- the pastor of a single cell or small congregation (1 for 50-200)
- The battalion leader -- the pastor of a multiple staff congregation or a regional leader (1 for 200-5000)
- The army leader -- a national / international denominational leader (1 for 5000+)

How to do it. The how is a technical issue. As missiological educators we must be careful about the technologies we seek to use. As one who has been interested in a range of educational technologies for more than thirty years, I am urging caution to be both relevant and bold to address the needs.

Instructional technology includes the design, development, administration, and evaluation of processes and resources for learning. Instructional technologies range across the use of all of the senses, simple technologies like the 16th century scholar's board to highly complex computer based interactive teleconferencing. Instructional technologies may include different uses of the same media such as information mapping or programmed instruction in a print medium. They may include multiple processes and resources as with the use of data projectors with lecturing.

As we equip women and men for ministries, we will be using various forms of technology. We sometimes are misled into the idea that the only technology we may use is linked to computers, the web or electronic gadgetry.

The technologies we use will affect the learning outcomes. We should select the technologies we will use on the bases of the desired outcomes, not on the bases of the newest, flashiest or "most powerful." Some technologies serve one kind of outcome better while other technologies serve other projected outcomes. The newest technology may not always serve every need better than older established means.

The following set of technologies and applications is by no means complete, but rather is intended to be suggestive.

From these tables one can clearly see that a given educational / instructional technology may or may not suit the purpose of the instruction. To be optimally effective one may well require a combination of technologies so the weaknesses of one will be compensated by the strengths of another.

Another set of variables greatly conditions these factors' potential impact / learning level of a person. These variables may be understood in terms of one's culture and relationships. Hofstede's four sets of variables provide one useful window to look at the potentials for these instructional technologies (Hofstede 1980:42-63). Another window through which one could look is through a set of worldview themes such as how a person sees categorizing the world, causality, the relation of a person to a group, the relation of a person to the physical world, and time. These worldview patterns provide the conceptual grids through which one's learning style emerges. The result is that in one culture where orality is high, visually recorded information is less needed, e.g., the Maasai. However, where orality is low and literacy is high, visually recorded information (e.g., books, class notes, meeting minutes) is very important.

TABLE 6
EDUCATIONAL MEDIA

Medium	Audio	Visual	Audio-visual	Simulations	Tele-conferencing	Com-puter Based	Web Based
Examples	Lecture, radio, tele-phone, audio-cassette	Print, photos, art, black/white boards slide projec-tors, overhead projec-tors	Motion pictures, Video tapes, televi-sion, CDs, DVD	"Word problems" Role plays, social system simulations	Audio only, audio-visual	Interac-tive tutorials, CD ROM with audio, video, text	Print based, graphics, streaming audio / video, 2-way text. Audio. Video, "branched" pro-grams

Medium	Audio	Visual	Audio-visual	Simulations	Tele-conferencing	Computer Based	Web Based
Advantages	Low cost, easy to do, Synchronous or Asynchronous	More information can be presented more quickly "A picture is worth 1000 words" Synchronous or Asynchronous, may be self-paced	Potentially highly engaging, wide potential Synchronous or Asynchronous, minimal skills required to use,	Adds personal discovery and higher emotive potential, Synchronous	Synchronous without space limits, may reach vast audience potentials	Asynchronous, synchronous may be self-paced, may be done individually or with a learning cadre	Synchronous or Asynchronous, may be interactive, may be self-paced, may be individualized or with a cadre
Disadvantages	Needs high redundancy to facilitate memory, single sense engagement	Expensive, single sense engagement need exegetical skills, requires equipment	Costly to produce, high level skills needed to produce, requires equipment	Requires debriefing skills	Requires technical support team, expensive to produce	Expensive to produce, requires equipment, requires equipment and moderate skill level	Expensive to produce, requires equipment, requires equipment and moderate skill level

TABLE 7
TYPES OF EDUCATIONAL MEDIA

Medium	Audio	Visual	Audio-visual	Simulations	Tele-conferencing	Computer Based	Web Based
Applications							
Expected Level of Cognitive Learning[1]	1-2	1-2	1-2	1-6	1-2	1-4	1-4
Expected Formation / Attitude-Development[2]	1-3	1	1	1-4	1-2	1-2	1-2

[1] Cognitive Taxonomy: 1. Knowledge, 2. Comprehension, 3. Application, 4. Analysis, 5. Synthesis (See Bloom 1956)
[2] Affective Taxonomy: 1. Receiving, 2. Responding, 3. Valuing, 4. Organizing, 5. Characterization by a value or value complex (world view change) See David R. Krathwohl (1964).

Conclusion

The future of effective missiological education depends on careful attention both to the foundational issues and appropriate delivery approaches. We dare not ignore the profound change that is occurring in each of the foundational areas I have mentioned. To ignore change is to allow it to rise up to bite us. However, to accept the change uncritically and fail to address the implications in our institutions will set us on the same course as the ancient cathedrals of medieval Europe. Only relics remain. Will our schools of the present become like the monasteries that still exist--museums of past accomplishment. Or, will our equipping programs continue with the dynamism inherent in them.

Bibliography

Albrecht, Robert and Gary Bardsley
    1994   "Strategic Planning and Academic Planning for Distance Education," In Barry Willis (ed.) *Distance Education Strategies and Tools.* Englewood Cliffs, NJ: Educational Technology Publications. pp. 67-86.

Association of Evangelicals in Africa
    1997   Training God's Servants: A Compendium of the Papers and Findings of a Workshop on Training for Missions in Africa. Nairobi: Association of Evangelicals in Africa.

Barna, George
    1995   *Generation Next.* Ventura, CA: Regal Books.

Blanch, Gregory
> 1994 Don't All Faculty Want Their Own TV Show?
> Barriers to Faculty Participation in Distance
> Education," *Deosnews. DEOS --The Distance*
> *Education Online Symposium.* Published in
> collaboration with the *American Journal of*
> *Distance Education* and the American Center
> for the Study of Distance Education, The Penn-
> sylvvania State University. 4:1.

Brace, Sylvia Bedwell and Gina Roberts
> 1997 "When Payup Becomes Payback: A University's
> Return on Instructional Technology Invest-
> ment," Syllabus97 Conference. Sonoma State
> University, Rohnert Park, CA. July 28-31.

Brown, F. Barry and Yvonne Brown
> 1994 "Distance Education Around the World," In
> Barry Willis (ed.) *Distance Education Strategies*
> *and Tools.* Englewood Cliffs, NJ: Educational
> Technology Publications. pp. 3-40.

Clinton, J. Robert
> 1995 *Leadership Emergence Theory.* Altadena, CA:
> Barnabas Publishers.

Cole, Victor Babajide
> 1997 "Missiological Factors Involved in Designing A
> Curriculum for an Adequately Rounded Theo-
> logical Training in Africa." In Training God's
> Servants: A Compendium of the Papers and
> Findings of a Workshop on Training for Mis-
> sions in Africa. Nairobi: Association of Evan-
> gelicals in Africa. Pp. 133-150.

Dede, Chris
    1993   "Trends and Forecasts in Distance Education," Educom Review. November / December 28:6. EDUCOM, 1112 16th St., N.W., Suite 600, Washington, DC 20036; 202 872-4200; via e-mail: EDUCOM@BITNIC.EDUCOM.EDU.

Doll, Ronald C.
    1996   *Curriculum Improvement Decision Making and Process.* (9th ed.). Boston: Allyn and Bacon.

Eastmond, Nick
    1994   "Assessing Needs, Developing Instruction, and Evaluating Resultsin Distance Education," In Barry Willis (ed.) *Distance Education Strategies and Tools.* Englewood Cliffs, NJ: Educational Technology Publications. pp. 87-108.

Elliston, Edgar J.
    1992   *Home Grown Leaders.* Pasadena: William Carey Library.

    1996   "Moving Forward from Where We are in Missiological Education," In J. Dudley Woodberry, Charles E. Van Engen and Edgar J. Elliston. *Missiological Education in the 21st Century.* Maryknoll, NY: Orbis Books. Pp. 232-256.

    1997   "Developing Leaders at a Distance: Contextualizing Leadership Development." Professorial Inaugural Address, Fuller Theological Seminary, October.

Elmer, Duane and Lois McKinney, (eds)
    1996   *With an Eye on the Future: Development and Mission in the 21st Century.* Monrovia: MARC.

Evangelical Lutheran Church
   1995   *Faithful Leaders for a Changing World:*
           Theological Education for Mission in the ECLA.
           Evangelical Church of America.
Ferris, Robert W. (ed)
   1996   *Establishing Ministry Training: A Manual for*
           Programme Developers. Pasadena: William
           Carey Library.
Frishberg, Nancy
   1997   "Technology Coupon Cutting: Faculty Support
           on a Shoestring," Syllabus97 Conference. So-
           noma State University, Rohnert Park, CA. July
           28-31.
Gerber, Vergil
   1980   *Discipling Through TEE.* Chicago: Moody
           Press. Pp. 171-191
Goulet, Daniel and Randall P. Peelen
   1997   "It Takes More than Two to Tango: A "Team
           Building" Model for Educational Technology,"
           Syllabus97 Conference. Sonoma State Univer-
           sity, Rohnert Park, CA. July 28-31.
Hammett, Paula
   1997   "Information Literacy and the Evaluation of
           Web-based Resources," Syllabus97 Confer-
           ence. Sonoma State University, Rohnert Park,
           CA. July 28-31.
Harley, C. David
           Preparing to Serve: Training for Cross-Cultural
           Mission. Pasadena: William Carey Library.
Harry, K. J. and D. Keegan (eds.).
   1993   *Distance Education: New Perspectives.* London:
           Routledge.

Hofstede, Geert
    1983   "Motivation, Leadership and Organization: Do
           American Theories Apply Abroad?" *Organiza-*
           tional Dynamics, Summer, AMACOM a divi-
           sion of American Management Association. pp.
           42-63.

Holmberg, B.
    1993   "Key Issues in Distance Education: An Aca-
           demic Viewpoint," In Harry, K., J., and
           Keegan, D (eds.). *Distance Education*: New
           Perspectives. London: Routledge. pp. 330-341

Jewett, Frank
    1997   "Case Study Manual Evaluating the Benefits
           and Costs of Mediated Instruction and Distrib-
           uted Learning," Syllabus97 Conference. So-
           noma State University, Rohnert Park, CA. July
           28-31.

Kearsley, Greg and William Lynch (eds.)
    1994   *Educational Technology Leadership Perspec-*
           tives. Englewood Cliffs, NJ: Educational
           Technology Publicatioins.

Keegan, D. O.
    1990   "A Theory of Distance Education," In Michael
           G. Moore (ed.), *Contemporary Issues in Ameri-*
           can Distance Education. Oxford, UK: Per-
           gamon Press. pp. 327-332

Kemp, Stephen
    1996   "A Silent Success: Church-Based Seminary
           Extension Education," *Access Newsletter*. De-
           cember, 10:1:1-3.

Kendall, Janet Ross and Muriel Oaks

    1992   "Evaluation of Perceived Teaching Effective-
ness: Course Delivery Via Interactive Video
Technology Versus Traditional Classroom
Methods," *Deosnews. DEOS --The Distance
Education Online Symposium.* Published in
collaboration with the American Journal of
Distance Education and the American Center for
the Study of Distance Education, The Penn-
sylvvania State University. 2:5.

Knowles, Malcolm

    1990   *The Adult Learner A Neglected Species.* (4th
Ed.). Houston: Gulf Publishing Company.

Kore, Danfulani

    1997   "The Role of the Theologian and of the Pastor in
Accomplishing the Missionary Mandate in Af-
rica." Training God's Servants: A Compendium
of the Papers and Findings of a Workshop on
Training for Missions in Africa. Nairobi: Association of Evangelicals in Africa. Pp. 21-32.

Krathwohl, David R. et. al.

    1964   *Taxonomy of Educational Objectives The
Classification of Educational Goals Handbook
II: Affective Domain.* New York, David McKay
Company, Inc.

Lauzon, Allan C. and George A. B. Moore

    1989   "A Fourth Generation Distance Education
System: Integrating Computer Assisted learn-
ing and Computer Conferencing" Journal of
Distance Education, 3:1:38-49.

McGavran, Donald A.
    1969   "Five Kinds of Leaders." A lecture delivered at
            Columbia Bible College
McGill, Mollie A. and Sally M. Johnstone
    1994   "Distance Education: An Opportunity for
            Cooperation and Resource Sharing," In Barry
            Willis (ed.) *Distance Education Strategies and
            Tools.* Englewood Cliffs, NJ: Educational
            Technology Publications. pp. 258-264.

McKinney, Lois
    1980   "Leadership: Key to the Growth of the
            Church," In Vergil Gerber, *Discipling Through
            TEE.* Chicago: Moody Press., Pp. 171-191

McMahan, Martin Alan
    1998   "Training Turn-Around Leaders: Systemic
            Approaches to Reinstating Growth in Plateaued
            Churches." Ph.D. Dissertation, Fuller Theologi-
            cal Seminary.

Miller, Gary E.
    1992   "Long-Term Trends in Distance Education,"
            *Deosnews. DEOS --The Distance Education
            Online Symposium.* Published in collaboration
            with the American Journal of Distance Educa-
            tion and the American Center for the Study of
            Distance Education, The Pennsylvania State
            University. 2:23.

Moore, Michael G. (ed.)
    1990   *Contemporary Issues in American Distance
            Education.* Oxford, UK: Pergamon Press. pp.
            327-332
    1990   "Recent Contributions to the Theory of Distance
            Education," *Open Learning.* 5:3:10-15.

1991   "Theory of Distance Education." Paper pre-
        sented at The Second American Symposium on
        Research in Distance Education, May 22-24,
        The Pennsylvania State University, University
        Park, PA.

Murphy, K.
    n.d.   "Introducing Teleconferencing to Turkey --
            Partnership That Work!" *The Australian Journal
            of Educational Technology*, 5:1: 14-22.

Oettinger, Anthony G.
    1993   "Information Age Choices: The Ecstacy and the
            Agony." Asia-Pacific Conference on Commu-
            nications, Taejon, Korea, August 25.

Patterson, Elizabeth
    1996   "The Questions of Distance Education,"
            Theological Education. 33:1:59-74.

Paulsen, Morten Flate
    1993   "The Hexagon of Cooperative Freedom: A
            Distance Education Theory Attuned to Com-
            puter Conferencing," *Deosnews. DEOS --The
            Distance Education Online Symposium* Pub-
            lished in collaboration with the American Jour-
            nal of Distance Education and the American
            Center for the Study of Distance Education, The
            Pennsylvania State University. 2:23

Peters, O.
    1993   "Understanding Distance Education," In K. J.
            Harry, and D. Keegan (eds.). *Distance Educa-
            tion: New Perspectives.* London: Routledge. pp.
            10-18.

Peterson, Mark L.
> 1997   "Providing Effective Technical Support in a
>   Distance Learning Environment," Syllabus97
>   Conference. Sonoma State University, Rohnert
>   Park, CA. July 28-31.

Roxburgh, Alan J.
> 1997   *The Missionary Congregation, Leadership and
>   Liminality.* Harrisburg, PA: Trinity Press In-
>   ternational.

Saba, F.
> 1990   "Integrated Telecommunication Systems and
>   Instructional Transaction." In M. G. Moore
>   (ed.), *Contemporary issues In American Dis-
>   tance Education.* Oxford, UK: Pergamon Press.
>   pp. 344-352
>
> 1994   "Educational Radio and Television of Iran: A
>   Retrospective, 1973-1978. *Educational Tech-
>   nology Research and Development*, 42:2:73-84.
>
> 1994b "From Development Communication to Sys-
>   tems Thinking: A Post-modern Analysis of
>   Distance Education in the International Arena."
>   In Conference Proceedings of the International
>   Distance Education Conference, June 1994,
>   University Park, PA.

Saba, F., and Shearer, R. L.
> 1994   "Verifying Key Theoretical Concepts in a
>   Dynamic Model of Distance Education." *The
>   American Journal of Distance Education*,
>   8:1:36-59.

Saba, F. and Twitchell, D.
>1988 "Research in Distance Education: A System Modeling Approach," *The American Journal of Distance Education.* 2:1:9-24.
>
>1988/89 "Integrated Services Digital Networks: How It Can Be Used For Distance Education," *Journal of Educational Technology Systems.* 17:1:15-25.

Shale, D.
>1990 "Toward a Reconceptualization of Distance Education. In Michael. G. Moore (ed.), *Contemporary Issues in American Distance Education.* Oxford, UK: Pergamon Press. pp. 333-343.

Skinner, Bob
>1997 "Instructional Computing at SMU," Syllabus97 Conference. Sonoma State University, Rohnert Park, CA. July 28-31.

Tanner, Daniel and Laurel Tanner
>1995 *Curriculum Development: Theory into Practice.* (3rd ed.). Englewood Cliffs: Prentice Hall.

Taylor, William D. (ed.)
>1996 *To Valuable to Lose: Exploring the Causes and Cures of Missionary Attrition.* Pasadena: William Carey Library.

Threlkeld, Robert and Karen Brzoska
>1994 "Research in Distance Education," In Barry Willis (ed.) *Distance Education Strategies and Tools.* Englewood Cliffs, NJ: Educational Technology Publications. pp. 41-66.

Verduin, John R., Jr. and Thomas A. Clark

   1991   *Distance Education: The Foundations of Effective Practice.* San Francisco: Jossey-Bass Publishers.

Villafañe, Eldin and Bruce W. Jackson (eds.)

   1996   *The Urban Theological Education Curriculum.* Gordon-Conwell Theological Seminary.

Vines, Diane

   1997   "Larger Scale Distance Learning Initiatives," Syllabus97 Conference. Sonoma State University, Rohnert Park, CA. July 28-31.

Walls, Francine and Jim Shuman

   1997   "Learning How To Learn," Syllabus97 Conference. Sonoma State University, Rohnert Park, CA. July 28-31.

Ward, Ted W.

   1984   *Living Overseas: A Book of Preparations.* New York: The Free Press.

   1994   "Integrity of Method and Objective," *Access Newsletter.* November, 8:2:1,4-5.

   1996   "Servants, Leaders, and Tyrants," in Duane Elmer and Lois McKinney, (eds), *With an Eye on the Future: Development and Mission in the 21st Century.* Monrovia: MARC, pp. 27-32.

Willis, Barry

   1993   *Distance Education A Practical Guide.* Englewood Cliffs, NJ: Educational Technology Publications.

   1994   "Enhancing Faculty Effectiveness in Distance Education," In Barry Willis (ed*.) Distance Education Strategies and Tools.* Englewood Cliffs,

NJ: Educational Technology Publications. pp. 277-290.

Willis, Barry (ed.)

1994 *Distance Education Strategies and Tools.* Englewood Cliffs, NJ: Educational Technology Publications.

Woodberry, J. Dudley, Charles E. Van Engen and Edgar J. Elliston

1996 *Missiological Education in the 21st Century.* Maryknoll, NY: Orbis Books.

Working Group Three

1997 "Minimum Essential Curriculum." *Training God's Servants: A Compendium of the Papers and Findings of a Workshop on Training for Missions in Africa.* Nairobi: Association of Evangelicals in Africa. Pp. 161-172.

Working Group Two

1997 "Patterns for Theological and Missions Training in Africa." In *Training God's Servants: A Compendium of the Papers and Findings of a Workshop on Training for Missions in Africa. Nairobi:* Association of Evangelicals in Africa. Pp. 123-132.

BIOGRAPHICAL SKETCHES

Kenneth B. Mulholland

Kenneth B. Mulholland is Professor and Dean of the Graduate School of World Mission at Columbia International University. He served as the president of the Evangelical Missiological Society for 1998 when the papers for this volume were presented in EMS conferences.. He served as a missionary in Guatemala.

John Piper

John Piper is senior pastor of Bethlehem Baptist Church in Minneapolis. He earned his Dr. Theol. at the University of Munich. He is author of *The ! Justification of God, Desiring God, Let the Nations Be Glad!* and *"Love Your Enemies": Jesus' Love Command in the Synoptic Gospels* and the *Early Christian Paraenesis.*

Michael J. Wilkins

Michael J. Wilkins is Dean of the Faculty and Professor of New Testament Language and Literature at Talbot School of Theology, Biola University, La Mirada, California. Ordained in the Evangelical Free Church, he pastored two churches prior to serving on the faculty at Talbot (1983-present). His research specializations (Ph.D. in New Testament, Fuller Theological Seminary) focus on the gospels, including master-disciple relationships in the ancient world and Christology. He has lectured on biblical discipleship in mission settings around the world. Among his publications are *Discipleship in the Ancient World and Matthew's Gospel* (E.J. Brill/Baker 1988/1995), *Following the Master: A Biblical Theology of Discipleship* (Zondervan, 1992), *Jesus Under Fire* (Zondervan, 1995), and *In His Image: Reflecting Christ in Everyday Life* (NavPress, 1997). He is currently writing two commentaries on Matthew's gospel. He lives in San Clemente, CA with his wife Lynne, and has two grown daughters, Michelle and Wendy.

Rick Love

Rick Love serves as the General Director of Frontiers, a mission that is committed to Muslim evangelism. He completed his Ph.D. in Intercultural Studies at Fuller Theological Seminary.

Sherwood G. Lingenfelter

Sherwood G. Lingenfelter is Professor and Dean of the School of World Mission at Fuller Theological Seminary. Prior to his appointment at Fuller he served as Professor of

Intercultural Studies and Provost and Senior Vice President at Biola University, La Mirada, CA. He holds the Ph.D. in Anthropology from the University of Pittsburgh. His field research includes three years in the Yap Islands of Micronesia, and shorter team research projects with the Summer Institute of Linguistics in Brazil, Cameroon, and Suriname. He has served as consultant to SIL over the last two decades in Papua New Guinea, Borneo, Philippines, Africa and Latin America. He also contributes regularly to mission conferences and to missionary candidate training for other evangelical mission organizations. His publications on missions include *Ministering Cross-Culturally* (1986), *Transforming Culture* (1992, 1998) and *Agents of Transformation* (1996).

Larry Poston

Larry Poston is Professor of Religion at Nyack College in Nyack, New York. He served with Greater Europe Mission from 1980 to 1984 as a professor at the Nordic Bible Institute in Saffle, Sweden, and holds a Ph.D. in the History and Literature of Religions from Northwestern University, Evanston, Illinois.

Jonathan Campbell

Jonathan helped start Life Community, a fellowship of churches in southern California. He has served since 1994 as a missionary and coach for church planting teams through Baton Networks, a global fellowship serving indigenous movements in a variety of cultures from Los Angeles, California to Ulanbattur, Mongolia.

From 1992 to 1999 Jonathan served as church planter strategist for the greater Los Angeles area with the North American Mission Board and as adjunct professor at Golden Gate Baptist Theological Seminary. His Ph.D. is from the School of World Mission, Fuller Seminary, where he studied mission to postmodern cultures.

In 1999, Jonathan began working in Seattle as Vice President of Ingram Labs, LLC, an interactive media company designed as a tentmaking company to enable the partners to fulfill their missionary calling in the Northwest and beyond. Jonathan and Jennifer live with their four children on Bainbridge Island, Washington.

Rick Sessoms

Rick Sessoms was a missionary educator in Indonesia and senior pastor of C&MA churches in Pennsylvania and New York. Currently he serves as Vice President of Spiritual Formation at Simpson College in Redding, California. He completed an M.Div. at Columbia International University and a D.Min. at Trinity International University. He is pursuing Ph.D. studies in leadership development at Fuller School of World Mission. Rick is a frequent conference speaker for churches and mission organizations around the world.

Abdella Usman Muktar

Abdella Usman Muktar was born and raised in Ethiopia. As an Oromo convert from Islam to Christ he served in relief and development responsibilities with NGOs in Ethiopia. He completed his M.A. in Inter-Cultural Studies at

Fuller Theological Seminary and is currently working on a Ph.D. program with a focus in international development.

Edgar J. Elliston

Edgar J. Elliston served as missionary in Ethiopia and Kenya with Christian Missionary Fellowship for eighteen years during which time he engaged in evangelism and training of both national leaders and missionaries at Daystar University in Nairobi. He then spent thirteen years at the School of World Mission, Fuller Theological Seminary where among other responsibilities as Professor of Leadership and Development, he served as the Director of Doctoral Programs and the Associate Dean for Academic Affairs. Currently, he is the Provost and Vice-President for Academic Affairs at Hope International University. He is married with three married children. He currently resides in Fullerton, California.

Some of his books include: *Relief and Development: Developing Leaders for Effective Ministries, Home Grown Leaders, Developing Leaders for Urban Ministries*, and *Completing the Task*(edited with Stephen Burris) and *Missiological Education in the Twenty-First Century* (edited with J. Dudley Woodberry and Charles Van Engen).

INDEX

OTHER TITLES IN EMS SERIES

#1 SCRIPTURE AND STRATEGY: The Use of the Bible in Postmodern Church and Mission, by David J. Hesselgrave

#2 CHRISTIANITY AND THE RELIGIONS: A Biblical Theology of World Religions, Edward Rommen and Harold Netland, Editors

#3 SPIRITUAL POWER AND MISSIONS: Raising the Issues, Edward Rommen, Editor

#4 MISSIOLOGY AND THE SOCIAL SCIENCES: Contributions, Cautions and Conclusions, Edward Rommen and Gary Corwin, Editors

#5 THE HOLY SPIRIT AND MISSION DYNAMICS, C. Douglas McConnell, Editor

#6 REACHING THE RESISTANT: Barriers and Bridges for Mission, J. Dudley Woodberry, Editor